# Springer Series on Cultural Computing

Cultural Computing is an exciting, emerging field of Human Computer Interaction, which covers the cultural impact of computing and the technological influences and requirements for the support of cultural innovation. Using support technologies such as artificial intelligence, machine learning, location-based systems, mixed/virtual/augmented reality, cloud computing, pervasive technologies and human-data interaction, researchers can explore the differences across a variety of cultures and cultural production to provide the knowledge and skills necessary to overcome cultural issues and expand human creativity.

This series presents monographs, edited collections and advanced textbooks on the current research and knowledge of a broad range of topics including creativity support systems, creative computing, digital communities, the interactive arts, cultural heritage, digital culture and intercultural collaboration.

This Series is abstracted/indexed in Scopus.

Stefania Stellacci · Serdar Aydin
Editors

# Endangered Heritage Sites

## Enhanced Representations for Informed Solutions

Springer

*Editors*
Stefania Stellacci
ISCTE—University Institute of Lisbon
(ISCTE-IUL)
Lisbon, Portugal

Serdar Aydin
Mardin Artuklu University
Mardin, Türkiye

ISSN 2195-9056 ISSN 2195-9064 (electronic)
Springer Series on Cultural Computing
ISBN 978-3-031-91948-0 ISBN 978-3-031-91949-7 (eBook)
https://doi.org/10.1007/978-3-031-91949-7



This Springer imprint is published by the registered company Springer Nature Switzerland AG
The registered company address is: Gewerbestrasse 11, 6330 Cham, Switzerland

# Preface: From Traditional Eidotypes to Enriched Representations in Cultural Heritage

## Introduction

For many years, the documentation and analysis of historical buildings and sites have relied on eidotypes, a practice that continues to evolve with the advent of digital technologies. Today, the preservation and management of cultural heritage face new challenges that demand a paradigm shift in how we document information, analyze data, and disseminate knowledge. Contemporary research and praxis move beyond purely visual and single-sensory approaches, embracing multi-dimensional formats and innovative methods. Historically, this evolution has been unpredictable, with post-war computational advancements in museology playing a crucial role in shaping new approaches. One early example can be traced to the 1960s, when Virginia Burton, working at IBM's New York Scientific Center, used a light pen on a Cathode Ray Tube (CRT) to digitally redraw the patterns of Egyptian vessels (Ellin, 1968).

Since then, computational transformation has accelerated and expanded into novel means of digitalization for the representation and further processes of architectural heritage. This is particularly evident in the ability to overlay, systematize, cross-reference, interpret, and simulate multi-layered digital information while preserving the physical integrity of the artifact(s). From the early use of CRT displays in museology to Kenderdine's (2015) integrated immersive multisensory installations, both successful and unsuccessful applications of computational tools have significantly contributed to the advancement of multidisciplinary scholarship. As such, Huhtamo's (2002) account brings attention to earlier examples of early CD-ROMs within museums for visitors, whereas a decade earlier, Ioannides (1993) had already pushed the field forward with advancements in 4D laser scanning. This technology-driven shift has emerged through the exploration and convergence of methods from various scientific disciplines, incorporating advanced analytical techniques such as thermography, laser scanning, and chemico-physical analysis. Additionally, tools such as remote sensing, semantic segmentation, deep learning, heritage building information modeling (HBIM), and gamification enable a comprehensive examination of the intricate layers that shape heritage sites worldwide, including those at risk of disappearance.

Alongside material degradation—a physical and unavoidable condition that has long been a central concern for restoration specialists and theorists, particularly since the Renaissance (sixteenth century) and later with the development of Brandian theories—it is increasingly clear that new challenges are emerging. These include the impact of climate change and the growing demand for cross-disciplinary documentation, underpinned by co-engagement design, which is now being widely shared and debated on a global scale (Europa Nostra Finland, 2018).

The dramatic global geopolitical landscape, as highlighted in the works recently compiled by Falk and Lopez-Claros (2024), calls for a unified global effort and shines a spotlight on the vast range of structures and cultures, whose memories and physical traces are at risk of being irreversibly lost. The List of World Heritage in Danger is extensive, updated by the active participation of dedicated members to oversee the implementation of the World Heritage Convention and other initiatives. Beyond this official list, there exists a vast, unofficial compilation of heritage sites relevant for local communities at risk of disappearing, threatened by factors such as bombings, floods, neglect, over-tourism, and more.

As highlighted in *A Guidebook for Action on the List of World Heritage in Danger* (UNESCO, 2024), to address specific Sustainable Development Goals, such as Climate Action and Life on Land, conservation and communication efforts must be tailored. Given the speed, scale, and negative impact of these challenges, collective reflection, dialog, and transnational efforts are thus essential to support local authorities—often caught in a vice between funding shortages and the prioritization of socio-humanitarian actions.

## Book Contents

The heritage sites analyzed in this book vary in type, ranging from archeological, military, and ecclesiastical remains to industrial heritage. Geographically, they span across Europe (including Portugal, France, and Poland) extending to the Turkish basin, then down the narrow Lebanese strip into Israel, before reaching Pakistan and further into China, near the country's border with Kyrgyzstan and Tajikistan. The fact that, beyond the diversity of the heritage sites and the contexts in which they were shaped, each faces threats from both natural hazards and anthropogenic disasters, may seem to make interpretation even more difficult, with conclusions potentially being even more misleading. This editorial project focuses less on presenting a collection of case studies or detailing corrective actions and more on broader data-driven interpretation and insights. It aims to contribute to the existing body of knowledge by sharing methods and ongoing efforts being applied and tested to analyze and safeguard endangered sites.

This book explores three key interrelated dimensions of digital heritage research: smart heritage information systems, heritage forensics, and interactive participation via virtual heritage applications. Part I delves into *Smart Heritage Information*, examining how digital technology, data, and intelligent systems enhance the management, preservation, and promotion of cultural heritage. Part II, *Digital Heritage Forensics*, investigates methods for assessing damage, revealing hidden details, and supporting strategies underpinning conservation efforts. Part III, *Interactive Virtual Heritage*, analyzes broader, co-creative engagement, emphasizing public participation, collaborative feedback, and evaluation.

Part I explores the processing and management of data for heritage conservation, with Chap. 1 introducing the concept of *smart heritage*. It examines how governance and policy frameworks influence cultural heritage preservation through digital technologies, using case studies from Suzhou, Notre Dame, Amsterdam, and Abu Dhabi. As a means that can potentially undermine *authorized heritage narratives, smart heritage* is discussed with an emphasis on the challenges of interdisciplinary collaboration and the need for policies that balance innovation with cultural integrity and sustainability. Chapter 2 examines an archeological site based on the water channels, exploring the ancient baths of Nero in Turkey. From a practical perspective, the authors demonstrate how to integrate 4D (time) and 5D (cost) modeling to digitally simulate and optimize archeological conservation efforts. Chapters 2 and 3 examine archeological sites, each employing distinct methodologies: laser scanning data and graph-based data models, respectively. Chapter 2 explores an archeological site in Israel, characterized by its water channels and challenging accessibility due to ongoing conflicts. Using laser scanning data, the authors demonstrate the potential for site monitoring and heritage preservation while also offering valuable insights for tourism. Chapter 3 focuses on the application of Knowledge Graphs and Labeled Property Graphs to streamline the analysis of diverse data formats and integrate information from multiple sources, with a particular focus on megalithic monuments and the surrounding in Portugal.

The second group of contributions explores the application of *digital forensics* in heritage studies, with Part II focusing on sites at risk due to environmental disasters or human-induced damage. Chapter 4 applies remote sensing methods to analyze flood-prone areas, using the 2022 Pakistan Floods as a case study. By leveraging satellite data, it assesses the disaster's impact on heritage sites across a vast geographic area. Chapter 5 introduces a data-driven forensic approach to two major recent natural disasters—the 2020 Beirut Port Explosion and the 2021 Quad State Tornado. It underscores the role of structural analysis in both pre-disaster documentation and post-event planning, proposing a process model for integrating disaster mission data. Chapter 6 shifts to a more recent historical context, examining how digital technologies, particularly generative design and Reflectance Transformation Imaging (RTI), are shaping narratives of destruction and reconstruction. It focuses on the 2019 fire at Notre Dame in Paris, drawing comparisons to the 1984 fire at York Minster.

Part III of this book delves into participatory approaches to *virtual heritage* with a specific focus on tourists, students, or other key stakeholders, considered as active interlocutors rather than passive recipients of information. Chapter 7 tackles a highly debated topic: the application of circular economy principles to adaptive reuse and the social awareness of industrial heritage, with a case study from Poland. This research emphasizes the importance of social connections and the need for new teaching methods. The heritage journey continues in Chap. 8, set in Istanbul at the Yedikule Fortresses, where audio accompaniment and gamification enhance the visitor experience through augmented and mixed reality. This study examines the quality of the information provided, the design of the visitor route, and the integration of game elements to bring the site's history to life. Chapter 9 shifts focus to the analysis of water channels at an archaeological site in Israel, using laser scanning data to explore a location that is both remote and difficult to access due to ongoing conflicts. It highlights the potential of this technology for monitoring heritage sites and providing information for tourists. Finally, Chap. 10 takes us to the old town of Kashgar in China, where the research underscores the generative potential of architectural heritage. It shows that digital engagement not only offers descriptive insights that link heritage to the past but also fosters a more dynamic and creative interaction with the present.

These contributions make it clear that shared methodological and programmatic challenges in diagnostic knowledge and intervention practices extend beyond cultural and geographical boundaries, impacting distinct regions with similar issues. In fact, key challenges include site inaccessibility, limited visibility of architectural and archaeological remains, and constraints on investigative efforts due to logistical and financial limitations—issues that are even more exacerbated in conflict zones and economically unstable areas. Additionally, fragmented and hard-to-access data, along with time-consuming operational processes, continue to complicate these efforts.

Beyond the diversity of cases studied and methodologies used, all selected contributions share the common goal of uncovering hidden narratives, preserving collective values, and reshaping perspectives on cultural heritage in the digital age.

Heritage at risk presents both a significant opportunity and a critical area of study, offering a pathway to address the challenges that amplify the fragility and the perishable nature of both physical and intangible data. We hope that, particularly for emerging heritage stewards and the younger generation, the transition from traditional two- and three-dimensional designs to contemporary explorations—where social media, communication, and interdisciplinary analyses intersect in multilayered representations and integrated approaches—will significantly contribute to methodological, epistemological, and practical advancements in digital humanities and heritage management.

Lisbon, Portugal Stefania Stellacci
Mardin, Türkiye Serdar Aydin

## References


Ellin E (1968) An international survey of museum computer activity. Comput Humanit 3(2):65–86

Europa Nostra Finland (2018) Heritage is ours: citizens participating in decision making. [Online]. https://www.europanostra.org/wp-content/uploads/2018/03/2018-heritage-is-ours.pdf

Falk R, Lopez-Claros A (Eds) (2024) Global governance and international cooperation: managing global catastrophic risks in the 21st century, 1st edn. Routledge India. https://doi.org/10.4324/9781032699028

Huhtamo E (2002) On the origins of the virtual museum. In: Nobel symposium (NS 120): virtual museums and public understanding of science and culture, Stockholm, Sweden, May 26–29

Ioannides M (1993) 3D object reconstruction using 4D-laser digitalizing. In: Rix J, Schlechtendahl EG (eds) Proceedings of the IFIP TC5/WG5.10 working conference on interfaces in industrial systems for production engineering, Darmstadt, Germany, Mar 15–17, 1993 (pp. 257–266)

Kenderdine S (2015) Embodiment, entanglement, and immersion in digital cultural heritage. In: Schreibman S, Siemens R, Unsworth J (eds) A new companion to digital humanities. Wiley, pp 22–41. https://doi.org/10.1002/9781118680605.ch2

UNESCO (2024) Implementing new visions: a guidebook for action on the List of World Heritage in Danger. United Nations Educational, Scientific and Cultural Organization. https://unesdoc.unesco.org/ark:/48223/pf0000390450

# Acknowledgments

We express our gratitude to all contributors of this editorial project for their dedication and commitment throughout the publication process. We thank Bruno Andrade (University Portucalense), Leman Figen Gül (Istanbul Technical University), Derya Güleç Özer (Istanbul Technical University), Tane Moleta (Wellington School of Architecture), and Marc Aurel Schnabel (Xi'an Jiaotong-Liverpool University), for their valuable assistance to the editors during the review process.

This work was supported by the *Fundação para a Ciência e a Tecnologia* through ISTAR Projects with grant numbers UIDB/04466/2020 and UIDP/04466/2020.

# Contents

# Part I
# Smart Heritage Information

# Chapter 1
# The Emergence and Implications of Smart Heritage

**Marc Aurel Schnabel and David Batchelor**

**Abstract** This study examines how governance, policy frameworks, and key stakeholders influence cultural heritage preservation through digital advancements. Drawing on existing literature and research findings, this research evaluates the integration of digital technologies within governance practices across four case studies: Suzhou, Paris' Notre Dame, Amsterdam, and Abu Dhabi, representing the possibilities of implementing digital heritage technologies and policies across various cultural and geographical contexts. It explores the implications of emerging technologies, including the metaverse, Web3, semantic data analysis, artificial intelligence, and heritage-building information modelling, in supporting risk-informed governance frameworks that enhance resilience to human and environmental threats while ensuring inclusivity and cultural integrity. This research identifies limitations in governance frameworks and cross-sector partnerships by analysing policies, governance structures, interdisciplinary collaborations, and stakeholder engagement, highlighting the need for policies that align digital tools with heritage conservation's socio-cultural and ethical imperatives. It concludes that governance, policy, and stakeholder participation are crucial for integrating innovation with the responsibility to safeguard cultural heritage for future generations. Without well-structured governance systems prioritizing data transparency, cultural sustainability, and proactive risk mitigation, digital heritage technologies will remain underutilized, leaving vulnerable sites increasingly at risk amid escalating global challenges.

**Keywords** Smart heritage governance · Digital heritage ethics · Heritage risk management · Artificial intelligence in conservation · Policy and cultural sustainability

---

M. A. Schnabel (✉)
Design School, Xi'an Jiaotong Liverpool University, Suzhou, China
e-mail: MarcAurel.Schnabel@xjtlu.edu.cn

D. Batchelor
Faculty of Science and Engineering, Anglia Ruskin University, Cambridge, England
e-mail: David.batchelor@aru.ac.uk

 
S. Stellacci and S. Aydin (eds.), *Endangered Heritage Sites*, Springer Series on Cultural Computing, https://doi.org/10.1007/978-3-031-91949-7_1

## 1.1 Introduction

Good governance and policy frameworks are crucial to guide and include digital technologies to manage and safeguard heritage, whether endangered or not. Preserving cultural heritage exceeds any technological development. Integrating digital methodologies and resources within governance systems is essential to prioritize cultural sustainability, risk management, and inclusive engagement. Although digital instruments, like metaverse, Web3, Artificial Intelligence (AI), heritage information modelling, and predictive analytics, are now becoming popular, their application within established heritage policies is non-existent or inconsistent. This inconsistency is frequently caused by unaligned different sets of policies, bureaucratic resistance, financial constraints, authenticity, personal or political bias, and ethical considerations (UNESCO 2021).

The complexities involved in aligning policy frameworks with digital innovation have been extensively explored within heritage studies. For example, Fatorić and Daly (2023) stated that adaptive governance structures are crucial for ensuring that technological developments meet the goals of the long-term sustainability of cultural heritage rather than leading to unconnected and underutilized efforts. Likewise, Raevskikh et al. (2024) argued that heritage policies must include and connect cultural values with digital technologies to address and reduce institutional biases and strengthen prevailing narratives.

This study presents four real-world cases from around the world: Suzhou, Paris, Amsterdam, and Abu Dhabi. These cities successfully implemented digital heritage technologies and policies to effectively manage, finance, and formalize practices related to digital heritage that mitigate risks, achieve sustainability, and involve the community.

With the aligned sets of strategic plans, legal structures, and funding strategies, shortcomings in policy execution and governance can have a positive impact in combining technological developments with cultural principles and societal requirements. In their research on Smart Heritage, Batchelor et al. (2021) presented that the conjunction of digital transformation and heritage governance necessitates a high-level approach that recognizes both the possibilities offered by technology and the constraints imposed by political contexts.

Smart Heritage governance operates as a preservation method and arena for meeting technological priorities, political agendas, and cultural values. The extent to which digital innovation facilitates more effective heritage and smart city policies raises important questions about whether these technologies inadvertently privilege certain narratives,[1] institutional structures, or economic interests over others. Addressing the governance of Smart Heritage requires adaptability, ethical oversight, and interdisciplinary collaboration to ensure technologically progressive and culturally responsible policies.

[1] Smith and Waterton (2012) introduced this issue in general without specifically referencing the power or disadvantages of technological applications.

Implementing policies and governance structures determines how digital heritage technologies will be used as accessible, sustainable practices or become isolated solutions. Stronger forward-thinking systems are necessary within current and future governance structures to appropriately connect innovation with heritage preservation in an era of accelerating global change.

This study expands on the critical analysis of existing governance models and technology-led heritage initiatives. It evaluates the effectiveness of policies that include technological developments for heritage and conservation. The study is structured as follows: first, it provides a comprehensive literature review on Smart Heritage research, tracing its evolution and theoretical foundations. This is followed by examining governance policies and frameworks in different regions and analysing how they incorporate digital tools for heritage conservation. The four real-world case studies demonstrate how digital heritage policies have been implemented successfully so far. Finally, a critical reflection is presented on future challenges, ethical considerations, and the role of global institutions in shaping Smart Heritage policies before concluding with recommendations for policy advancements and governance innovations.

## 1.2 Literature Review on Smart Heritage Research to Date

### *1.2.1 A Brief Overview of the Contributing Discourses*

Academic literature traces the iterative development of the Smart Heritage discourse, evolving from a hypothesized extension of the smart city and heritage discourses in 2013 to structured policy frameworks and refined definitions a few years later to, more recently, a distinct field. The following literature review provides a brief overview of the smart city and digital heritage origins that contextualize the discourse and a synthesis of the key contributions to the Smart Heritage discourse, tracing its evolution and theoretical and practical development.

#### 1.2.1.1 Smart City Origins

Since the start of the twenty-first century, innovators have envisioned a city where automated and autonomous technologies operate, sustain, and enhance urban places and living conditions. Bowerman et al. (2000) portrayed a city that monitors the conditions of its infrastructure and major buildings to optimize these resources, plan maintenance, and monitor security while maximizing services to citizens. Ishido (2002) described 'digital cities' as arenas that integrate real-time urban information into public spaces. Partridge (2004) proposed a place where information technologies strengthened freedom of speech and the accessibility to public information and services. These and other early visions of smart cities emphasized technologies' physicality and practical utility within urban spaces, retaining the innovative city as subservient to human control.

As the century progressed, the smart city discipline expanded beyond physical infrastructure as it was applied to address social, governance, and economic issues. Smart city commentators during this period often contextualized the smart city as a solution for the increased demand for government services and the need to provide tailored and targeted services for a diversifying population. Giffinger et al. (2007) defined the smart city as delivering a combination of economic, governance, mobility, environment, people, and living solutions that are underpinned and enhanced by technologies that allow for openness, vitality, and integration. Harrison et al. (2012) saw collective intelligence as a result of the intertwining of human capital, information technology infrastructure, and business activity. San Diego's 'City of the Future' and Ottawa's 'Smart Capital' projects sought to enhance business and governance functions (Hollands 2008). Townsend (2013, p. 15) provided a prominent definition from this period in the seminal book *Smart Cities: Big Data, Civic Hackers, and the Quest for a New Utopia*, "places where information technology is combined with infrastructure, architecture, everyday objects, and even our bodies to address social, economic, and environmental problems".

The Smart City discourse later expanded to form a holistic system encompassing the urban experience's complex facets. Lara et al. (2016, p. 9) described a smart city as "a community that systematically promotes the overall wellbeing for all of its members, and flexible enough to proactively and sustainably become an increasingly better place to live, work and play". Yigitcanlar et al. (2018) outlined the smart city as a system with three main drivers: community, policy, and technology, which are interlinked to deliver productivity, sustainability, accessibility, well-being, liveability, and governance outcomes. They described the smart city system as a means, not an end; instead, it supports the social and humanistic condition. As such, the influence of smart technology appeared within tourism, social equality, privacy, ethics, and other discussions (Khan et al. 2017; Kempin Reuter 2019; Lung-Amam et al. 2021). At the end of the second decade of the twenty-first century, the concept of the Smart City had expanded from a physical place to a holistic sphere where technology disrupted, transformed, and led the experience of the city, establishing its ability to intersect with the heritage discourse. The implications of this holistic smart city discourse began to permeate into previously non-technological industries, discussions, and visions of cities, where automation acted before humans, mediating their actions, decisions, and experiences, rather than posed a solution for a human-first environment.

#### 1.2.1.2 The Evolution of Heritage: Conceptual Foundations and the Shift Towards Digital Realms

Heritage comprises a contested discourse that is charged with political, historical, ethnographical, national, and individual experiences (Smith and Waterton 2012). These contestations speak to the richness of the content and the mature state of the ongoing discourse.

Academic literature positions heritage as an abstract thought or idea that is unique for individuals and collectives rather than a physical form, building, or object. Larkham (1995, p. 85) stated that heritage is "all things to all people", with its definition appearing through the definer's eyes and thereby avoiding claiming a standardized description or value. Johnson and Thomas (1998, p. 170) emphasized the link between the past and its interpreter, stating that heritage is "virtually anything by which some kind of link, however tenuous or false, may be forged with the past". Lowenthal (2006, p. 81) added that "heritage denotes everything we suppose has been handed down to us from the past". Other commentators identify how this abstraction may be applied. Urry (1990) argued that heritage is the leisure consumption of the past that offers individuals contemporary escapism. Uzzell (2009, p. 1) described heritage as a resource and source of inspiration, meaning, identity, and commercial profit, "a social construction, an empty box, waiting to be filled with our values, beliefs, desires." Commentators identify the complexities of the concept. Winter (2012, p. 5) recorded that "heritage is both enmeshed in and constituted by complex, entangled and contradictory processes". Janssen et al. (2017, p. 1) stated that heritage is "constantly in flux and whose substance and meaning are continuously being redefined by society". In its fundamental form, heritage is an abstract and subjective valuing process for interpreting the past.

Organizations categorize heritage through the imposition of governance documents and definitions as part of valuing and interpreting the past. Each heritage category embodies a political purpose, jurisdiction, and specific heritage interpretation and, in turn, justifies the organization's function, authority, and reading of the past. Co-dependency forms between the heritage category and the organization. Fredheim and Khalaf (2016) recognized that heritage categories often distinguish themselves by adding prefixes to the discipline. These prefixes and focuses are typically associated with a discernible quality of the heritage, such as physicality, age, cultural group, or period. Ahamd (2006) noted that heritage categories use concise language to build a discourse that supports its focus and enables practitioners to claim a specific expertise area. Through concise jargon, the categories become independent research areas, identities, and professional services. Their adoption in academic literature, governance documents, and practitioner membership associations defend and normalize their claimed area of expertise.

There are many examples of these categories in governance and professional literature. Historic England, a non-departmental public body of the British Government, (2008, p. 71) described heritage as "all inherited resources which people value for reasons beyond mere utility". The Heritage Council (2021) in the Republic of Ireland stated that heritage is "our tangible, intangible and natural heritage and all the associated myths, legends, traditions, and memories provide us with a common language and insight that enables us to communicate on a deep level with each other and to express ourselves in a unique way to the outside world". The numerous International Council on Monuments and Sites charters identify historic gardens, historic towns, built vernacular and architectural heritage.

Academic and professional literature contains countless categories and supporting definitions, including social heritage, urban heritage, and virtual heritage (e.g., Reber et al. 2009; Orbasli 2000; Roussou 2002). The definitions distinguish and promote each unique heritage lens, serving as a rampart to preserve a particular heritage category and as a platform from which organizations and distinct expertise can be formed. Notably, each category does not alter the broader heritage discipline, nor does it resist the claim of adjacent or related categories of heritage. For example, built heritage may include architectural and industrial heritage, and all three categories may be relevant to the same site. The lack of contention against new categories speaks to the discipline's abstractness and subjectivity.

Digital Heritage was officially categorized in 2003 by adopting the United Nations Educational, Scientific and Cultural Organization (UNESCO) *Charter on the Preservation of Digital Heritage*. The Charter states (2003, p. 1):

> Digital heritage consists of unique resources of human knowledge and expression. It embraces cultural, educational, scientific and administrative resources, as well as technical, legal, medical and other kinds of information created digitally or converted into digital form from existing analogue resources. Where resources are "born digital", there is no other format but the digital object.

The Charter seeks to preserve digital materials, including texts, databases, still and moving images, audio, software, webpages, and other digital formats. A central tenet within the definition is its framing of digital heritage as a passive store of resources from which people can access. It regards technology as an archival tool for displaying stored historical data through screens and projections. Under this characterization, humans are to remain the decision-makers, choosing what, when, and how to archive, display, and use digital resources, with the technology being the subservient actor. This categorization aligns with the internet's popularization, expansion, and evolution in the early twenty-first century as the first digital resources were replaced with updated content, and culture started to become 'online' but remained a reflection of real-world experiences.

Since the expansion of the Smart City concept into socially complex areas and industry advancements that allow technology to have a more active role in decision-making, the Digital Heritage categorization is losing applicability. The Internet has been reframed from many static resources to become an ecosystem in flux, where online experiences occur disconnected from real-world events. This conceptual shift allowed researchers, policymakers, and practitioners to converge heritage and autonomous technologies like Smart Infrastructure, Smart Buildings, and other smart fields. The following section details the emergence of Smart Heritage as a distinct discourse.

## 1.3 Key Contributions to the Smart Heritage Discourse

### *1.3.1 A Hypothesized New Discourse*

Smart Heritage emerged as a theoretical discourse in the second decade of the twenty-first century, driven by the expectation that smart city and heritage frameworks would increasingly converge. The first reference to Smart Heritage was by Thwaites (2013, p. 341), who described 'Smart Heritage and cultural futures' as "hybrid virtual-real worlds rich in detail, interpretation, and aesthetic impact" that was aided by animation, narratives and immersive sound and vision technologies. Thwaites proposed that smart technologies were to create immersive experiences that interacted with digitalized historical sites, artworks, and objects in museums, galleries, and controlled public spaces. The theoretical underpinnings of this concept were still to be formed. However, this initial reference to Smart Heritage signalled the shift to a new paradigm where technology actively curates the past.

Chianese and Piccialli (2014) conceptually applied Smart Heritage to outline a smart 'Cultural Heritage Environment' within museums and static heritage spaces. This environment would use the Internet of Things to monitor cultural objects' health within an exhibition space, such as measuring moisture and structural strength. While initially focusing on authorized museums and controlled cultural spaces, Chianese and Piccialli identified that smart technology has further applications for enhancing the valorization, knowledge diffusion, fruition, and growth of a positive and engaging heritage experience through active and unscripted interaction with museum visitors. They stated, "We can imagine a situation in which a user is walking within a museum among several art objects, and when he is particularly close to one of them, its mobile device (e.g. a smartphone or a tablet) is detected by the object [...] the object begins to talk about itself, its story and its status by means of multimedia content and facilities".

Qiu et al. (2015) theorized a Smart Heritage platform when seeking to enhance the experience at a national archaeological site and park in China. This platform involved the management and analysis of data, site management, 3-O (online-offline-onsite) services, and digital explanation to create a complete service circle of the historic site. Referring to this platform as Smart Heritage, the platform would automatically share historical site data with asset managers and visitors in real-time data and collect data on the user in online, onsite, and offline settings through in-situ and mobile device sensors. Qiu et al. (2015, p. 260) stated that the platform "expands the limitations of traditional and single-site area [heritage] consumption" by transforming physically independent cultural sites into a broader cultural landscape. They projected the potential for economic and social opportunities through the novel convergence of heritage and visitors' data. For example, analyzing tourist behaviour and cultural and economic patterns assists in designing, promoting, and managing heritage places.

### 1.3.2 Novel Smart Heritage Pilots

Angelidou et al. (2017) referred to "cultural heritage in smart city environments" in investigating how local government smart city policy can support the historical and cultural heritage of Barcelona, Amsterdam, and London. The policy analysis compared smart city and cultural heritage documentation in the three case studies and found mutual interests between the disciplines regarding cultural heritage preservation and promotion outcomes. The analysis concluded that government policy did not exploit or recognize these opportunities. As such, the researchers advocated for a unified interdisciplinary discourse in local government strategies to better incorporate "cultural heritage objectives in technology-led urban development. Angelidou and Stylianidis (2020) updated this earlier research with a similar policy analysis of Tarragona in Spain, Budapest in Hungry, and Karlsruhe in Germany. They found that there are nascent connections between the Smart City and heritage disciplines' strategic documentation, mainly serving tourism outcomes. They stated, "[i]t could be argued that we are in front of a new generation of smart city initiatives in which cultural heritage is of increasing importance."

Borda and Bowen (2017) referred to Smart Heritage in a review of museum and heritage installations from Australia, the United States of America, the United Kingdom, South Africa, Spain, and China. While most applications employed augmented and virtual reality technologies and intranet-connected devices, which are often categorized as digital and other forms of innovative heritage, some applications comprised smart technologies. *The Collection Wall* in the Cleveland Museum of Art, Ohio, automatically updated and rearranged a historical image exhibition based on users 'liking' of art. Borda and Bowen stated, "Smart Heritage focuses on adopting more participatory and collaborative approaches, making cultural data freely available, and consequently increasing the opportunities for interpretation, digital curation, and innovation" networks. However, Borda and Bowen recognized that heritage organizations typically lack the technical knowledge and funding resources to enlist smart technology.

Mar et al. (2018) reported the 'Smart Heritage City' project,[2] which utilized a network of sensors and an algorithmic computer system to aid the maintenance, conservation, energy savings, and tourist management in the historical city of Avila, Spain. It offered a centralized smart system for heritage site managers called 'SHCity-Manager' that diagnosed issues with heritage assets and attractions, such as overcrowding and failures of protective measures for objects. The project also featured a mobile device system called 'SHCity-Tourist', which curated an optimized visit sequence tour of the city for visitors based on a short questionnaire of personal preferences, such as accessibility restraints and interest. The system compared each user's responses against the real-time wait times at attractions, the user's location, and the distance to the attraction to maximize the time spent there. The mobile device SHCity-Tourist application highlighted the individualistic curatorial capabilities of

[2] http://shcity.eu/

Smart Heritage in a novel tourist user context, while the SHCity-Manager showed its operational and governance application.

### 1.3.3 Smart Heritage Discourse

In the recent years, a concise understanding and definition of Smart Heritage has materialized in the academic literature. Brusaporci (2020) described Smart Heritage as a conceptual and operative relationship between the technology and heritage disciplines, producing seamless interactions between the disciplines in a personal, continuous, and multidirectional manner. This framing constituted a conceptual leap as it aligned with the smart city's holistic system approach, contrasted with the previous separate management of the disciplines in earlier accounts of the discourse, and identified a singular Smart Heritage discourse. Brusaporci stated that Smart Heritage is a "cultural turn, about which a Smart City becomes able to innovate its development dynamics in a cultural sense and a sustainability perspective."

In *Smart Heritage: Defining the Discourse*, Batchelor et al. (2021) comprehensively reviewed the emergent Smart Heritage discourse for the first time in the academic literature and offered a definition considering the contributing disciplines. It defined Smart Heritage as an independent discourse that intertwines smart technologies' autonomous and automatic capabilities and innovation with the contextual and subjective interpretation of the past. This definition framed Smart Heritage within the singular discourse. Within the discourse, the smart city discipline gains historical context and subjective value as it draws on humans' connection to the past as novel data resources, and the heritage discipline adopts autonomous and automatic capabilities that advance it from the previous technology and heritage confluences, such as Digital Heritage and Virtual Heritage. Batchelor et al. identified that tensions between the contributing disciplines remain within the discourse. The technocratic and user-experience focus of the smart city discipline may clash with the subjectivity and governance aspects within the heritage experience.

Since the definition of Smart Heritage as a distinct discourse, academic literature on the topic has increased. Das et al. (2024) documented the development of Varanasi, India, as a 'Smart Heritage City' through India's Smart Cities Mission, an urban renewal and retrofitting initiative led by the Government of India to create 100 Smart Cities nationally. The city's supporting policy within the national initiative targeted using smart technology to enrich heritage, culture, spirituality, and traditions through innovative social and financial inclusions. The researchers recorded improvements to infrastructure, transportation, surveillance, and built heritage and interpretation. They recognize that Smart Heritage lags behind the established Smart Infrastructure and Smart Mobility discourses regarding funding and implementation. The authors also note that, in this instance, weak institutional coordination and corruption serve as major obstacles to material Smart Heritage initiatives.

Geng et al. (2024) investigated how Smart Heritage may be implemented in Chinatown in Melbourne, Australia. This research interviewed community development, built environment, and heritage conservation experts. It found that tourism and gentrification, cultural evolution regarding migrant-to-tourist demographic and commercial shifts, and community-driven efforts were key forces in shaping the precinct's identity and considering its future. Geng et al. note how the unique socio-cultural dimension of Smart Heritage sets the discourse apart from techno-centric smart city paradigms and that augmented reality, virtual reality, and data analytics can enhance visitor engagement and improve the management of heritage assets. Nevertheless, adequate funding, planning regulations concerning heritage assets, and cross-discipline collaboration methods, resources, and expertise are industry gaps in implementing Smart Heritage at scale. Other researchers have engaged Smart Heritage in novel ways. McLennan and Brown (2021) applied a Smart Heritage system to re-generate designs of nineteenth Century timber churches in New Zealand. Song and Selim (2022) reviewed smart heritage in the light of sustainable development policies and definitions. Shiran et al. (2024) examined how Smart Heritage influenced the heritage precinct identity of Chinatown Melbourne and identified the enablers and challenges of implementing the discourse.

## 1.4 Real-World Examples of Smart Heritage in Action

Smart Heritage preservation policies have become crucial for managing risks and mitigation in endangered cultural heritage sites. These policies go beyond incorporating advanced technologies into their governance frameworks to mitigate risks, achieve sustainability, and involve the community. Using four recent samples of Smart Heritage policy changes, this section explores how a transformative technology shift can be successfully enacted and implemented into heritage policies: (i) Suzhou's Smart Heritage initiative, showcasing how governance and digital tools can protect cultural heritage; (ii) the digital restoration of Notre Dame Cathedral, where proactive data regulations were essential in the process; (iii) Amsterdam's Smart Heritage strategies, where AI plays a role in practical risk mitigation; and (iv) Abu Dhabi's value-driven approach to policymaking that aligns value, heritage conservation, and sustainable development objectives.

### *1.4.1 Smart Heritage in Suzhou: Governance and Policies Addressing Heritage at Risk*

The city of Suzhou, China, has developed effective governance and policy frameworks to safeguard heritage sites at risk while simultaneously managing urban growth in a city known for its historic canals and classical gardens. The key to this balance lies in the city's comprehensive 'smart city cluster,' which combines modernization with heritage preservation. This management integrates real-time monitoring, informed policymaking, and adaptive governance to address potential threats to its historic assets (Huawei 2023).

At the core of the Smart Heritage governance structure is the "City Operations Linkage Center", which oversees the historic old town of Suzhou called 'Gusu'. The centre uses digital technologies to assess heritage sites for structural weaknesses and unauthorized modifications. Policies have been established to facilitate prompt actions when threats are identified, thereby incorporating heritage conservation into broader urban management strategies. These measures effectively weave technological advancements into governance practices, ensuring that conservation efforts are proactive and responsive (Huawei 2023; UNESCO 2021).

Public involvement also plays a vital role in Suzhou's heritage governance. The city has adopted immersive digital platforms, including virtual reality (VR) initiatives, to boost cultural awareness and appreciation. A recent example by Xu et al. (2020) is translating an eighteenth-century handscroll painting called 'Prosperous Suzhou' into an interactive VR experience, demonstrating how policies can foster innovation while maintaining cultural narratives. Such initiatives align with policy objectives to promote inclusivity and make heritage accessible to various audiences.

Suzhou's methodology highlights the significance of governance frameworks focused on heritage risk management. By incorporating real-time monitoring, adaptive policies, and community engagement, the city has established a model for sustainable heritage governance. This comprehensive approach ensures the preservation of Suzhou's cultural assets for future generations, providing a valuable template for other cities aiming to tackle heritage risks through innovative policy solutions.

### *1.4.2 Digital Reconstruction of Notre Dame Cathedral: Policy Lessons from Emergency Heritage Response*

The fire of Notre Dame Cathedral in 2019 highlighted the pressing necessity for heritage policies that are prepared for disasters. The reconstruction efforts employed the 3D laser scans created by Andrew Tallon, which were developed independently as part of his academic research (Tallon 2015; National Geographic 2019). These scans were crucial to guiding the restoration process, demonstrating the importance of digital documentation, and showing gaps in policy approaches to heritage risk management.

The French government enacted new policies addressing these deficiencies in the aftermath of the fire. In the after sight, these new policies take into account the importance of proactive digital documentation of heritage sites through innovative technologies, ensuring that essential structural and aesthetic attributes are preserved for potential future crises (UNESCO 2021; Sabour et al. 2024). By incorporating Tallon's scans into an official restoration framework, these data sets became the basis for policy change. They established a benchmark for how to use (existing) digital data in managing heritage during emergencies.

Public access, collaborative data sharing, and promotion of transparency and inclusivity enhanced the policies and strengthened the efforts to preserve heritage.

The digital archives of Notre Dame were made available to international experts to enable a global collaborative approach to the reconstruction efforts (Hong 2024; Manžuch 2017). Nevertheless, data ownership and governance challenges remain, particularly concerning who has authority over digital archives and the ethical and secure use of this data (UNESCO 2021).

This process and methodology illustrate that integrating digital documentation into comprehensive heritage policies benefits all stakeholders and offers novel solutions to preserve heritage at risk. These policies should include the proactive archiving of vulnerable sites, balance the principles of open access with security considerations, and encourage collaborative frameworks that facilitate rapid and accurate restoration in response to disasters.

### *1.4.3 Smart Heritage in Amsterdam: AI as a Policy Tool for Risk Mitigation*

Amsterdam has positioned itself as a leader in Smart Heritage policy by embedding AI-driven predictive maintenance into its urban conservation strategies (European Commission 2023; Gemeente Amsterdam 2023). Through sensor networks and real-time structural monitoring, the city ensures that historic canal-side buildings receive timely interventions to prevent collapse (European Commission 2023). These proactive policies mitigate risks associated with climate change and infrastructure deterioration.

The policy significance of Amsterdam's Smart Heritage initiative lies in its governance model. The city's approach demonstrates how AI can be institutionalized as a decision-support tool in urban heritage planning. However, challenges remain in defining accountability—such as the governance of AI-driven heritage decisions and their regulations. Policies must ensure transparency in AI applications while safeguarding against over-reliance on automated decision-making (UNESCO 2021; Sabour et al. 2024).

Amsterdam also provides a model for community participation in Smart Heritage policies. Here, citizens can contribute to digital heritage mapping projects, allowing policymaking to reflect local cultural values (Gemeente Amsterdam 2023; European Commission 2023). This policy model offers Smart Heritage frameworks to be integrated into public engagement, enhancing cultural sustainability and civic inclusion.

### *1.4.4 Value-Based Policymaking in Abu Dhabi: Sustainability as a Heritage Governance Strategy*

Abu Dhabi's approach to Smart Heritage is characterized by a policy-oriented strategy contrasting the technology-centric models prevalent in many European cities. Rather than concentrating exclusively on digital solutions, Abu Dhabi has established a governance framework grounded in values that harmonize heritage conservation with sustainable development objectives (Raevskikh et al. 2024). This policy structure includes indicators assessing heritage's socio-cultural, environmental, and economic effects, ensuring conservation initiatives bolster long-term community resilience.

This framework presents the potential for policy instruments to weave intangible heritage into risk management practices. Nonetheless, the dependence on quantifiable indicators for assessing heritage value poses specific challenges, as the cultural significance of heritage is often elusive and not easily measured. To enhance future Smart Heritage initiatives, adopting a hybrid governance model that integrates quantitative sustainability measures with qualitative cultural evaluations is advisable, fostering a more comprehensive understanding of heritage preservation.

## 1.5 AI in Smart Heritage Policymaking: Moving Towards Policy-Driven Smart Heritage Governance

AI is increasingly integrated into heritage policymaking, offering predictive tools for risk assessment, conservation prioritization, and funding allocation. Cities like Singapore have deployed AI-driven analytics to determine which heritage sites are most vulnerable to climate change and infrastructure failure. These data-driven insights inform urban development policies, ensuring heritage assets receive timely interventions (European Commission 2023).

However, policy gaps remain in AI governance and ethical oversight. Bias in AI training data could lead to excluding underrepresented heritage narratives. Additionally, adopting AI in policymaking raises concerns about decision-making accountability—if an AI system determines which heritage sites receive conservation funding, how are ethical considerations incorporated? Policies must include regulatory frameworks that ensure AI applications in heritage remain transparent, fair, and culturally inclusive (UNESCO 2021; Sabour et al. 2024).

Future policy development should also explore AI's potential in heritage risk forecasting. Machine learning models could analyze historical conservation data to predict which heritage assets will likely deteriorate, allowing policymakers to implement preventive measures before irreversible damage occurs.

The future of Smart Heritage governance hinges on developing adaptable, inclusive, and flexible frameworks that respond to evolving risks while remaining anchored in cultural authenticity and value-driven principles. Governance models should emphasize transparency by leveraging open-source tools and platforms, ensuring technological advancements are accessible to all stakeholders, including policymakers and local communities. Such openness promotes collaboration and cultivates a sense of shared ownership in preserving heritage.

An adaptable governance approach is crucial for addressing emerging challenges such as climate change, rapid urbanization, and socio-political instability (Fatorić and Daly 2023). Implementing real-time monitoring systems and policy-oriented decision-making in Suzhou exemplifies how flexible frameworks can effectively reduce risks to heritage assets. By incorporating digital tools into broader governance strategies, Suzhou illustrates the significance of proactive measures over reactive ones in managing heritage risks.

Inclusivity is a fundamental element of successful Smart Heritage governance. Initiatives like participatory mapping in Amsterdam highlight the importance of involving local communities in developing heritage policies. Such initiatives ensure that diverse voices are represented in decision-making processes, fostering a collective sense of responsibility and cultural identity.

Maintaining the cultural integrity of heritage sites relies heavily on authenticity and value-based governance principles. Abu Dhabi's alignment of its heritage policies with sustainable development goals is a model for integrating tangible and intangible cultural aspects. This approach helps to prevent the commodification of heritage and ensures that preservation efforts resonate with the lived experiences of local communities (Raevskikh et al. 2024).

The effectiveness of Smart Heritage governance depends on its capacity to merge technological innovation with inclusive practices. By promoting transparency, adaptability, and community involvement, policies can ensure that heritage preservation initiatives are resilient against risks and capable of enriching cultural narratives for future generations.

## 1.6 Ethical Challenges of Smart Heritage Curating the Past

Smart Heritage has the potential to generate ethical challenges for society. While its initial applications showcased tourism and economic opportunities managed within controlled research and museum settings, the rise and dispersal of artificial intelligence increases the likelihood that the automation of heritage processes will challenge how we engage with the past. This section provides a forward-thinking hypothesis of the risks of Smart Heritage and how may resolve them.

### *1.6.1 Risks for Authorized Heritage Dismantling Authorized Heritage Discourse*

Smart Heritage can undermine *authorized heritage* narratives and the organizations that often serve as the gatekeepers and certifiers to the past (Smith 2006). Authorized heritage is a critical framing of the heritage policies that views socio-politically powerful organizations as reinforcing approved understandings of heritage by repeating or uplifting certain historical narratives that fit with organizational, cultural, and national identities while ignoring other narratives. They generate heritage through issuing research grants on selected topics, providing access to national archives and historical assets, and curating specific educational and experience content for the public. They are seen to define the past through lists or registers of heritage assets that are supported by prescribed definitions in legalization or professional guidance documents. These organizations also sustain their versions of the past by advocating for their prescribed definitions to be used in legal and policy frameworks and for them to be a consultee on heritage matters, establishing their procedures as the professional standard, and preserving select historical assets and narratives.

The ability of smart technology to collect and survey text and images could expedite historical research processes and reduce costs, lowering the technical and financial barrier to entry for researchers. This outcome aligns with the well-documented democratization of heritage through Digital Heritage initiatives (Taylor and Gibson 2017). However, the novel ability of smart technologies to further assess and synthesize knowledge from historical text and images risks generating misconstrued or false histories. Non-expert researchers and experts who rely on the accuracy of the technology may not identify these errors. AI-based commercial initiatives, such as DALL-E,[3] Stable Diffusion,[4] and Midjourney,[5] are already drawing on digitalized historical resources to generate hyper-realistic heritage-inspired videos and images, including fake 'vintage' photographs and documentary-style videos from various time periods, that convey historical narratives (Wasielewski 2024).[6] Users generate these images through text-to-image prompt-interfaces that fabricate content. The content is often created without citation to sources and shared on social media without disclosures that they are synthetic, making it unclear whether the content is historically accurate or meant to be interpreted as interpolations of the past.

Authorized heritage organizations are also already exploring the use of smart technology to generate heritage narratives. The European Commission (2022) encourages the use of smart technology to tag and classify historical objects and process, analyse, and interpret text, resulting in new knowledge. A project titled HAZEL between the University of Edinburgh and Historic England is investigating how a pilot generative AI chatbot can summarize text and undertake analysis to assist authors preparing Historic England's guidance literature (Heritage Minds 2024). However, academic researchers have raised concerns regarding the generation of heritage information. Spennemann (2023) tasked ChatGPT to write 36 essays that discuss the nature of values used in the assessment of cultural heritage with references. Spennemann reported that the essays asserted an authoritive position through claims to expert opinions, drawing on scholarly literature, and adhering to industry best practice, but contained a small number of genuine references, with most references being fictional. Only one essay had a disclaimer that the references were false. The research also

[3] https://openai.com/index/dall-E-3/

[4] https://stability.ai/stable-image

[5] https://www.midjourney.com/home

[6] https://website.beacons.ai/histairy_films

finds that ChatGPT lacks the combined effects of socialization and lived experiences to interpret and contextualize factual and historical information. Other researchers have also raised concerns regarding the inaccuracies of the technology to generate historical knowledge and the need to educate experts and the public about these shortcomings (Giannini and Makri 2023). As such, Smart Heritage may risk historical accuracy from outside and within the authorized heritage process.

Subsequent events that challenge the defining and sustaining aspects of authorized heritage and their organizations could result from the generation of alternative or inaccurate histories. Questioning of the authority of national and organizational heritage lists and registers, such as lists of nationally listed buildings, and heritage policies could occur if evidence employs artificial intelligence to justify the protection of assets. List and policymakers may also encounter false counter research produced by artificial intelligence that influences their decision-making. While occurrences of such events are not recorded currently and the socio-political of authorized narratives appear to be stable, scepticism of artificial intelligence creates a fertile environment for doubt to be cast over authorized heritage.

To address the challenges to authorized heritage and the organizations that serve the sector, it is essential to enhance transparency and accountability by requiring clear labelling of artificial intelligence-generated content, ensuring citation of sources, and utilizing digital watermarking to prevent the spread of misleading narratives. Authorized heritage organizations also must play a proactive role in Smart Heritage governance by setting best practices, forming partnerships with artificial intelligence developers and policymakers, and implementing human oversight to validate artificial intelligence-generated research. Additionally, heritage professionals and researchers should be trained to prevent AI-generated misinformation from influencing heritage decisions and policies. By integrating these strategies, heritage organizations could mitigate Smart Heritage risks while harnessing its potential.

### 1.6.2 Impacts of Synthetic Heritage Content

Synthetic heritage content, being AI-generated material, follows the trajectory of artificial and deepfake content that is now somewhat normalized in present political and social situations (Slater 2025). Deceptive content is claimed to have influenced elections and tarnished personal reputations (Jones 2023).

However, due to the intangible and subjective valuing process within heritage, synthetic heritage content could pose a greater risk to society. The abstract nature of heritage, as it operates as an intangible interpretation process, poses a challenge for correcting misunderstandings and false narratives. Unlike social and political fake news that can be disproven through ubiquitous access to digital fact-checking websites and real-time news reports, heritage often does not benefit from highly accessible and user-friendly information sources. Historical information is frequently mediated through institutions such as museums, cultural organizations, and educational institutions that require membership and knowledge of databases. They also rely on expert interpretations and nuance that struggle to hold attention in popular discourses. As such, misleading reconstructions, oversimplified historical narratives, and nationalistic reinterpretations of the past can gain traction, making it even more difficult to challenge entrenched misunderstandings.

The subjective aspect of heritage, which involves valuing processes and the forming of personal and group identities, creates issues regarding how to challenge false understandings and risks societal togetherness. Since heritage is deeply intertwined with identity, correcting misconceptions or countering fabricated narratives can be perceived as an attack on personal or collective beliefs. This challenge is further compounded by the current social condition of heritage valuing, otherwise framed as interest biases, where individuals and groups value selected stories for the purpose of safeguarding and advocating for them without ill regard to others. Also, when competing interpretations emerge—whether due to political agendas, misinformation, or digital distortions—they can create division rather than unity. Without clear frameworks for evaluating authenticity and historical accuracy, conflicting heritage claims can fuel societal tensions, leading to the exclusion, disconnection, or alienation of particular groups.

Efforts should be made to increase the accessibility and visibility of accurate heritage interpretations. Digital tools such as publicly accessible and engaging archives, open-access scholarly research, and accurate and engaging virtual heritage reconstructions could help make nuanced narratives more widely sought by the public over false historical experiences. Improving media and communities' access to heritage experts, fostering interdisciplinary discussions between those who make synthetic heritage content and heritage experts, and promoting critical engagement with heritage narratives could curtail the creation and dispersal of false and inaccurate histories.

### *1.6.3 A More Equitable Future for Smart Heritage*

The future of Smart Heritage lies in balancing technological innovation with ethical responsibility. While digital tools can enhance heritage conservation, they must be implemented through well-structured policies that address transparency, equity, and sustainability. Without strong governance frameworks, digital heritage risks becoming fragmented, commercialized, or controlled by select groups rather than serving as a tool for inclusive, long-term preservation.

The integration of smart technologies into heritage should be approached with caution. Heritage governance should not merely respond to technological trends but actively shape them to ensure that preservation efforts remain ethical, sustainable, and representative of diverse cultural narratives. If policies are not carefully designed, the future of Smart Heritage may serve only a privileged few while leaving vulnerable sites increasingly at risk in the face of global challenges.

## 1.7 Final Remarks

The intersection of governance, policy, and digital heritage presents opportunities and challenges for preserving cultural assets in an era of technological transformation. As explored throughout this study, digital tools such as artificial intelligence, heritage-building information modelling, and predictive analytics have reshaped the strategies available for heritage conservation. However, their integration into existing governance frameworks remains uneven, hindered by fragmented policy implementation, funding constraints, and ethical dilemmas. Addressing these challenges requires a coordinated effort across multiple governance levels and NGOs.

International bodies such as UNESCO could be more proactive in mandating policy reforms, fostering cross-border cooperation, and establishing enforceable global heritage conservation standards. Simultaneously, national governments and agencies could ensure that heritage policies are adequately funded, adaptable to emerging digital innovations, and effectively implemented. Regional entities, such as the European Union, have the capacity to lead regulatory precedents, financing digital heritage initiatives, and facilitating knowledge exchange to drive global adoption of Smart Heritage policies. At the same time, privately owned buildings, where real estate interests may challenge preservation efforts, proactive policy incentives are necessary. Without clear stewardship and regulatory oversight, the potential of digital heritage technologies risks being constrained by inconsistent governance and limited cross-border collaboration.

A critical analysis of governance structures highlights the need for policy coherence to ensure digital heritage technologies translate into effective, sustainable, and ethically responsible preservation strategies. Examining strategic documents, legal frameworks, and real-world applications has demonstrated that digital innovations alone are insufficient without structured regulatory mechanisms that address transparency, accessibility, and cultural authenticity. As highlighted in prior research by Batchelor et al. (2021), policies must be adaptable, interdisciplinary, and aligned with the socio-political contexts in which heritage assets exist.

Future policy approaches must move beyond reactive measures and towards proactive, forward-thinking strategies that integrate technological advancements while maintaining ethical integrity. Ensuring digital heritage remains a public good rather than a privatized commodity will be crucial in maintaining equitable access and representation.

As AI generates predictive scenarios, ranging from climate risk simulations, infrastructure deterioration, and societal value shifts, how these are defined and who controls these narratives is crucial to safeguard diverse cultural perspectives. It is essential to start now with an open discourse of how these technologies will shape and define our future and, with these, how we or the technologies will interpret and value our past.

Ultimately, the governance of Smart Heritage must evolve alongside technology, ensuring that heritage conservation efforts are not only technologically advanced but also ethically sound, culturally inclusive, and sustainable for future generations.

## References

Ahmad Y (2006) The scope and definitions of heritage: from tangible to intangible. Int J Herit Stud 12(3):292–300

Angelidou M, Stylianidis E (2020) Cultural heritage in smart city environments: the update. In: Proceedings of the ISPRS annals of the photogrammetry, remote sensing and spatial information sciences. ISPRS, pp 957–964

Angelidou M, Karachaliou E, Angelidou T, Stylianidis E (2017) Cultural heritage in smart city environments. In: Proceedings of the international archives of the photogrammetry, remote sensing and spatial information sciences. ISPRS, pp 27–31

Batchelor D, Schnabel MA, Dudding M (2021) Smart heritage: defining the discourse. Heritage 4(2):1005–1015. https://doi.org/10.3390/heritage4020055

Borda A, Bowen JP (2017) Smart cities and cultural heritage—a review of developments and future opportunities. EVA London 2017: electronic visualisation & the arts, pp 9–18

Bowerman B, Braverman J, Taylor J, Todosow H, Wimmersperg U (2000) The vision of a smart city. In: 2nd International life extension technology workshop

Brusaporci S (2020) Towards smart heritage: cultural challenges in digital built heritage. In: Pavlidis G (ed) Applying innovative technologies in heritage science. IGI Global, pp 271–296

Chianese A, Piccialli F (2014) Designing a smart museum: when cultural heritage joins IoT. In: 2014 Eighth international conference on next generation mobile apps, services and technologies, pp 300–306

Das D, Chowdhary BK, Mishra SV, Aditi A (2024) Varanasi—the making of a smart heritage city. Environ Urban ASIA 15(1):141–155. https://doi.org/10.1177/09754253241230588

European Commission: Directorate-General for Communications Networks, Content and Technology, Izsak, K., Terrier, A., Kreutzer, S., Strähle, T., Roche, C., Moretto, M., Sorensen, S., Hartung, M., Knaving, K., Johansson, M., Ericsson, M., & Tomchak, D. (2022). Opportunities and challenges of artificial intelligence technologies for the cultural and creative sectors, Publications Office of the European Union. https://data.europa.eu/doi/https://doi.org/10.2759/144212

European Commission. (2023). Urban Agenda for the EU Partnership on Culture /Cultural Heritage

Fatorić S, Daly C (2023) Towards a climate-smart cultural heritage management. WIREs Climate Change 14(6). https://doi.org/10.1002/wcc.855. Final Action Plan. Retrieved from https://ec.europa.eu/futurium/en/system/files/ged/master_final_action_plan_culture_cultural_heritage_v2.pdf

Fredheim L, Khalaf M (2016) The significance of values: heritage value typologies re-examined. Int J Herit Stud 22(6):466–481

Gemeente Amsterdam (2023) Participatory mapping initiatives in heritage preservation. Retrieved from https://www.amsterdam.nl

Geng S, Chau H-W, Jamei E, Vrcelj Z (2024) Enablers and challenges of Smart Heritage implementation—the case of Chinatown Melbourne. Smart Sustain Built Environ. https://doi.org/10.1108/SASBE-07-2024-0275

Giannini E, Makri E (2023) Cultural heritage protection and artificial intelligence; the future of our historical past. In: Moropoulou A, Georgopoulos A, Loannides M, Doulamis A, Lampropoulos K, Ronchi A (eds) Transdisciplinary multispectral modeling and cooperation for the preservation of cultural heritage. TMM_CH 2023. Communications in computer and information science, vol 1889. Springer, Cham. https://doi.org/10.1007/978-3-031-42300-0_32

Giffinger R, Fertner C, Kramar H, Kalasek R, Pichler-Milanovic N, Meijers E (2007) Smart cities: ranking of European medium-sized cities. Vienna University of Technology

Harrison R (2012) Heritage: critical approaches. Routledge

Heritage Minds (2024) Project Announcement: HAZEL, a pilot generative artificial intelligence (AI) guidance assistant for Historic England. Accessed 7 Feb 2025 https://www.heritageminds.org/post/project-announcement-hazel-a-pilot-generative-artificial-intelligence-ai-guidance-assistant-for

Historic England (2008) Conservation principles policies and guidance for the sustainable management of the historic environment
Hollands R (2008) Will the real smart city please stand up? City 12(3):303–320
Hong L (2024) Digital documentation of the reconstruction of Notre Dame de Paris. Int J Comput Sci Inf Technol 2(1):492–503. https://doi.org/10.62051/ijcsit.v2n1.52
Huawei (2023) Smart city cluster: how suzhou built a smart city cluster. Retrieved from https://e.huawei.com/eu/ict-insights/global/ict_insights/ict31-digital-government/success-stories/ancient-city-suzhou-built-smart-city-cluster
Ishido T (2002) Digital city Kyoto. Commun ACM 45(7):78–81
Janssen J, Luiten E, Renes H, Stegmeijer E (2017) Heritage as sector, factor and vector: conceptualizing the shifting relationship between heritage management and spatial planning. Eur Plan Stud 25(9):1654–1672
Johnson P, Thomas B (1998) Heritage as a business. In: Lowenthal D (ed) The heritage crusade and the spoils of history. Cambridge University Press, pp 170–190
Jones N (2023) How to stop AI deepfakes from sinking society—and science. Nature (London) 621(7980):676–679. https://doi.org/10.1038/d41586-023-02990-y
Kempin Reuter T (2019) Human rights and the city: including marginalized communities in urban development and smart cities. J Hum Rights 18(4):382–402
Khan M, Woo M, Nam K, Chathoth P (2017) Smart city and smart tourism: a case of Dubai. Sustainability 9(12)
Lara AP, Da Costa E, Furlani T, Yigitcanlar T (2016) Smartness that matters: towards a comprehensive and human-centred characterisation of smart cities. J Open Innov: Technol, Mark, Complex 2(1):1–13
Larkham P (1995) Heritage as planned and conserved. In: Herbert D (ed) Heritage, tourism and society. Mansell, pp 85–116
Lowenthal D (2006) Natural and cultural heritage. Int J Herit Stud 11(1):81–92
Lung-Amam W, Bierbaum AH, Parks S, Knaap GJ, Sunderman G, Stamm L (2021) Toward engaged, equitable, and smart communities: lessons from west baltimore. Hous Policy Debate 31(1):93–111
Manžuch Z (2017) Ethical issues in the digitisation of cultural heritage. J Contemp Arch Stud 4(4). Available at https://elischolar.library.yale.edu/jcas/vol4/iss2/4
Mar A, Monteiro F, Pereira P, Martins J (2018) An application to improve smart heritage city experience. In: Ioannides M, Martins J, Žarnić R, Lim V (eds) Advances in digital cultural heritage. Springer International Publishing, pp 89–103
McLennan S, Brown A (2021) A smart heritage system to re-generate New Zealand's 19th century timber churches. Heritage 4(4):4040–4055. https://doi.org/10.3390/heritage4040222
National Geographic (2019) How 3D laser mapping helped save Notre-Dame Cathedral. Retrieved from https://www.nationalgeographic.com/magazine/graphics/notre-dame-after-the-fire-feature
Orbasli A (2000) Tourists in historic towns. Taylor & Francis
Partridge H (2004) Developing a human perspective to the digital divide in the smart city. In: Australian library and information association biennial conference
Qiu J, Li J, Sun H (2015) Innovative and applied research on big data platforms of smart heritage. In: 25th international CIPA symposium, pp 257–261
Raevskikh E, Di Mauro G, Jaffré M (2024) From living heritage values to value-based policy-making: exploring new indicators for Abu Dhabi's sustainable development. Humanities Soc Sci Commun 11:1311. https://doi.org/10.1057/s41599-024-03841-5
Reber A, Rhiannon A, Reber E (2009) The Penguin dictionary of psychology. Penguin Books Ltd
Roussou M (2002) Virtual heritage: from the research lab to the broad public. In: Virtual archaeology: proceedings of the VAST 2000 Euroconference. Archaeopress, pp 93–101
Sabour S, Megarry W, Ferguson S, Paterno T, Potts A, Soares Silva JP, Ronsin-Quechon D, Bouaziz K, Polanco J, Snyder M, Carpio E, Herrmann V (2024) The preserving legacies guiding principles

and framework for assessing climate change risk to heritage places (Project Report). Charenton-le-Pont & Paris: ICOMOS & Preserving Legacies. Retrieved from http://openarchive.icomos.org/id/eprint/3341/

Shiran G, Chau HW, Jamei E, Vrcelj Z (2024) Enablers and challenges of Smart Heritage implementation—the case of Chinatown Melbourne. Smart Sustain Built Environ 1–27. https://doi.org/10.1108/SASBE-07-2024-0275

Slater A (2025) Critical response IV: this photo does not exist: generativity and the AI gaze. Crit Inq 51(2):416–422. https://doi.org/10.1086/732925

Smith, L. (2006). Uses of Heritage. Routledge.

Smith L, Waterton E (2012) Constrained by commonsense: the authorized heritage discourse in contemporary debates. In Skeates R, McDavid C, Carman J (eds) The Oxford handbook of public archaeology, pp 153–171

Song H, Selim G (2022) Smart heritage for urban sustainability: a review of current definitions and future developments. J Contemp Urban Aff 6(2):175–192. https://doi.org/10.25034/ijcua.2022.v6n2-5

Spennemann DHR (2023) ChatGPT and the generation of digitally born "knowledge": how does a generative AI language model interpret cultural heritage values? Knowledge 3(3):480–512. https://doi.org/10.3390/knowledge3030032

Tallon A (2015) Divining proportions in the information age. Arch Hist 2(1), Art. 15. https://doi.org/10.5334/ah.bo

Taylor J, Gibson LK (2017) Digitisation, digital interaction and social media: embedded barriers to democratic heritage. Int J Herit Stud: IJHS 23(5):408–420. https://doi.org/10.1080/13527258.2016.1171245

The Heritage Council (2021) What is Heritage?. https://www.heritagecouncil.ie/what-is-heritage

Thwaites H (2013) Digital heritage: what happens when we digitize everything?. Ch'ng E, Gaffney V, Chapman H (eds) Visual heritage in the digital age. Springer London, pp 327–348

Townsend A (2013) Smart cities: big data, civic hackers, and the quest for a new utopia. W.W Norton & Company

UNESCO (2021) Digital archiving and heritage preservation: challenges and best practices. Retrieved from https://unesdoc.unesco.org/ark%3A/48223/pf0000130071

United Nations Educational, Scientific and Cultural Organisation (2003) Charter on the preservation of digital heritage

Urry J (1990) The tourist gaze: leisure and travel in contemporary societies. Sage

Uzzell D (2009) Where is the discipline in heritage studies? a view from environmental psychology. In: Sorensen M, Carman J (eds) Heritage studies: methods and approaches. Routledge, pp 326–333

Wasielewski A (2024) Unnatural images: on AI-generated photographs. Crit Inq 51(1):1–29. https://doi.org/10.1086/731729

Winter T (2012) Clarifying the critical in critical heritage studies. Int J Herit Stud 19(6):532–545

Xu Q, Brown A, Moleta T, Schnabel MA, Rogers M (2020) Inhabiting 'Prosperous Suzhou' through smart VR: interrogating an ancient artwork and documents to manifest tangible and intangible heritage. In: Holzer D, Nakapan W, Globa A, Koh I (eds) RE: anthropocene—design in the age of humans. CAADRIA, Bangkok, pp 173–182. https://doi.org/10.52842/conf.caadria.2020.2.173

Yigitcanlar T, Kamruzzaman M, Buys L, Loppolo G, Sabatini-Marques J, da Costa E, Yun J (2018) Understanding 'smart cities': intertwining development drivers with desired outcomes in a multidimensional framework. Cities 81:145–160

# Chapter 2
# Anastylosis of the Frigidarium in Patara Ancient City Using HBIM Methodology

**Merve Şule Yörük, Salih Ofluoğlu, and Mustafa Koçak**

**Abstract** This study, applied to the Nero Bath in the Patara Ancient City, combines Heritage Building Information Modeling (HBIM) with 4D (time) and 5D (cost) modeling to digitally simulate, optimize, and coordinate archeological conservation efforts. This approach facilitates efficient, data-driven decision-making and a seamless transition from virtual planning to physical restoration. A point cloud model was created using data from Light Detection and Ranging (LIDAR) scans and drone imagery of the Nero Bath. A 3D mesh model was created using geometric modeling software, with the proposed reconstruction interventions for the walls, roof, and partial ground initially modeled as NURBS surfaces. Then, architectural and archeological data, such as structural damages, required completion elements, and support systems, were incorporated into the model using BIM authoring software. To plan the post-excavation reconstruction process in a virtual environment, the excavation period, intervention decisions and cost calculations were transferred to a BIM coordination program. The resulting database demonstrated how the process could be tracked across the 4D (time) and 5D (cost) dimensions by defining tasks, timeframes, and cost allocations for the bath's reconstruction. This approach provides a preview of potential conservation actions, helping to prepare the digital heritage for its eventual physical implementation.

**Keywords** Data management · HBIM in archeology · Patara ancient city · NURBS surfaces · Frigidarium · Nero bath

M. Ş. Yörük (✉) · S. Ofluoğlu · M. Koçak
Faculty of Fine Arts and Architecture, Antalya Bilim Üniversitesi, Antalya, Türkiye
e-mail: ysule.yoruk@std.antalya.edu.tr

S. Ofluoğlu
e-mail: salih.ofluoglu@antalya.edu.tr

M. Koçak
e-mail: mustafa.kocak@antalya.edu.tr

 
S. Stellacci and S. Aydin (eds.), *Endangered Heritage Sites*, Springer Series on Cultural Computing, https://doi.org/10.1007/978-3-031-91949-7_2

## 2.1 Introduction

Conservation practices have increasingly focused on systematic preservation strategies and research designed to anticipate potential risks, moving beyond traditional activities like documentation, reconstruction, and restoration (Penjor et al. 2024). With the advent of digital tools, the establishment of a sustainable preservation infrastructure for heritage marks a significant advancement in the field.

While the focus on systematic preservation strategies and digital tools marks a significant advancement in the field, the reconstruction process remains deeply rooted in traditional methods. Reconstruction is defined as rebuilding a historical structure that has been lost, damaged, or destroyed over time by its original state (Güven 2024). Traditional methods involve identifying the geometries of structural elements, extracting metric information, and creating two-dimensional drawings based on horizontal and vertical references in the space (Korumaz et al. 2011). These drawing techniques can be time-consuming. In contrast, digital tools streamline relevant tasks, such as creating geometric models of heritage structures, accurately scaling with references, and producing two-dimensional drawings (Georgopoulos and Stathopoulou 2017).

The use of Heritage Building Information Modeling (HBIM) technology has played a key role in analyzing and carrying out conservation efforts. While the use of BIM mainly pertains to modern constructions, providing substantial digital levels of detail regarding the physical and functional characteristics of a building, HBIM applies those principles to the conservation and management of historic structures. BIM enables the creation of precise 3D models and contains semantically rich alphanumerical data that extends beyond visual representations, unlike traditional Computer-Aided Design (CAD) methods. It not only captures the current state by modeling the geometries of each structure and its components but also supports the management of construction techniques, material properties, and process coordination, among others (Oostwegel 2022). HBIM also plays a significant role in project management, planning, and monitoring, enabling heritage projects to be carried out within time and budget constraints by facilitating risk and change analysis, as discussed by Karaçar et al. (2022). In archeological excavations, the application of 4D (3D + time) and 5D (3D + time + cost) planning methodologies supports the management of critical parameters such as resource allocation and delay detection. This method enables the visualization of planning and cost management, allowing the process conditions to be anticipated and worked with effectively (Wan Abdul Basir et al. 2023).

Building on such developments, Sewasew (2024) underscored the importance of integrating the building-level material archive into the HBIM model for holistic material record creation. Though data collection and processing are challenging, a comprehensive documentation can be provided to support proactive decision-making on rehabilitation, renovation, renewal, demolition planning, defect detection, and disaster management. Moreover, the 4D planning capability of HBIM significantly enhances the management and conservation of heritage sites. For example, the rehabilitation and reuse of the De Simone factory (in Naples, Italy), a nineteenth century industrial archeology site, were supported by 4D planning. The HBIM model facilitates site structuring in a way for seamless adaptation to further developments, as discussed in literature (e.g., Mazzei et al. 2024).

## 2.2 Digital Heritage Documentation Using HBIM

In conservation and restoration studies, data for application can be integrated into the 3D morphological model by identifying the existing building features (Maietti 2023). A detailed and accurate documentation that identifies the architectural details and any existing interventions over time serves as a guide for future works. Digital documentation allows the information in question to be recorded in a shared database as reports, technical drawings, photogrammetry, planning, and cost documentation. The fact that the information is accessible within a centralized, networked space, such as the cloud, and can be utilized by different disciplines makes the process fast and reliable, as outlined by Quintero et al. (2020).

The first step in creating a HBIM is to gather all information recorded from the time the heritage structure was built to the present (e.g., textual documents, two-dimensional drawings and visual documents, such as archival photographs). The second step is to document the current state of the building or environment. The point cloud of the structure is produced by selecting the scanning method appropriate for the physical conditions of the structure (e.g., LIDAR—Light Detection and Ranging scanning or photogrammetry). Since the physical geometry can be realistically reflected in terms of form and material, the use of LIDAR and photogrammetry methods as digital modeling tools has become widespread. Several studies demonstrate the importance of these techniques in transferring physical data to the digital environment and use it as a 3D model infrastructure in BIM and HBIM methods (Ulvi and Hamal 2024).

Scanning is carried out along the horizontal and vertical routes within the interior and exterior space of the structure. The recorded scanning data generates a point cloud model of the structure. This point cloud data is further transformed into mesh surfaces through photogrammetry or 3D modeling software, giving a 3D solid model (Kushwaha et al. 2020). 3D model data obtained from LIDAR scanning provides more accurate results than those derived from photogrammetric scanning methods (Karslı et al. 2022).

In this study, human-scale scanning was carried out using mobile devices' LIDAR feature, while point cloud data was conducted using drone-captured photographs from hard-to-reach heights. The generated point cloud, therefore, forms the basis for coherently reconstructing coordination, serving as a reference on which to define the heritage structure and carry out an in-depth situational analysis.

### 2.2.1 Nero Bath Structure

This study focuses on Nero Bath structure, located in the Ancient City of Patara in Antalya, Turkey (Öner 1997). In antiquity, Patara held a significant position as the administrative center of the Lycian region. The city, bordering Sinus Glaucos (Fethiye Bay) to the west and Mare Pamphylium (Gulf of Antalya) to the east, possessed a port facilitating commercial interactions for the northern Mediterranean. By the fifteenth and sixteenth centuries AD, the port was filled and turned into a swamp due to the alluvium carried by the Xanthos River. Patara lost its vitality with the port becoming unusable (İşkan and Halifeoglu 2020).

The Nero Bath, the first of the five baths uncovered in Patara, is thought to have been built in the 60 s AD (Orhan 2023). Bath structures hold significant social and cultural functions in ancient cities and historical settlements. In antiquity, although the primary purpose of baths was hygiene, they also served as social meeting spaces (İşkan and Halifeoglu 2020). The structure covers an area of approximately 1270 square meters, with a west–east axis of 47 m and a north–south axis of 27 m. The building has three main spaces: Frigidarium, Tepidarium and Caldarium (Fig. 2.1). When examining the bath structure, it is evident that most of the walls have been well-preserved (Ergül 2023).

Upon entering the Nero Bath structure, the first area encountered is the Apoditerium, the dressing area and the storage space for personal belongings, where an attendant usually oversees the security of clothes and items. After leaving the Apoditerium, one moves to the Palaestra section to exercise before bathing. Next, in the Tepidarium, the body would be cleansed using olive oil. The bathing ritual then continues with a visit to the Caldarium or sweating room. For those wishing to cool

**Fig. 2.1** Southeast perspective in Nero Bath (photo by Yoruk 2025)

down or swim after cleansing, the Frigidarium with its cold-water pool offers a refreshing end to process. Thus, the full bath ritual is completed (Erkoç 2020). The best-preserved section of the bath is the Frigidarium, which is the focus of this study.

#### 2.2.1.1 Analysis of the Frigidarium in Nero Bath

The Frigidarium measures approximately 9.5 × 19 m and features a cold-water pool at its northern end (Fig. 2.2). The entrance and exit doors to the Tepidarium are on the east wall, while two additional doorways are on the west wall. Across the entire bath complex, each section is equipped with entrance and exit doors as well as large windows. When originally constructed, the east wall of the building measured 14.5 m.

Over time, as the number of users increased and their needs changed, the Tepidarium and Caldarium were expanded by 10.5 m to the north. In Fig. 2.3, the damaged

**Fig. 2.2** Axonometric view of the Frigidarium in Nero Baths (image by M. Yoruk)

areas of the wall are highlighted in yellow, while the yellow dashed line outlines the first stage of the wall and purple highlighting marks the extended section of the wall. The lintel of the doorway leading to the Tepidarium and some of the stones comprising the wall has partially collapsed.

As shown in Fig. 2.4 (*top*), the north wall of the building, measuring 13.5 m in length, features two windows that remain sufficiently intact. The heights of these openings were estimated based on comparable bath structures and spatial requirements. Restoration plans for the north wall include completing it to match the existing wall heights, taking into account the window openings.

The remains also indicate that the roof of the Frigidarium section was constructed with a vaulted ceiling approximately 10 m in diameter. Compared with other known examples of Roman bath architecture, an analysis of the side walls also suggests that

**Fig. 2.3** East wall of the Frigidarium in Nero Baths (image by M. Yoruk)

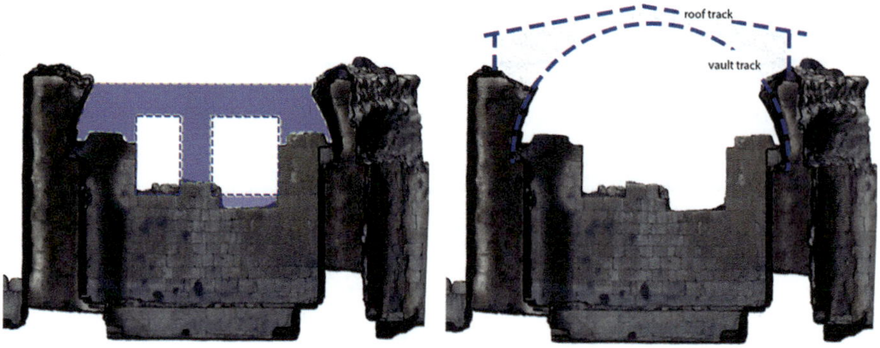


**Fig. 2.4** North wall of the Frigidarium in Nero Baths (image by M. Yoruk)

a barrel-shaped roof enclosed the vault. It is likely that the roof incorporated a tile covering supported by wooden beams (Fig. 2.4, *bottom*).

## 2.3 Existing Condition of the Worksite

Archeological excavations of the Nero Bath structure are ongoing with the work being carried out by different archeological teams. Simple repairs to the wall and floor were completed during the excavations of the Frigidarium section in 2018. Protective measures were implemented through a two-stage intervention based on the degradation analysis data: temporary interventions for immediate stabilization and long-term interventions for sustained preservation. Temporary interventions involved using support elements, usually made of wood or steel, in the damaged area to prevent the collapse of structural elements such as walls, floors or roofs in the early stages of the excavation. As shown in Fig. 2.5, these supports were applied to protect the wall from external factors that could exacerbate the damage during the excavation works. With the disintegration of the lintel, a crucial component of the door opening, shifts were observed in the surrounding blocks. To maintain the structural integrity under vertical loads, wooden elements were used to replace the original lintel. Additionally, steel elements were employed to support the masonry blocks (Fig. 2.5).

## 2.4 3D Modeling Workflow

The Nero Bath structure was scanned using LIDAR technology with an iPad Pro tablet. The scanning process involved repetitive movements along specific $X$ and $Y$ planes, beginning from the building's exterior and progressing inward. The collected data was processed through 3D Scanner software, resulting in a mesh model created by integrating physical data. The LIDAR method produced high-resolution models, especially for the ground and human-scale wall heights. However, resolution and accuracy were limited in the upper parts of the structure or areas requiring scanning at a 90-degree angle.

Additionally, the structure was modeled using photographs taken automatically at regular intervals to reduce the chances of human error in the process. This technique produced better results than LIDAR in higher and more complex areas. In this way, a digital model of the structure was created using both techniques, and the results were compared. Although LIDAR is excellent in terms of speed in data collection and processing, its resolution and coverage were compromised by the limitations of manual scanning.

More extensive data was captured using Unmanned Aerial Vehicles (UAV). Drone shots were taken to give a bird's-eye view of the whole structure. The shooting, done in the morning hours to avoid being affected by sunlight, spanned three days and resulted in 705 images. These photos were processed in Agisoft Metashape™

**Fig. 2.5** Temporary support application in the east wall of the Frigidarium in Nero Bath (photo by Yoruk 2025)

and Autodesk ReCap Pro™ software to create point clouds and mesh models. The processed data yielded a 4.91 GB point cloud used for the 3D simulation models (Fig. 2.6). Throughout these stages, the software's automatic processing features have made the documentation and modeling processes practical.

In the first stage of the modeling process, the load-bearing structure of the building based on the stone masonry system was analyzed, comparing it with other architectural buildings of the same period. The main framework of the building consists of vertical supports such as walls and columns, with stone blocks, mortar, and filling materials used to enhance the strength of load-bearing elements. For modeling this construction system, the dimensions of the blocks were extracted from the mesh model and copies of these blocks were created. A Non-uniform rational B-spline (NURBS), set of rational curves defined on non-uniform surfaces based on the preset curves, was drawn on the mesh model to extract block samples. Using the block geometries created in the 3D model and the mesh surface as a reference, NURBS curves were drawn. These curves were then converted to NURBS surfaces, and the

**Fig. 2.6** Point cloud model of the Nero Bath (image by M. Yoruk)

volume was added to form 3D block objects of these surfaces. Figure 2.7 (*top*) illustrates the completion of the northern wall of the Frigidarium section using block objects on the mesh model. The block geometries were aligned with the surviving stone wall, and the joint distances between the blocks were modeled to correspond with the mesh structural element. The slope of the vault was calculated by referring to the width of the space and supporting the curve at the stirrup points on the wall. Building elements were created by replicating cut stone blocks along this curve.

In addition to the load-bearing elements of the building, there are cold water and hot water pools among the parts that continue to function as spaces. In order to complete the mesh model of the pool in the Frigidarium section of the building, the edge blocks forming the pool wall were first produced. Blocks of varying sizes were adjusted using the traces on the ground as a reference. The same principle of producing stone wall blocks is repeated to model pool blocks. Following the traces on the ground, the NURBS curve was drawn and then translated onto the surface. Thickness was added to the surfaces by considering the height of the existing blocks. Figure 2.7 (*bottom*) depicts a column arrangement believed to be part of the structure.

Photographs of the column base findings were imported into the Rhinoceros™ program, where a cross section of the base was created and then converted into a 3D object. The column bases, placed on the completed blocks at the perimeter, were finished by modeling column pieces based on the photographs as references.

The process indicates the foundational framework for reconstruction management in a digital environment. Initially, the digital reconstruction applications of the building were created in Autodesk Revit,™ the BIM authoring software. Although the mesh model obtained from the point cloud could be opened in Revit, the program does not allow interventions on the model. Basic commands (e.g., cut or displace) were not allowed within the mesh model opened in the software's mass modeling

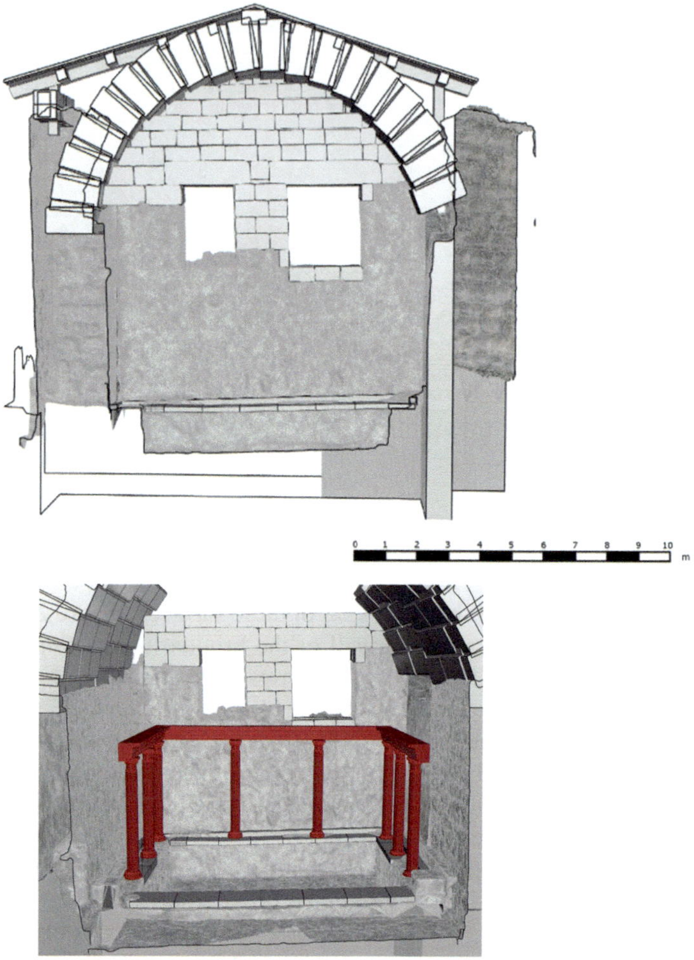


**Fig. 2.7** Simulation of analystilos (*top*) and 3d model of cold-water pool in the Frigidarium in Nero Bath (*bottom*) (images by M. Yoruk)

environment. Besides, smooth navigation within the program was not possible, which was considered as a parameter that would slow down the modeling process. In addition, since it was impossible to define a texture in this mesh model, areas that needed to be intervened could not be processed, such as completing the wall structure. The 3D model of the Frigidarium section was transferred back to Revit, where the roof structure was re-created as BIM families (Fig. 2.8).

Following the HBIM methodology, a table in the BIM model is created for processing the qualitative and quantitative data of the designed element, referred to as an 'identity card' (Fig. 2.8). The table shows, among other things, the type,

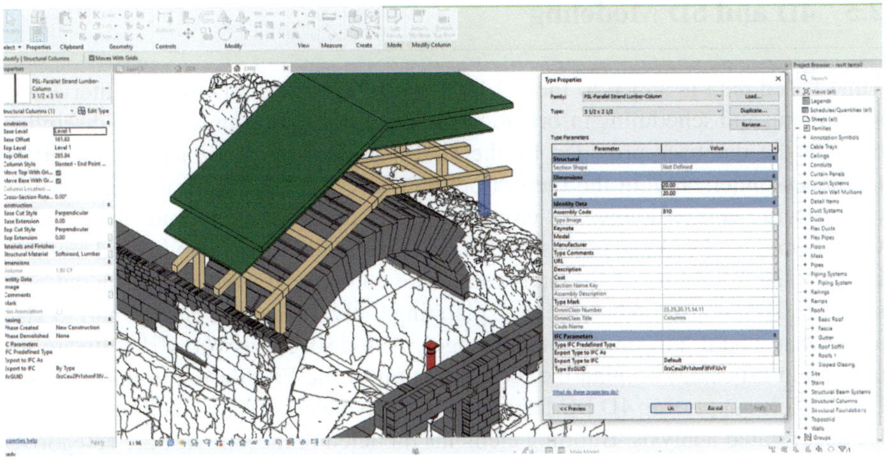

**Fig. 2.8** Roof structure of the Frigidarium in Nero Bath using Revit (image by M. Yoruk)

dimensions, and material of each building element, and textual data related to interventions applied to the model and restoration periods can be processed. Moreover, visual data can be attached to the table. The intervention processing capability of the form allows switching between the current and original form of the element.

The HBIM methodology customizes the parametric data for cataloging information. Architectural elements used in the structure are modeled considering the peculiar characteristics, creating a library for the heritage building. Further, the possibility of updating such a library in the future through interventions on single building elements or the whole structure shows that HBIM is a scalable and interoperable method for documentation and conservation, with application in archeology as well. Figure 2.9 shows the reconstruction of the Frigidarium section through the point cloud model.

**Fig. 2.9** 3D model of Frigidarium in Nero Bath (image by M. Yoruk)

## 2.5 4D and 5D Modeling

Time-based data is added to the 3D BIM model to have a 4D model. Intervention sequencing and scheduling information can be obtained for conservation disciplines through the database provided by the HBIM system to monitor progress. HBIM facilitates understanding the reconstruction process while offering various advantages for projects. It allows for easier coordination of time and budget by making visually distinct tasks and processes that are sometimes blurry in traditional methods. Besides, the feasibility of alternative scenarios can be analyzed to reach an optimum solution. This is also updated in time planning tools such as the Gantt Chart to visualize what would happen after the changes. Autodesk Navisworks™ software was utilized in this study to plan the reconstruction of the Frigidarium section of Nero Bath. While supporting 4D BIM applications, Navisworks™ also facilitates 5D BIM for cost-related analysis. Building elements modeled in the software are categorized based on intervention decisions, while material, labor, and equipment costs are used to calculate total costs (Inzerillo et al. 2024; Tarak and Agnihotri 2021).

There are a limited number of studies on the use of 4D and 5D planning in existing heritage structures as such, the BIMLegacy system, developed for coordinating the conservation process of the historic San Juan del Hospital site in Valencia, Spain, was u The Evolution of Heritage: Conceptual Foundations and the Shift Toward Digital Realms for the fourth dimension (Palomar et al. 2020). The standardization of given work processes is foreseen to offer long-term economic benefits by supporting heritage teams to organize data and processes within the conservation discipline (Jordan-Palomar et al. 2018). A similar study on the management of heritage buildings was conducted on the NED Heritage Building in Karachi (Pakistan). After producing a 3D BIM model of the building, three different application scenarios were created and tested using Navisworks™ software. Simulations were analyzed to select the most cost-effective and quickly applicable scenario (Khan et al. 2022).

The generated 3D model was transferred to Navisworks™ software, used for 4D and 5D construction management, as shown in Fig. 2.10, *top*. In the Navisworks™ timeliner tab, the planned reconstruction steps were defined by providing the necessary information. The object group corresponding to each action was added to the action row. Also, in the simulation section of the timeliner tab, the software automatically generates a visual and textual simulation of the entered data. The timeliner tab can be revised by adding new parameters based on the needs of the heritage structure from the available settings (Fig. 2.10, *bottom*). 25 tasks have been defined and grouped into 'repair', 'reconstruction', 'temporary construction', and 'demolition'. This allows for faster decision-making regarding time and cost for the application items while also making it easier to monitor. The parameter 'cost' is cataloged for 'material', 'subcontractor', and 'total'. In this way, tracking the material stock allocated for each task and the number of subcontractors is possible, thus preventing time losses and allowing the process to continue smoothly. Excavation works are currently ongoing in this area, so cost information could be then integrated into the database, or it can be indicated according to current market data.

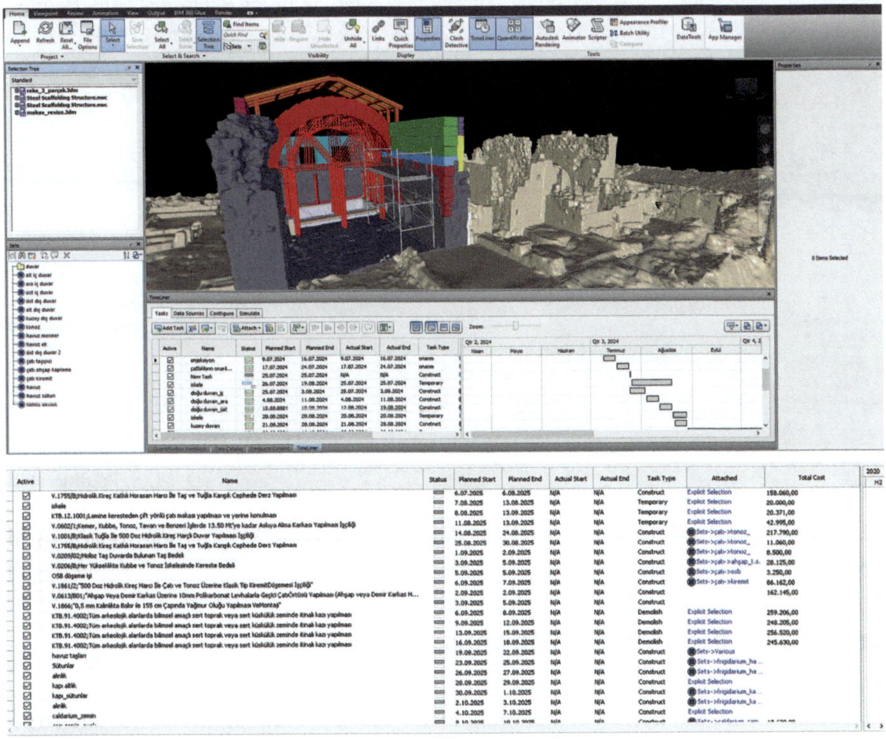

**Fig. 2.10** HBIM model (*top*) and timeline tasks defined on Navisworks™ software (*bottom*) (images by M. Yoruk)

Using in Navisworks™ software, the simulation shows the planned sequence of the conservation actions, specifying the days spent, application weeks, and cost information. If there is a repair function before the conservation action, the architectural element on which the application will be made is represented briefly in green. Then, temporary component such as scaffolding, or support elements are placed in the required area. As shown in the figure, three truss systems and the steel legs supporting them before the vault roof application were added to the desired area of the Frigidarium at a distance of 1 m. Afterward, the reconstruction of the vault was simulated with the excavated stones on the support. The tile roof and wooden carrier system that will be placed on the vault have been added to the simulation as planned in practice (Fig. 2.11). The scaffolding system was recorded in the timeline task list to be removed from the simulation at the end of the planned period for the vault roof application. Although reconstruction decisions for the entire structure have not yet been implemented, the simulation of conservation activities in the BIM environment helps identify possible design scenarios. Future works are also planned for other sections of the Nero Bath.

**Fig. 2.11** 3D simulated Model of Nero Bath structure on Navisworks™ software (image by M. Yoruk)

## 2.6 Discussion and Conclusions

Interventions in built heritage, including anastylosis, present architectural and structural challenges that are not typically encountered in modern constructions, due to the difficulties to analyze details such as the damage to excavated structural elements' internal and external surfaces, their strength, or resistance to external loads, among others. These analyses are relevant for taking decisions on necessary reconstruction or retrofitting activities. In line with this information, conservation activities should be properly planned and different process steps should be clearly defined by a multidisciplinary team. In reconstruction projects, the coordination of 4D (time) and 5D (cost) is relevant to ensure effective planning of activities to preserve historical structures and their components. Integrating traditional tools into the HBIM system offers the opportunity to organize the budget and time allocated to the project process more effectively. Comparing the conservation work carried out in Türkiye and other countries, as well as the exchange processes of data, can provide an opportunity to develop the necessary groundwork for the planned reconstruction. Processing the existing structural data on this groundwork will enable the derivation of results from the proposed hypotheses.

HBIM digitally brings together historical buildings' geometric and qualitative data, helping to analyze the building elements in detail and make informed conservation decisions. NURBS geometries and BIM artifacts analyzed in this study constitute the basis for reconstruction simulation. A digital scenario was created for the Nero Baths by processing plant cleaning, structural repairs, and reconstruction applications with time (4D) and cost (5D) dimensions to evaluate potential consequences of interventions and minimize associated risks. As shown in this study, the HBIM method offers an effective solution compared to traditional methods by allowing simultaneous management of both field applications and digital documents. The broader adoption of the HBIM method will be possible through the development of modeling tools designed to the unique characteristics of historical structures. In the future, increasing the availability of plugins to streamline data transfer between across software platforms will further support this progress.

## References

Ergül PC (2023) Patara Antik Kentinin Etnomimari Açıdan İncelenmesi [Published Master's Thesis], Ankara Üniversitesi

Erkoç S (2020) Yıkanma Kültürü ve Hamamlar. Lykia'nın Akdeniz'e Açılan Kapısı Patara, Kültür Ve Turizm Bakanlığı 1:67–73

Georgopoulos A, Stathopoulou EK (2017) Data acquisition for 3D geometric recording: state of the art and recent innovations. In: Heritage and archaeology in the digitalage, quantitative methods in the humanities and social sciences, pp 1–2. https://doi.org/10.1007/978-3-319-65370-9_1

Güleç Korumaz A, Dülgerler ON, Yakar M (2011) Kültürel Mirasin Belgelenmesinde Dijital Yaklaşımlar. Selçuk Üniversitesi Mühendislik, Bilim ve Teknoloji Dergisi 26(3):67–83

Güven Ö (2024) Anıtsal yapıların rekonstrüksiyon uygulamalarının incelenmesi ve Ayasofya Fatih Medresesi örneği (M.Sc. Thesis) İstanbul Aydın University

Inzerillo L, Acuto F, Pisciotta A, Mantalovas K, Mino G (2024) Exploring 4D and 5D analysis in BIM environment for infrastructures: a case study. The international archives of the photogrammetry, remote sensing and spatial information sciences, XLVIII-2/W4–2024, pp 233–240. https://doi.org/10.5194/isprs-archives-XLVIII-2-W4-2024-233-2024

Işik N, Halifeoglu F (2020) The Importance of Material Analysis in Determining the Structural Problems of the Historical Deva Bath, Livre de Lyon publications.Işkan, H. (2020). Likya Birliği ve Eyaleti Başkenti: Patara. Lukkadan Likyaya: Sarpedon ve Aziz Nikolaosun Ülkesi (2.Baskı). Yapı Kredi Yayınları

Jordan-Palomar I, Tzortzopoulos P, García-Valldecabres J, Pellicer E (2018) Miras Bina Bilgi Modellemesi (HBIM) Kullanılarak Miras Bina Müdahalelerini Yönetme Protokolü. Sürdürülebilirlik 10(4):908. https://doi.org/10.3390/su10040908

Karaçar P, Benli G, Güner A (2022) Heritage building information system (HBIM) in project management of cultural heritage buildings. In: 7th international project and construction management conference (IPCMC2022). Yildiz Technical University, İstanbul, Turkey, pp 288–296

Karslı B, Yilmazturk F, Bahadir M, Ozdemir E, ve Karsli F (2022, 17–19, Kasım) Görüntü Eşleştirme ve LİDAR Tabanlı Nokta Bulutu Üzerinden Otomatik Bina Çıkarımı ve Sayısallaştırma. VIII. Uzaktan algılama-cbs sempozyumu, Ankara

Kaya R, Arda Ü, Kale E (2023) Serbest zaman ve wellness perspektifinden eski Roma hamamları [Ancient Roman baths from leisure time and wellness perspective]. Ankara Üniversitesi Beden Eğitimi ve Spor Yüksekokulu Spormetre Beden Eğitimi ve Spor Bilimleri Dergisi, 13–23. https://doi.org/10.33689/spormetre.1175886

Khan MS, Khan M, Bughio M, Talpur B, Kim I, Seo J (2022) An integrated HBIM framework for the management of heritage buildings. Buildings 12:964. https://doi.org/10.3390/buildings12070964

Kushwaha SKP, Dayal KR, Sachi S, Raghavendra S, Pande H, Tiwari P, Agarwal S, Srivastav S (2020) 3D digital documentation of a cultural heritage site using terrestrial laser scanner a case study. https://doi.org/10.1007/978-981-13-7067-0_3

Maietti F (2023) Heritage enhancement through digital tools for sustainable fruition: a conceptual framework. https://doi.org/10.20944/preprints202305.1283.v1

Mazzei A, Martinelli L, Empler T, Cessari L, Gigliarelli E (2024) Modelling for uncertainty in HBIM processes. Vitruvio—Int J Arch Technol Sustain 9. https://doi.org/10.4995/vitruvio-ijats.2024.22093

Orhan S (2023) Patara Nero Hamamı Tepidarium Kapısı. Akdeniz İnsani Bilimler Dergisi 13:231–248. https://doi.org/10.13114/MJH.2023.603

Öner E (1997) Eşen Çayı Taslun-Delta Ovasının Jeomorfolojisi ve Antik Patara Limanı. Ege Coğrafya Dergisi 9(1)

Oostwegel L JN, Jaud Š, Muhič S, Malovrh Rebec K (2022) Digitalization of culturally significant buildings: ensuring high-quality data exchanges in the heritage domain using OpenBIM. Heritage Sci 10(1):10

Palomar JI, Valldecabres GJ, Tzortzopoulos P, Pellicer E (2020) An online platform to unify and synchronise heritage architecture information. Autom Constr 110:1–17. https://doi.org/10.1016/j.autcon.2019.103008

Penjor T, Banihashemi S, Hajirasouli A, Golzad H (2024) Heritage building information modeling (HBIM) for heritage conservation: framework of challenges, gaps, and existing limitations of HBIM. Digit Appl Archaeol Cult Herit 35:e00366. https://doi.org/10.1016/j.daach.2024.e00366

Quintero M, Awad R, Barazetti L (2020) Harnessing digital workflows for the understanding, promotion and participation in the conservation of heritage sites by meeting both ethical and technical challenges. Built Herit 4:6. https://doi.org/10.1186/s43238-020-00005-7

Sewasew Y (2024) Historic building information modeling (HBIM) supported material passport for sustainable urban heritage conservation: case study of Massawa, Eritrea

Tarak G, Agnihotri V (2021) Digital conservation: the application of advanced technologies in heritage conservation

Ulvi A, Hamal SNG (2024) A new technology for documentation cultural heritage with fast, practical, and cost-effective methods IPAD Pro LİDAR and data fusion. Research Square. https://doi.org/10.21203/rs.3.rs-4400658/v1

Wan Abdul Basir W, Ujang U, Majid Z (2023) Adaptation 4D and 5D BIM for BIM/GIS data integration in construction project management. In: IOP conference series: earth and environmental science, vol 1274, pp 012002. https://doi.org/10.1088/1755-1315/1274/1/012002

Yoruk MS (2025) Dijital mirasın rekonstrüksiyonu sürecinde HBIM metodolojisine dayanan bir yaklaşım önerisi. [Master's thesis, Antalya Bilim University]. National Thesis Center of Turkey

# Chapter 3
# Representing Spatial and Contextual Information About Megalithic Monuments and the Landscape: A Knowledge-Graph Approach

**Ariele Câmara, Ana de Almeida, and João Oliveira**

**Abstract** Vectorized Topographic Maps (VTMs) offer standardized and comprehensive information crucial for researchers across various disciplines, including the social and natural sciences. With VTMs, it is possible to delineate both natural and man-made features over time and space, encompassing water lines, relief areas, soil types, and soil uses. Understanding spatial environments is integral for the recognition and preservation of cultural heritage. Despite digitization, analyzing archaeological data alongside topographic maps remains labor-intensive. Knowledge Graphs represent, organize, and semantically link diverse data types, offering a solution and facilitating semantic querying for enhanced analysis. A method to integrate vector geographic features and archaeological data into a labeled property graph is proposed. This study uses CIDOC-CRM and GeoSPARQL ontologies as the backbone to enable easy querying and visualization to discern patterns related to monument localization. The approach is validated using megalithic monuments—dolmens—in Pavia-Mora (Portugal), and official VTMs from various national organizations. This study demonstrates the effective representation and querying of multiple data types, thus contributing to the discovery of patterns and the inference of knowledge about the dolmens localizations. This, in turn, could be instrumental in improving the recognition and preservation of these monuments.

---

A. Câmara (✉) · A. de Almeida · J. Oliveira
Instituto Universitário de Lisboa (ISCTE-IUL), ISTAR, Lisbon, Portugal
e-mail: acaer@iscte-iul.pt

A. de Almeida
e-mail: ana.almeida@iscte-iul.pt

J. Oliveira
e-mail: joao.p.oliveira@iscte-iul.pt

A. de Almeida
Centre for Informatics and Systems of the University of Coimbra (CISUC), Coimbra, Portugal

J. Oliveira
Instituto de Telecomunicações, Lisboa, Portugal

 
S. Stellacci and S. Aydin (eds.), *Endangered Heritage Sites*, Springer Series on Cultural Computing, https://doi.org/10.1007/978-3-031-91949-7_3

**Keywords** Vectorized topographic maps · Archaeological remains · Megalithic monuments · Knowledge graphs · Digital humanities · Pavia-Mora

## 3.1 Introduction

Integrating contextual information with geospatial data on cultural heritage and landscape entails understanding and connecting diverse datasets (Verdonck et al. 2019). Knowledge Graphs (KGs) and Labeled Property Graphs (LPGs) can significantly enhance this process by facilitating the analysis of various data formats and information from multiple sources. They enable the representation and exploration of relationships between the context and spatial relations of all geographic entities represented (Câmara et al. 2022). Geospatial data can be classified into two primary types: raster data, such as satellite imagery or elevation models, and vector data, representing discrete features, and are commonly analyzed using Geographic Information Systems (GIS) (Shbita et al. 2022). On the other hand, archaeological information is typically accessed in semantic form, which involves understanding and categorizing artefacts, structures, and historical records, often represented in a non-structured or semi-structured format.

Furthermore, it is crucial to emphasize that both cultural heritage and landscape representations utilize vector data to capture precise spatial locations (Câmara and Batista 2017). Vector data plays a crucial role in representing discrete features of the landscape from the real world, such as rivers, elevations, soil types, and archaeological monuments. These data are commonly packaged into Vectorized Topographic Maps (VTMs), facilitating efficient storage and transmission for web mapping applications. VTMs encode features as geometries, including points, lines, and polygons. Points represent individual geographic locations, while lines represent linear features such as rivers. Polygons, on the other hand, represent enclosed areas like water bodies (Shbita et al. 2022). However, despite the effectiveness of GIS in analyzing and manipulating geospatial data, they have limitations in handling unstructured or semantic data. Moreover, GIS may lack adequate support for reasoning and inference, limiting their ability to uncover hidden patterns or make predictions about complex phenomena. One promising approach to address these limitations is to generate and interlink geospatial entities from vector data with external entities that provide contextual and semantic information. By presenting spatial features semantically with contextual information about cultural heritage in a linked and structured way, a deeper understanding of the relationships of the object with the landscape can be achieved.

This research presents an approach to represent VTMs within LPGs and extends the LPG implemented in Câmara et al. (2024), which represents the semantic information about dolmens in Pavia, in the Mora region of Portugal. For this extension, various vector maps covering the total area of Pavia (185 $km^2$) depicting landscape details of this Portuguese city have been used. The maps contain spatial information and feature descriptions about local hydrography, hypsometry, soil types, border contour, soil use, and the locations of dolmens. This approach was tailored to represent landscape entities characterized as important for the recognition of dolmens within the analyzed Area Of Interest (AOI), where classification keys were defined to recognize dolmens through photointerpretation, as delineated in a previous work by Câmara (2017). Once the VTMs are converted into linked data, it is possible to identify spatial–temporal and or contextual patterns or changes between the entities, gaining a deeper understanding of the entities represented.

This approach enables the quick obtention of answers to complex queries, such as investigating the interrelationships between the monuments, the surrounding landscape, and the evolution of land use over time, offering valuable insights for identifying patterns that facilitate the recognition of AOIs that could be its monument. Using this approach, it is possible to access geospatial data and contextualized information about the geographic features represented, and queries can be handled using both types of data. This enables the extraction of insights to be used, for example, to identify areas with a higher likelihood of containing additional monuments, thereby guiding fieldwork efforts such as the prospecting for unidentified monuments. Additionally, this approach can also be utilized to preserve and manage cultural heritage.

## 3.2 Knowledge Graph to Represent Archaeological and Landscape Data

To represent spatial information, GIS systems have been used for decades to represent and analyze cultural-historical and archaeological data, but they have typically prioritized visual symbols over integrating rich contextual object descriptions. Conversely, archives, libraries, and museums store contextual information, with detailed historical records yet with limited spatial determination, relying on the language of the source or local context. This poses challenges when users need both types of data to use in the implementation of automated systems, "*The fact that "people know quite well where the Parthenon lies" or "you'll see it when you go to Athens" is not helpful for today's IT systems*" (Hiebel et al. 2017, p. 272). The separation and lack of integration between spatial data and contextual information on the same object poses significant challenges for the analysis and interpretation of these data and the extraction of knowledge. The use of knowledge-based models to represent spatial and contextual knowledge as linked data is an effective approach in remote sensing and cultural heritage and have been applied to standardize information and improve accessibility and interoperability.

Knowledge graphs are a powerful framework for representing knowledge in a semantically structured and interconnected manner. At its core, a KG consists of nodes representing entities and relationships representing connections between these entities. Each entity is uniquely identified within the graph and may have associated attributes or properties which describe specific characteristics or qualities. Properties enrich the representation by providing additional context and information about the entities and relationships. The relationships between entities capture semantic connections, defining the context and meaning of the entities within the graph. This can be formally symbolized by KG = $(V,E,A)$, where $V$ represents the set of or nodes or vertices, $E$ represents the set of or relationships formally known as edges, and $A$ represents the set of attributes associated with the $V$ and $E$ in an LPG. Instances of these entities and relationships populate the KG, forming a rich interconnected web of information, enabling sophisticated querying, reasoning, and inference, facilitating comprehensive exploration and insights derived from the interconnected information (Robinson et al. 2015).

Central to this initiative is the development of ontologies, which are conceptual frameworks that define classes and relationships within specific domains. Notably, ontologies primarily focus on metadata—the structure and semantics of the data—rather than specific data instances. Separate ontologies have emerged to address the unique characteristics of each data type: spatial and cultural. For instance, the CIDOC Conceptual Reference Model (CIDOC-CRM) ontology (Bekiari et al. 2021), an ISO standard, was tailored for cultural heritage information, while the GeoSPARQL ontology (Perry and Herring 2012), also an ISO standard, was designed for spatial information. The CRMgeo (Hiebel et al. 2017) is an extension of the CIDOC-CRM ontology that facilitates its integration with GeoSPARQL. The CIDOC-CRM and its extensions have been successfully applied to represent archaeological buildings by knowledge graphs, in several studies, by Garozzo et al. (2017); Gergatsoulis et al. (2021); Santos et al. (2022); and Câmara et al. (2024). Filzwieser and Eichert (2020) developed a model focusing on representing geospatial and archaeological data. The use of these three ontologies has been successfully applied to deal with spatio-temporal reasoning of cultural heritage data (Doer et al. 2013; Nys et al. 2018). On the other hand, to access information about the landscape there are already popular general knowledge graphs such as Wikidata (Hernández et al. 2016), DBpedia, and OpenStreetMap, which contain data on geographic entities and much more. Additionally, several other knowledge graphs have been recently implemented to represent landscape features, such as GeoLink[1] (Cheatham et al. 2018), Geonames[2] (GeoNames n.d.), KnowWhereGraph[3] (Janowicz et al. 2022), and LinkedGeoData.[4] However, their coverage of geographic information is limited, as they may not offer the same level of granularity as national/local VTMs, particularly regarding detailed landscape features and local context. Semantic representations of vector maps as a knowledge graph present inherent challenges due to the large, heterogeneous, and

[1] GeoLink addresses the challenges of integrating and accessing disparate geoscience datasets by developing a unified semantic framework, for representing earth science knowledge.

[2] Geonames provides access to information about geographic features but lacks detailed information about terrain features such as soil use, relief, and water lines.

[3] KnowWhereGraph focuses solely on the United States and its territories, supporting pilot scenarios in disaster relief, agricultural land use, and food-related supply chains.

[4] LinkedGeoData aims to create a comprehensive spatial knowledge graph by converting OpenStreetMap data into RDF format.

ambiguous schema, and several recent projects are addressing this issue (Dsouza et al. 2021; Mai et al. 2022; Shbita et al. 2022; Wang et al. 2019; Zhang et al. 2022).

All the diverse implementations illustrate the growing interest and efforts in using KGs to represent contextual and spatial knowledge about archaeological monuments, addressing the challenges of data heterogeneity and interoperability. However, to the best of our knowledge, no other work has focused on the joint representation of geospatial data with contextual information of archaeological monuments with landscape elements obtained from texts and VTMs data, as proposed. Compared to other studies undertaken by the authors, this study focuses on the representation of spatial features and their descriptions extracted from the VTMs pertaining to landscape elements and dolmen points.

## 3.3 Methodology

This section delves into the methodological approach, emphasizing the integration and representation of geospatial data sourced from VTMs with the semantic context of archaeological monuments, specifically dolmens. The approach builds upon the model outlined by Câmara et al. (2024), but expands its scope by incorporating spatial information primarily sourced from VTMs. The primary motivation behind correlating landscape data with archaeological information, with a focus on spatial relationships and conceptual descriptions of each element, is to provide a framework for understanding the surrounding environment of each monument across large areas. The overarching objective is to construct a comprehensive LPG that encapsulates the multidimensional aspects of different entity types, focusing on understanding how they are related. The AOI and the VTM data used in this research are also outlined. Next, the LPG is presented, encompassing the schema model, ontologies, and information retrieval and findings. These elements collectively improve the ability to analyze the data effectively.

### *3.3.1 Area of Interest*

The region of Pavia in the municipality of Mora in Portugal's Alentejo region stands out as the study area. Renowned for hosting one of the highest concentrations of megalithic monuments in Europe, this region has garnered significant attention in recent years, particularly regarding the preservation of these monuments. This concern has prompted action, with an order issued to classify and protect them, proposing the classification of 2049 monuments spread across neighboring municipalities (Official Gazette No. 39/2022, Series 2 of 25/02/2022). Among these monuments are dolmens, which are characterized by a chamber formed by orthostats supporting capstones, often encased in earth and stone to create burial mounds. In

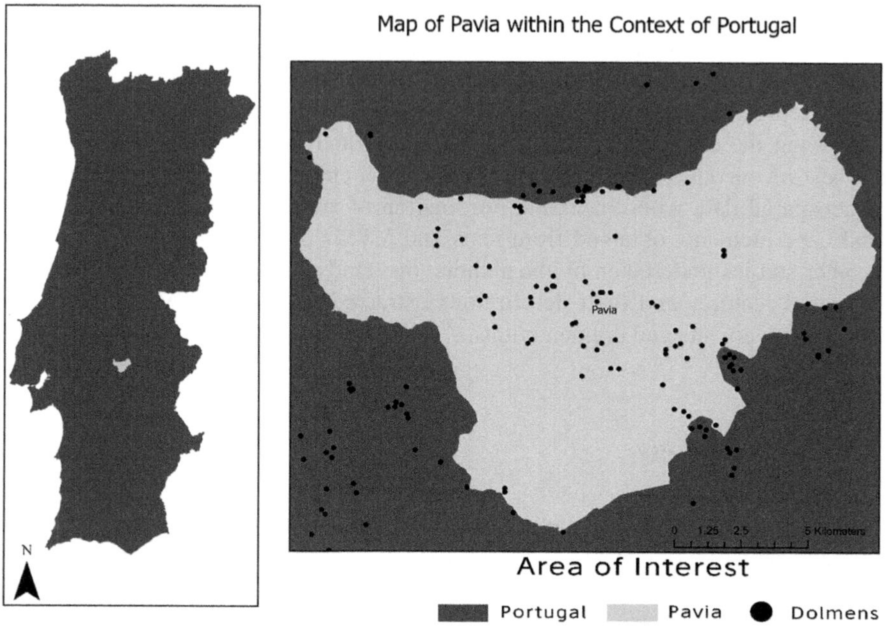


**Fig. 3.1** Map of Portugal and the locations of dolmens in Pavia (own elaboration)

the Alentejo region, these structures typically span 2–5 m in diameter and are predominantly crafted from granite or schist (Câmara 2017, 2024). In this work, 94 unique dolmens were identified (Fig. 3.1).

The Pavia region boasts a diverse geological and geomorphological landscape, comprising mainly granitic and schistose rocks interspersed with quartzites and metamorphic formations, making it one of Portugal's most expansive plateau regions (Rocha 1999; Zbyszewski et al. 1979). This area features a relatively uniform topography, with elevation levels ranging between 50 to 300 m and an average altitude of approximately 200 m, sculpted over time by gradual erosion caused by water currents (Ferreira 2000). The landscape is characterized by elongated relief features, gentle slopes, and meandering watercourses, interspersed with agricultural lands predominantly cultivating cereal crops, olive groves, and vineyards. Hydrologically, the Central Alentejo region encompasses the three major river basins in southern Portugal (Tejo, Guadiana, and Sado), with the area under study primarily associated with the Tejo basin. This diverse landscape played a pivotal role in shaping the settlement patterns of prehistoric communities and influenced the construction of megalithic monuments (Câmara 2017).

**Table 3.1** Overview of the vectorized topographic maps (VTMs) used in this research

| VTMs Data | Data Description | Source | Format |
|---|---|---|---|
| Borders | The Official Administrative Map of Portugal 2023 | DGT[6] | Polygon |
| Soil use | The Land Use and Occupation Map (COS) of Portugal | DGT | MultiPolygon |
| Soil type | The Soil Type of southern Portugal | DGADR | MultiPolygon |
| Contour line | Map of the Mora from municipality of Mora | Municipality of Mora | Line |
| Water line | Water masses on mainland Portugal | SNIAmb[7] | Line |
| Monuments | Localization of dolmens | (Archaeologist's Portal n.d.) | Point |

### 3.3.2 *VTMs Data*

The selection of landscape elements to be analyzed was guided by previous research that established classification keys for identifying dolmens in the AOI through the interpretation of satellite images (Câmara 2017). Understanding natural elements such as hydrography, hypsometry, soil type, and land use within the landscape is crucial, as they often indicate areas with a higher likelihood of megalithic monuments' existence. The table remains also indicate that the roof of the Frigidarium section was constructed with a vaulted ceiling approximately 10 m in diameter. Compared with other known examples of Roman bath architecture, an analysis of the side walls also suggests that a barrel-shaped roof enclosed the vault. It is likely that the roof incorporated a tile covering supported by wooden beams (Fig. 2.4, *bottom*).

Table 3.1 provides an overview of the VTMs utilized in the project. Each VTM (.shp) was sourced from different databases, all of which are openly accessible, except for the chart map from DGADR[5] and the Municipality of Mora. The two VTMs that are not openly available were obtained and authorized for use in the project by the respective organizations.

The VTMs analyzed were acquired at a scale of 1:25,000, except for the vector map depicting contour lines, which was at a scale of 1:10,000. ArcGIS Pro Desktop was employed to extract the data from each VTM, providing seamless access to shapefile archives and streamlining the extraction of embedded cartographic knowledge. Each vector map contained spatial and detailed attribute information about the geographic features represented, enhancing the understanding of the landscape.

[5] Direção-Geral de Agricultura e Desenvolvimento Rural (DGADR) standing for General Directorate of Agriculture and Rural Development.

[6] Direção Geral do Território (DGT) standing for General Directorate for Territory.

[7] SNIAMB—Sistema Nacional de Informação Ambiental, meaning "National Environmental Information System". Other information: https://sniamb.apambiente.pt/.

A crucial aspect of this process involved consistently identifying and applying the ISO-8859-1 Unicode Encoding across all datasets. Additionally, for the Coordinate Reference System (CRS), the projection utilized was EPSG:3726 (WGS 84), ensuring standardization across all datasets.

### 3.3.3 Main Structure—LPG

As seen in the previous section (Sect. 3.5), the study analyzed each VTM, extracted its geometries, and mapped all feature descriptions. Subsequently, the LPG implementation presented in (Câmara et al. 2024) was extended to represent the spatial information extracted from the VTMs, with their feature descriptions as instances in a semantic and interconnected manner. LPGs encapsulate key-value pairs, known as properties, associated with nodes and relationships (Robinson et al. 2015), facilitating more concise queries compared to atomic-node RDF graphs and enabling seamless execution of queries involving multiple levels of relationships among instances (Stanescu 2021). Neo4J Desktop (version 1.5.6) was chosen for data integration. Neo4J is a schema-free native graph database management system (NGDB). It represents all information using its language, Cypher, for representation, search, and retrieval, supporting spatial geometry in the form of points linked to a specific CRS that needs to be represented as values in the Cartesian or WGS-84. All geometry data was represented as Well-Known Text (WKT) by converting all vertices into points and morphing them into arrays for representation in the LPG. To facilitate data transfer, it was converted it into a tabular format for bulk loading, aligning with the defined schema model.

### 3.3.4 Schema Definition

The LPG schema model is constructed using established ontologies, including CIDOC-CRM, its extension CRMgeo, and GeoSPARQL, as the foundation of the model. Predefined classes and relationships from these ontologies are utilized as labels within the LPG to maintain vocabulary consistency and enhance interoperability. In CIDOC-CRM and CRMgeo, classes and relationships (referred to as properties in CRM) are identified by numbers preceded by letters. For instance, classes in CIDOC-CRM are identified with the letter "E" (e.g., E28), while in CRMgeo, the letters "SP" are used. Relationship identifiers in CIDOC-CRM use the letter "P" (e.g., P1), whereas in CRMgeo, the letter "*Q*" is applied. Class names are formed using nominal groups with initial capitals (e.g., E28 Conceptual Object). In contrast, property names are written in lowercase as verbal phrases in both directions (e.g.,

P1 is identified by (P1 identifies)). Properties are named in parenthetical and non-parenthetical forms, with the non-parenthetical form indicating the domain-to-range direction and the parenthetical form indicating the range-to-domain direction.[8]

While primarily using classes from CIDOC-CRM, a limitation in geometry representation has been found, prompting the incorporation of three classes, one relationship from its CRMgeo extension, and two relationships from GeoSPARQL. This adaptation enabled the comprehensive representation of all aspects of geometry extracted from vector cartography. Additionally, addressing the absence of standards in these ontologies for denoting proximity, a custom relationship labeled '*nearby*' was introduced. This relationship allows for the representation of the distance between entity *X* and entity *Y*, as the goal is to retrieve the distance between geographic entities when disconnected. This bespoke relationship facilitates linking E94 Space Primitive entities that are spatially close to one another, enabling precise determination of spatial relationships, with nuanced characteristics inserted as properties of the relationships. Currently, the topological spatial relations are represented using "*Nearby*" and "*within*" which connect two nodes E94. The distance between each element can be calculated and inserted as a property of the relationship. To further enhance the representation of geospatial data contained within each VTM, including dimensions of areas, angles in the image, lengths, and vertex parts, a specific class labeled "*C1 Geometry Extract from Maps*" was created to maintain all knowledge pertaining to this data type. This class allows for the insertion of geometry descriptions from VTMs as properties, utilizing a set of eight key sets for data value insertion: Area_Hectares, Distance, Angle, Length, and Identification of vertex positions (Vertex_Index, Vertex_Part, Vertex_Part_Index)[9]—features that describe the geometric entities represented.

To represent the data from VTMs as instances in the LPG, three key components were employed: (i) *metadata definitions*; (ii) *general and individual concepts*; and (iii) *geometry* (as shown in Fig. 3.2). *Metadata definitions* are information regarding the sources from which the data originated. This is crucial for facilitating accessibility and proper data citation by other researchers, thereby promoting data reuse. When representing concepts, these were categorized into general and specific categories. *General concepts* serve as broad categories encompassing a diverse range of examples, providing a foundational framework for understanding various instances within their scope. For example, general concepts such as "*rivers*" were used in categorizing "Water Lines" types. Conversely, *individual concepts* denote specific occurrences of a general concept within the data model. They represent concrete entities, such as the "*Matalote River*" course, along with associated specifications/parameters like *dimension* and/or *chemical condition state*. Each concept, whether general or individual, was represented using terminology consistent with that found

[8] For further details on CIDOC-CRM refer to Bekiari et al. (2021), and for CRMgeo see Hiebel et al. (2017).

[9] Identification of vertex positions describes a vertex's position in a geometric shape, including the index in the sequence of vertices (Vertex_Index), the part of the geometric shape (Vertex_Part), and the position within that part (Vertex_Part_Index).

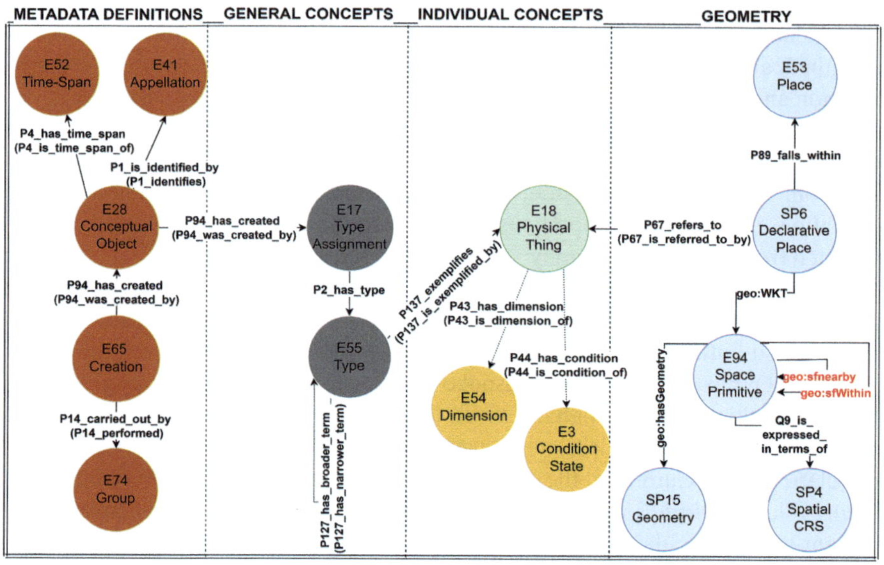


**Fig. 3.2** LPG model used in the study to represent the VTMs (own elaboration)

in the data source. Finally, the spatial data of each entity was incorporated into the LPG, including the designations assigned to locations by their respective sources, alongside coordinates extracted from geometries. Each geometry corresponds to a spatial description encoded as a WKT representation, either as a point, line, or polygon.

The schema devised for representing vector cartography data, as illustrated in Fig. 3.2 treats the VTM as a conceptual object (E28) designed to represent physical entities. Within this schema, instances within the cartography are regarded as physical objects (E18), allowing for the detailed representation of individual features. General concepts of the represented physical objects are described as type assignments (E17). To establish the relationship between the entities extracted from the VTM and their geometry, the SP6 class of CRMgeo is used to denote location as per the cartography, thereby extending to represent the geometry of the depicted objects. The schema design employs the E28 class and its surrounding classes (shown in orange in Fig. 3.2) for metadata definitions. In contrast, the E17 class and its adjacent classes (grey) are used for general concept representation. Individual concepts are represented using the E18 class (green), and the SP6 class and its neighboring classes are utilized for location representation (blue). This approach ensures a standardized representation of both geography and geometry for landscape data.

To thoroughly examine spatial relationships across the expansive study area, a structured grid methodology was implemented to segment and explore the AOI. The entire area was systematically divided into a consistent grid format, resulting in 150 individual cells. The grid was initially created in GIS and then transformed into a VTM, allowing for semantic representation in the LPG. This structured grid seamlessly integrates with landscape data, ensuring alignment with existing datasets and offering a comprehensive representation of the study region. This approach presents numerous advantages. Firstly, grid segmentation enables the analysis of spatial patterns and relationships at a granular resolution, facilitating the detection of subtle variations and localized phenomena within the study area. This methodology streamlines the analysis process by prioritizing searches within each grid cell or its vicinity, avoiding exhaustive searches across all entities and focusing instead on localized regions of interest. The uniform grid structure facilitates comparisons across different parts of the region, thereby enhancing the ability to identify spatial correlations between landscape features.

The geographical features within the landscape studied are intricately intertwined with the monuments through their spatial positioning. This holistic approach allows for detailed queries encompassing both spatial and contextual aspects, offering semantic descriptions of the archaeological monuments and landscape within the AOI. The spatial relationships provide valuable insights into how the monuments interact with their surrounding environment, highlighting their contextual significance. Moreover, this methodology is a robust foundation for conducting complex spatial analyses. Consequently, the model is utilized to identify patterns that aid in pinpointing areas more likely to contain these structures. To ensure the validity of the findings, the data analysis results are cross-referenced with photointerpretation of the monuments within the study area, ensuring consistency.

## 3.4 Information Retrieval

The provided LPG was implemented with the primary objective of analyzing spatial relationships among dolmens within their surrounding landscape. Serving as a repository for associated data sources of each general concept, the LPG facilitates comprehensive analysis and interpretation of these different layers of data—since each VTM is represented as a subgraph that can be connected with another subgraph that contains the information about the dolmens. The topological spatial interactions between the entities are derived from the analysis between the entities and represented as properties within the relationships. Embedding the relationships with information derived from the original data as properties ensures a clear distinction between raw data extracted from original sources—such as metadata definitions, general and individual concepts, and geometry (represented as properties within the nodes)—and derived information, such as the distances between two entities (represented as properties within the relationships). Thus, this LPG provides a clear demarcation between raw data and insights derived from subsequent analyses or inferences. Integrating derived topological spatial relationships into the LPG significantly enriches the model, allowing the correlation of all subgraphs through the localization of each entity represented by the CRS (E94). This is shown in Fig. 3.3, which displays information on how the dolmen Anta Capela de S. Dinis (D11) is related to the landscape.

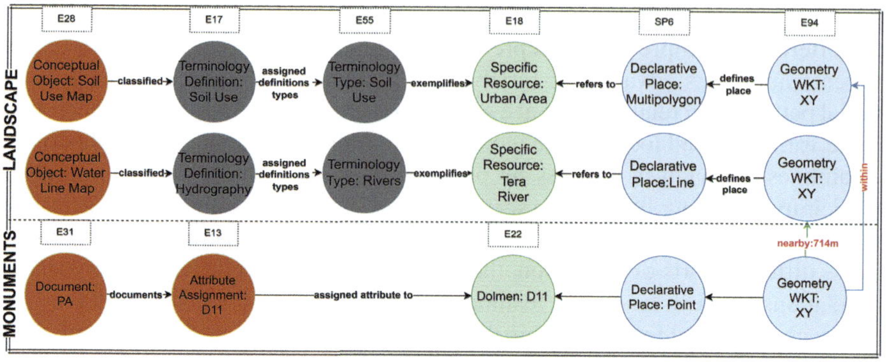


**Fig. 3.3** Graph representation at the instances level: In orange, the data source; in grey, the general concepts; in green, the individual concepts; and in blue, spatial location elements (own elaboration)

This color scheme applies to both monuments and landscape information. The key-value pair representing each node is shown in Fig. 3.3. Three subgraphs are connected spatially: one with archaeological monuments, one with waterline data, and one with local land use data.

The instances of D11, sourced from Archaeological Portal (PA) data, the instances of the water line next to D11, and the land use where D11 is situated, derived from vector cartographies, are retrieved, as indicated by the different colors (orange) on the left side. The spatial relationships are identified in red (*within* and *nearby*), reflecting the spatial connections between the entities, with the latter containing properties indicating the distance between nodes. The *within* relationships are created when an entity represented by a point is inside an entity represented by polygons, while n*earby* is created when an entity represented by a point is related to another entity represented by a point, line, or polygon when the domain entity is outside the range entity but nearby. The relationship of both instances of D11 with the surrounding landscape entities is consistent, as indicated by proximity to the Tera River at about 714 m from the dolmen and its location in an urban area, in Pavia center city. Additionally, the search could be extended to retrieve how a monument relates to other elements of the landscape, such as the local relief, land use in different time periods (1995, 2007, 2010, 2015, or 2018), soil types, or its relationship with other nearby monuments.

In the assessment of the LPG, its semantic capabilities for information retrieval were explored with the aim of understanding the intricate relationships that exist. By crafting queries with multiple relationships, nuanced connections within the data have been understood. Notably, regardless of the complexity of the relationships queried, all information was retrieved with remarkable speed and processed in mere milliseconds. For instance, using Cypher queries, it was possible to retrieve specific information about individual monuments, such as entity D11, as well as discover broader insights. This is exemplified by Query 1 (Table 3.2), where all dolmens described as "destroyed" were targeted to analyze the predominant soil types in which they are located. The findings revealed a predominant presence of these dolmens in

**Table 3.2** Query 1: Dolmen distribution by soil type for the 'destroyed' category

```
MATCH Dolmen=( E22DolmenDomain:E22_Human_Made_Object)-[P55Dolmen:P55_has_
current_location]->(SP6Dolmen:SP6_Declarative_Place)-[P168Dolmen:P168_place_is_
defined_by]->(E94Dolmen:E94_Space_Primitive),
DolmenDomainCondition=(E22DolmenDomain)-[P46DolmenDomain:P46_is_composed_
of]->(E22ChamberDolmenDomain:E22_Human_Made_Object)-[P44DolmenDomain:P44_
has_condition]->(E3DolmenDomain:E3_Condition_State),
SoilType=(:E17_Type_Assigment {E17TerminologyDefinition: "Tipo de Solo"})-[:P2A1_
assigned_definition_types]->(E55SoilType:E55_Type)-[:P137_is_exemplified_
by]->(E18SoilType:E18_Phisical_Thing)-[P67SoilType:P67_is_referred_to_
by]->(SP6SoilType:SP6_Declarative_Place)-[P168SoilType:P168_place_is_defined_
by]->(E94SoilType:E94_Space_Primitive)<-[SoilTypeWithin:sfWithin]-(E94Dolmen)
WHERE E54TypeOfDimensionDolmenDomain.E54TypeOfDimension="Diameter" AND
E22ChamberDolmenDomain.E22DolmenComponent="Chamber" AND
E3DolmenDomain.E3ConditionState="destroyed"
RETURN COLLECT (E22DolmenDomain.E22Dolmen) AS DolmenName, COUNT
(E22DolmenDomain) AS DolmenNumber, E18SoilType.E18SpecificResource AS SoilType,
E3DolmenDomain.E3ConditionState AS Condition
```

Gneiss or similar rocks, brown Mediterranean soils (pgn), and Lithic, Non-Humic, Slightly Unsaturated, Normal (pg), granite soils.

The results included dolmen names, the number of dolmens in each soil type, and corresponding soil types for detailed analysis, as shown in Table 3.3. The analyses identified the characteristics of the area of interest for the dolmens recorded as destroyed. Such insights can help understand distribution patterns across different soil types and their potential correlations with conservation status.

By representing domain knowledge in a linked manner and focusing on the representation of instances in a granular way, flexibility to explore the relationships among entities through both general and specific analyses is achieved, thanks to the granular nature of the knowledge representation. This approach transcends the confines of mere monument data and reveals intricate patterns in their interaction with the surrounding landscape by correlating contextual data about the monuments with geospatial data from vector maps. Consequently, it fosters a more comprehensive interpretation of the dynamic interplay between dolmens and their environmental context. Through this perspective, recurring patterns among dolmens are discerned, illuminating their intrinsic connection with the broader landscape.

## 3.5 Research Findings

Based on the information retrieval of dolmens' interactions with their environmental contexts, the findings indicate the entities with which dolmens are generally associated, considering the surrounding landscape. This enabled the identification of predominant patterns, such as the proximity of dolmen structures to each other, as well as their interactions with soil type, land use, elevation, and hydrography.

**Table 3.3** Query results: dolmen names, quantity of dolmen per soil type and soil type designation

| Dolmen name | No. dolmen | Soil code | Soil type description |
|---|---|---|---|
| ["Outeiro da Forca"] | 1 | "Pdg" | *Lightly Unsaturated Argilluviated Soils* Mediterranean, Brown Soils, from Non-Calcareous Materials, Para-Hydromorphic Soils, from Arkoses or Similar Rocks |
| ["Têra 4"] | 1 | "Pmg" | *Lightly Unsaturated Argilluviated Soils* Mediterranean, Brown Soils, from Non-Calcareous Materials, Normal, from Quartzodiorites |
| ["Entreáguas 4; Anta do Forno"] | 1 | "Sr" | *Lightly Unsaturated Argilluviated Soils* Mediterranean, Red or Yellow Soils, from Non-Calcareous Materials, Normal, from 'rañas' or Similar Deposits |
| ["Forca Velha"] | 1 | "Pm" | *Lightly Unsaturated Argilluviated Soils:* Mediterranean, Brown Soils, from Non-Calcareous Materials, Para-Clays, from Diorites, Quartzodiorites, or Similar Microphaneritic or Crystallophilic Rocks |
| ["Folha da Anta"] | 1 | "A" | *Incipient Soils:* Modern Alluviosols, Non-Calcareous, with Medium Texture |
| ["Entreáguas 3"] | 1 | "Vt" | *Litólicos, Não Húmicos, Pouco Insaturados Normais, de arenitos grosseiros* |
| ["Matalote 1", "Freixo"] | 2 | "Pg, Arg" | *Litholic, Non-Humic, Lightly Unsaturated Normal Soils, from Coarse Sandstones* |
| ["Pucícaros 2", "Pucícaros 1"] | 2 | "Pdc, Pdg" | *Lightly Unsaturated Argilluviated Soils*: Mediterranean, Brown Soils, from Non-Calcareous Materials, Para-Hydromorphic Soils, from Arkoses or Similar Rocks/Rock Outcrop of Granites or Quartzodiorites |
| ["Monte das Figueiras", "Têra 5", "Madre de Deus 1", "Casa Branca 2"] | 4 | "Pg" | *Lowly Unsaturated Argilluviated Soils:* Mediterranean, Brown Soils, Composed of Non-Calcareous Materials, Hydromorphic Soils, with Arcoses or Related Rocks |
| ["Oliveira 2; Anta do Cabeço da Anta", "Adua 5", "Gonçala 2", "Ferragial da Fonte"] | 4 | "Pgn" | *Lowly Unsaturated Argilluviated Soils*: Mediterranean, Brown Soils, Made of Non-Calcareous Materials, Hydromorphic Soils, with Arcoses or Related Rocks |

To verify the accuracy of the relationships represented in the graph, the graph was traversed in search of patterns to compare with a previous study conducted by Câmara (2017).

Firstly, the results indicate that dolmens are mainly situated at an average distance of 308 m from each other, with clustering being the norm, albeit with occasional isolated instances. Only four exceptions to this clustering pattern were observed within the AOI, where dolmens were found more than 1 km apart. Overall, an average of three dolmens per km area was found. Secondly, the analysis reveals a consistent association between dolmens and water sources, as well as specific soil types characterized by rock outcrops and relief areas. Dolmens are typically located within close proximity to natural water sources, with an average distance of 417 m. This underscores the significant role of water availability in the placement and contextualization of these structures. Moreover, the majority of dolmens (86%) are located within 1 km of drinkable water sources, indicating a prevalent pattern of water proximity. Such proximity often suggests the existence of potential dolmen clusters. However, it is important to acknowledge the dynamic nature of natural water lines over time, which may affect data interpretation.

The analysis of the relationship between dolmens and soil types reveals a strong preference for areas characterized by PG (Litholic Soils) and ARG (Rock Outcrops) soil types. These soil types are typically associated with granite substrates and rock outcrops, respectively, and are often found near dolmens. Even when dolmens are not directly situated within these soil types, they tend to be located within an average distance of less than 1 km. This preference for PG and ARG soils may be influenced by various practical and cultural factors, such as elevated vantage points, improved visibility, convenient access to rock materials, and reduced flood risks. On the other hand, the findings highlight a consistent trend wherein dolmens in Pavia are predominantly located at altitudes above 160 m. This distribution pattern corroborates longstanding theories suggesting prehistoric communities deliberately chose marginally elevated areas to erect their monuments. Reasons might include strategic visibility, cultural significance, or ritualistic practices linked to these slightly higher terrains.

Finally, the analysis of soil use patterns indicates that dolmens are frequently situated within areas characterized by vegetation, such as Holm Oak-based agroforestry systems and pastures. However, dense vegetation or forested regions may obscure the visibility of these ancient structures, posing challenges to their detection. Dolmens are rarely found in urban areas, likely due to modern construction layers or prior identification. Although the use of soil is not considered a definitive indicator of the presence of a monument, as these landscapes change rapidly, and dolmens are ancient structures, the information from land use maps represented as soil use can either facilitate or hinder the identification of these monuments. For example, if a monument is currently within a watercourse, it may no longer be visible. Furthermore, this information can be used for further analyses to understand if land use impacts archaeological monuments in any way.

In general, the LPG allows for delving into the broader context of dolmens, examining their interactions with the surrounding environment and shedding light on various aspects of dolmen positioning, including considerations of topographical features indicative of possible strategic significance, preferred soil types for construction, proximity to water sources, and relative dolmen density. By contextualizing all landscape elements relevant to monument recognition, these insights help uncover the factors that may have influenced the selection of the location of the dolmens or to recognize AOIs for analyzing and identifying previously unknown similar monuments. Furthermore, the model not only captures the common attributes of the monuments but also accentuates their unique individual features, offering a nuanced perspective on dolmen placement and its implications.

These findings were confirmed through a graph traversal within the implemented LPG, which involved a comprehensive analysis of all dolmen data and their relationships. The findings demonstrate that the results are similar, highlighting the advantage of this approach in swiftly comprehending the surrounding landscape when analyzing multiple monuments. While the previous work was time-consuming (Câmara 2017), this research enables the analysis of all spatial and contextual information using the graph in seconds. Actionable insights were derived by executing specific queries and conducting pattern analysis within the graph, and robust guidelines were established for recognizing and understanding dolmens within their environmental context. The traversal process entailed executing specific queries and conducting pattern analysis within the graph, allowing this information to be used as domain rules. Domain rules are sets of constraints that help to define the relations among different types of entities within a specific domain. Essentially, these rules act as a compass, guiding the integration, interpretation, and visualization of knowledge in an LPG, ensuring that the information is both coherent and contextually relevant. In the context of this study, the rules pertain to the relationships between landscape entities with the dolmens represented.

This model not only offers significant utility in representing data but also provides a robust framework for understanding how monuments relate to one another, guiding the analysis of archaeological monuments and their AOIs.

## 3.6 Conclusion and Future Works

The implementation of the LPG offers significant utility in contextualizing scenes and guiding the recognition of AOIs. For known monuments, the LPG provides invaluable insights into their features and potential visual limitations. For instance, when a monument represented in the LPG is known to be destroyed or submerged, it is understood that its visualization is not feasible. Similarly, it is known that only a mound of earth will be visible for monuments located beneath a burial mound. Conversely, in recognizing new monuments, the information stored in the LPG can be leveraged to identify AOIs where these monuments are most likely to be identified. Additionally, the LPG facilitates targeted searches for specific areas. For example, by analyzing a particular location, it can be determined if it exhibits similar patterns to other monuments, considered relevant entities that increase the likelihood of finding such an object. Using domain rules and insights from archaeological studies, the understanding of landscape characteristics is enhanced, and potential areas where dolmens are likely located are identified. This knowledge helps overcome limitations in visualization and contributes to more accurate and comprehensive analyses of archaeological sites.

In summary, the implementation of an LPG, grounded in widely accepted ontologies such as CIDOC-CRM, CRMgeo, and GeoSPARQL, demonstrated promising results for the integration of VTMs with semantic information related to archaeological monuments and their surrounding landscape. This LPG allows the possibility to query geographic features, general and individual concepts, and metadata definitions about archaeological monuments and landscape entities using spatial and contextual information. With these tools, it is possible to analyze different data types and spatiotemporal information semantically, enabling a comprehensive understanding of their interrelations. This approach facilitates efficient information retrieval and pattern analysis, enabling a nuanced understanding of how megalithic monuments are interconnected with landscape features.

The method effectively handles both geospatial and contextual data, providing valuable insights into monument interactions within their environmental context. This harmonization not only supports collaboration in cultural heritage preservation but also empowers archaeologists to analyze monument placement choices and their relationship with the natural landscape. Moreover, the approach offers significant potential beyond megalithic heritage, as the landscape information extracted from VTMs can be correlated with various entities represented in the LPG.

Moving forward, the integrated approach is designed to enhance scene contextualization and improve automated recognition accuracy. It provides a robust foundation for training automated systems using the knowledge embedded within the LPG.

**Acknowledgements** The authors would like to thank the municipality of Mora, Portugal, and to *Direção-Geral de Agricultura e Desenvolvimento Rura*l (DGADR) for their collaboration in providing access to the VTMs. These resources played a crucial role in enhancing the depth of the implemented Knowledge Graph.

This work was partially supported by *Fundação para a Ciência e Tecnologia* through ISTAR Projects with grant numbers UIDB/04466/2020 and UIDP/04466/2020 and through the scholarship UI/BD/151495/2021.

## References

Archaeologist's Portal (n.d.). Retrieved 4 Mar 2024, from https://arqueologia.patrimoniocultural.pt/

Bekiari C, Bruseker G, Doerr M, Ore CE, Stead S, Velios A (2021) Volume A: definition of the CIDOC conceptual reference model

Câmara A (2017) A fotointerpretação como recurso de prospeção arqueológica. Chaves para a identificação e interpretação de monumentos megalíticos no Alentejo: aplicação nos concelhos de Mora e Arraiolos [Universidade de Évora]. https://dspace.uevora.pt/rdpc/handle/10174/22054

Câmara A, de Almeida A, Caçador D, Oliveira J (2022) Automated methods for image detection of cultural heritage: overviews and perspectives. Archaeol Prospect. https://doi.org/10.1002/arp.1883

Câmara A, de Almeida A, Oliveira J (2024) Transforming the CIDOC-CRM model into a megalithic monument property graph. J Comput Appl Archaeol 7(1):213–224. https://doi.org/10.5334/jcaa.151

Cheatham M, Krisnadhi A, Amini R, Hitzler P, Janowicz K, Shepherd A, Narock T, Jones M, Ji P (2018) The GeoLink knowledge graph. Big Earth Data 2(2):131–143. https://doi.org/10.1080/20964471.2018.1469291

Doerr M, Hiebel G, Eide Ø (2013) CRMgeo: Linking the CIDOC CRM to geosparql through a spatiotemporal refinement. TECHNICAL REPORT: ICS-FORTH/TR-435

Dsouza A, Tempelmeier N, Yu R, Gottschalk S, Demidova E (2021) WorldKG: a world-scale geographic knowledge graph. In: Proceedings of the 30th ACM international conference on information & knowledge management, pp 4475–4484. https://doi.org/10.1145/3459637.3482023

Ferreira AMPJ (2000) Dados Geoquímicos de Base de Sedimentos Fluviais de Amostragem de Baixa Densidade de Portugal Continental: Estudo de Factores de Variação Regional. *Tese de Doutoramento. Universidade de Aveiro. Departamento de Geociências. Aveiro, I*(2)

Filzwieser R, Eichert S (2020) Towards an online database for archaeological landscapes. using the web based, open source software openatlas for the acquisition, analysis and dissemination of archaeological and historical data on a landscape basis. Heritage 3(4):1385–1401. https://doi.org/10.3390/heritage3040077

Garozzo R, Murabito F, Santagati C, Pino C, Spampinato C (2017) CULTO: an ontology-based annotation tool for data curation in cultural heritage. Int Arch Photogramm Remote Sens Spat Inf ScI. https://doi.org/10.5194/isprs-archives-XLII-2-W5-267-2017

GeoNames (n.d.). Retrieved 5 May 2024, from https://www.geonames.org/

Gergatsoulis M, Papaioannou G, Kalogeros E, Mpismpikopoulos I, Tsiouprou K, Carter R (2021) Modelling archaeological buildings using CIDOC-CRM and its extensions: the case of Fuwairit, Qatar. In Towards open and trustworthy digital societies 13133:357–372. https://doi.org/10.1007/978-3-030-91669-5_28/COVER

Hernández D, Hogan A, Riveros C, Rojas C, Zerega E (2016) Querying Wikidata: comparing SPARQL, relational and graph databases. In: Lecture notes in computer science (including subseries lecture notes in artificial intelligence and lecture notes in bioinformatics) 9982:88–103. https://doi.org/10.1007/978-3-319-46547-0_10/FIGURES/7

Hiebel G, Doerr M, Eide Ø (2017) CRMgeo: a spatiotemporal extension of CIDOC-CRM. Int J Digit Libr 18(4):271–279. https://doi.org/10.1007/S00799-016-0192-4/FIGURES/6

Janowicz K, Hitzler P, Li W, Rehberger D, Schildhauer M, Zhu R, Shimizu C, Fisher CK, Cai L, Mai G, Zalewski J, Zhou L, Stephen S, Gonzalez S, Mecum B, Lopez-Carr A, Schroeder A, Smith D, Wright D, Currier K (2022) Know, Know Where, Know Where Graph: a densely connected, cross-domain knowledge graph and geo-enrichment service stack for applications in environmental intelligence. AI Magazine 43(1). https://doi.org/10.1002/aaai.12043

Mai G, Huang W, Cai L, Zhu R, Lao N (2022) Narrative cartography with knowledge graphs. J Geovisualization Spat Anal 6(1). https://doi.org/10.1007/s41651-021-00097-4

Nys GA, Van Ruymbeke M, Billen R (2018) Spatio-temporal reasoning in CIDOC CRM: an hybrid ontology with GeoSPARQL and OWL-Time. In: CEUR workshop proceedings, vol 2230. RWTH Aachen University, Aachen, Germany

Perry M, Herring J (2012) OGC GeoSPARQL-A geographic query language for RDF data. OGC Candidate Implement Stand

Robinson I, Webber J, Eifrem E (2015) Graph databases—new opportunities for connected data. In: Joe Celko's Complete Guide to NoSQL

Rocha L (1999) Aspectos do Megalitismo da área de Pavia, Mora (Portugal). Revista Portuguesa de Arqueologia, 2(1). https://dspace.uevora.pt/rdpc/handle/10174/2248

Santos I, Vieira R, Trojahn C, Rocha L, Cuenca EC (2022) Megalithism representation in CIDOC-CRM. Commun Comput Inf Sci 1652:550–558. https://doi.org/10.1007/978-3-031-15743-1_50/COVER

Shbita B, Knoblock CA, Duan W, Chiang YY, Uhl JH, Leyk S (2022) Building spatio-temporal knowledge graphs from vectorized topographic historical maps. Semantic Web 1–23. https://doi.org/10.3233/SW-222918

Stanescu L (2021) A comparison between a relational and a graph database in the context of a recommendation system. In: 16th conference on computer science and intelligence systems, pp 133–139. https://doi.org/10.15439/2021F33

Verdonck L, De Smedt P, Verhegge J (2019) Making sense of anomalies: practices and challenges in the archaeological interpretation of geophysical data. Innov Near-Surf Geophys: Instrum, Appl, Data Process Methods 151–194. https://doi.org/10.1016/B978-0-12-812429-1.00006-4

Wang S, Zhang X, Ye P, Du M, Lu Y, Xue H (2019) Geographic knowledge graph (GeoKG): a formalized geographic knowledge representation. ISPRS Int J Geo-Inf 2019 8(4):184. https://doi.org/10.3390/IJGI8040184

Zbyszewski G, Da Veiga Ferreira O, Barros e Carvalhosa A (1979) *Carta Geológica de Portugal na escala 1/50.000, Folha 35-B (Mora) e respectiva notícia explicativa.* (1ª Edição). Serviços Geológicos de Portugal

Zhang X, Huang Y, Zhang C, Ye P (2022) Geoscience knowledge graph (GeoKG): development, construction and challenges. Trans GIS 26(6):2480–2494. https://doi.org/10.1111/TGIS.12985

# Part II
# Digital Heritage Forensics

# Chapter 4
# Endangered Cultural Heritage Sites in the Era of Changing Climate: Lessons Learnt from Pakistan's 2022 Floods Using Satellite Data and Field Observations

**Muhammad Younis Khan, Sher Muhammad, Federico Zaina, Shahid Naeem, and Deodato Tapete**

**Abstract** Climate change endangers heritage sites globally, particularly in Pakistan, ranking among the top ten countries most affected by its consequences. The low adaptation capacity to cope with climate change-related flooding events in Pakistan enhances the risk to endangered archaeological sites along the Indus River. The risk assessment to archaeological sites and monuments caused by the 2022 Pakistan floods remains limited. This study presents an integrated approach relying on remote sensing data (Sentinel-2 imagery) and field surveys to evaluate the impact of flood on severely affected UNESCO-recognized and unrecognized heritage sites. In this work, using digital tools and remote sensing data products with the provision of replication at other sites offer an opportunity for the local end-users to assess damage in post-disaster mapping. This study contributes to the decision-making regarding the official state of conservation reports, as well as national and international legislations aimed

M. Y. Khan (✉)
Department of Earth Sciences, College of Science, Sultan Qaboos University, Muscat, Oman
e-mail: m.khan1@squ.edu.om

S. Muhammad
International Centre for Integrated Mountain Development (ICIMOD), Kathmandu, Nepal
e-mail: sher.muhammad@icimod.org

F. Zaina
Fondazione Museo Delle Antichità Egizie di Torino, Turin, Italy
e-mail: federico.zaina@museoegizio.it

S. Naeem
College of Resources and Environment, Yangtze University, Wuhan, China
e-mail: shahidn@igsnrr.ac.cn

D. Tapete
Italian Space Agency (ASI), Rome, Italy
e-mail: deodato.tapete@asi.it



S. Stellacci and S. Aydin (eds.), *Endangered Heritage Sites*, Springer Series on Cultural Computing, https://doi.org/10.1007/978-3-031-91949-7_4

at assessing and preserving heritage sites due to the extreme events in the developing world.

**Keywords** Cultural heritage · Copernicus program · Sentinel · Flood risk · Pakistan

## 4.1 Introduction

Globally, natural, and human-induced disasters are dynamic periodic processes that pose serious threats to sustainable socio-economic development and daily life. In the twentieth century, earthquakes caused about 1.87 million fatalities between 1990 and 2010 (Khan et al. 2022; Blaikie et al. 2014). Despite huge investments, and significant progress in the form of strategies being developed for prevention and effective management in recent decades, floods are considered as the most devastating natural hazard globally (Munich Re 2015). Between 1980 and 2015, Asia experienced the largest share of losses of global flood losses (62%) compared to other regions, such as Europe (19%) and the Americas (15%) (Bubeck et al. 2017). The frequency and severity of the floods have been influenced by the changing climates worldwide. Furthermore, such drastic shifts in weather patterns have also ravaged the cultural properties across the globe (Nguyen and Baker 2023) and as reported by the international bodies, such as United Nations (2018) and World Bank (2016).

In the Asia, the vulnerability to climate change is particularly apparent, with countries like Pakistan, ranking among the top ten mostly affected by it, due to its geological and climatic characteristics. Like other countries in the world, these devastating flood events pose a threat to the cultural heritage in Pakistan (Khan et al. 2023b).[1] While the damage to the residential buildings and crops has been extensively studied (e.g., Haq et al. 2010, 2012; Memon et al. 2015), the impact on heritage related to extreme climate-change related events has received little attention. More focus is needed to understand the critical intersections between heritage and climate change, as stated in the literature (Kiani et al. 2021; Khan et al. 2023a, b). Understanding the relationships of climate change and heritage might contribute to the advancement of the heritage field of study in general (Terrill 2008).

This study provides a review of the climatic conditions, historic flood events and their adverse impacts with a focus on the 2022 floods on heritage sites in Pakistan. It also provides a brief description of the selected heritage sites followed by the Copernicus Program that provides satellite imagery (Sentinel-2 imagery). It sheds light on the ready-to-use digital tools and products with the provision of replication at other

[1] It is noteworthy that about 90% of flood-related damages are reported from developing nations with low resilience like Pakistan (Douben 2006). Over the last seven decades, on average of 4-year, Pakistan has experienced the worst floods that resulted in many casualties, the destruction of livestock, local infrastructures, and agricultural lands across the country (Rahman 2010; Canada et al. 2011). The 2022 summer floods in Pakistan represent the latest example resulting in the record-breaking rainfall in July and August.

sites in Pakistan as well as other countries in the world, offering an opportunity for the local end-users. The end-users include Directorate General of Archaeology and Museums, National Heritage and Culture Division, Islamabad, Pakistan, Directorate General of Archaeology and Museums, Government of Khyber Pakhtunkhwa, Directorate General of Antiquities and Archaeology Government of Sindh, and Departments of archaeology and geology, University of Peshawar to assess damage in the post-disaster phase that may be applied to the UNESCO Disaster Risk Management Cycle (UNESCO 2010).

The outcomes of this research may contribute to support in the decision-making process related to the national and international legislations aimed at protecting archaeological sites and monuments at risk of flooding events. Additionally, potential limitations or challenges related to the use of these datasets and tools in this context are discussed. Finally, a thorough analysis of procedures in place and related issue at the national institutions for tackling the causes and impacts of climate change-triggered natural hazards such as floods in countries is conducted. Finally, recommendations for improvements in the management practices aimed at the preservation of heritage sites, within the broader policy and institutional framework of cultural heritage management in Pakistan and in other parts of the world with similar hydrogeological and climatic conditions at heritage properties are provided.

**Cultural Heritage Preservation**

Cultural heritage is "the legacy of physical artefacts and intangible attributes of a group or society that are inherited from past generations, maintained in the present and bestowed for the benefit of future generations" (Nilson and Thorell 2018). Cultural heritage preservation aims to protect archaeological remains and deposits at site scale (Fairclough 2006). Due to the universal value and cultural significance of heritage, and changing climates, cultural heritage management is required to go through a process of change,[2] where more focus is placed on incorporating climate change considerations into the policy and preservation practices of cultural heritage management. However, in most cases the absence of such of planning programs and required financial resources for risk mitigation has enhanced the vulnerability of cultural heritage sites, and subsequent damage has been recorded worldwide as per the UNESCO policy documents (UNESCO 2024a, b; UNOSAT 2024).

Within this context, the main stakeholders responsible for the preservation and management of built heritage as well as academic institutions at the national level must play a role in studying the affected heritage sites during the post-flood phase. To investigate heritage sites and their surroundings affected by floods, remote sensing method has gained popularity due to its high resolution, extensive coverage in less time. The role of space-borne satellite imagery (remote sensing) for supporting cultural heritage management as a non-destructive tool has been successfully studied

[2] The impact of climate change on cultural heritage revealed that one in six cultural heritage properties is at risk (UNESCO 2021). In the early 2000s, UNESCO conducted studies and outlined several threats to cultural heritage including rising temperatures, increased levels of evaporation and groundwater, and catastrophic flooding events. These factors are equally important for the selected heritage properties in this study (UNESCO 2006; UNESCO 2007a).

in the recent past (Alexakis et al. 2009; Opitz and Herrmann 2018). Remote sensing techniques allow fast prospecting and mapping of heritage sites at multiple scales, rapid analysis of multisource datasets, dynamic monitoring of heritage sites, and their surrounding environments at low to zero cost involved in practical applications to heritage to ensure long-term protection. One of the most used programs that provides freely available and high resolution open-access satellite datasets is Copernicus (2020). The European Copernicus Programme provides both radar and optical satellite images with almost global coverage acquired from the earth observation sensors (Sentinel-1 and Sentinel-2). Literature shows a systemic review on the use of remote sensing technology in archaeological research and heritage sites management (Agapiou and Lysandrou 2015; Luo et al. 2019).

## 4.2 Cultural Heritage in the Changing Climate in Pakistan and Associated Hazards

Climate change is a global phenomenon, and Pakistan is not an exception. The high-altitude environment in the north of the country and a long coast along Arabian Sea in the south mark the significant altitudinal variations resulting in considerable climatic changes of precipitation, temperature, and related extreme events such as floods. Climate change, melting glaciers (Muhammad et al. 2019a, b, 2020), and extreme precipitation events may trigger flooding (Hussain et al. 2022), and hence endanger the infrastructure and livelihood as well as heritage. The frequency of extreme events due to the changing climate and their impacts in Pakistan has increased recently, particularly floods with devastating effects on the infrastructure, livelihood, and communities, as discussed by Muhammad et al. (2021). Climate change has exacerbated these extreme events with an increased frequency and severity both in Central and South Asia (IPCC 2021; Pachauri et al. 2014; Hoegh-Guldberg et al. 2018). In Pakistan, the costs of the impact caused by floods and mass movements in mountainous regions were the highest in the Hindu Kush Himalaya region, reaching 45 billion USD between 1985 and 2014 (McCallum et al. 2023). While Pakistan has experienced recurrent floods almost every decade since 1947, since the 2000s this trend increased, with a peak of destructive events in 2010, 2011, and 2012 which resulted in substantial human, economic, and environmental losses.[3]

[3] The 2010 floods alone inundated over 70,000 $km^2$ and affected approximately 900,000 households (Haq et al. 2010, 2012). Overall, roughly 55–60 million people were hit by these events with approximately 3500 deaths (NDMA 2013; Memon et al. 2015; World Bank 2023; Qamer et al. 2023). The 2011 floods inundated over 21,000 $km^2$, displaced 5.9 million people, and damaged critical infrastructure including roads, railways, forests, and agricultural lands (NDMA 2013; Haq et al. 2012). Similarly, the 2012 floods affected 13,157 $km^2$ across 22 districts, severely impacting agricultural production and infrastructure (Memon et al. 2015). A notable increase of 75% in heavy rainfall over 60 days in the Indus River basin has been observed, indicating an extreme weather event (Philip et al. 2023).

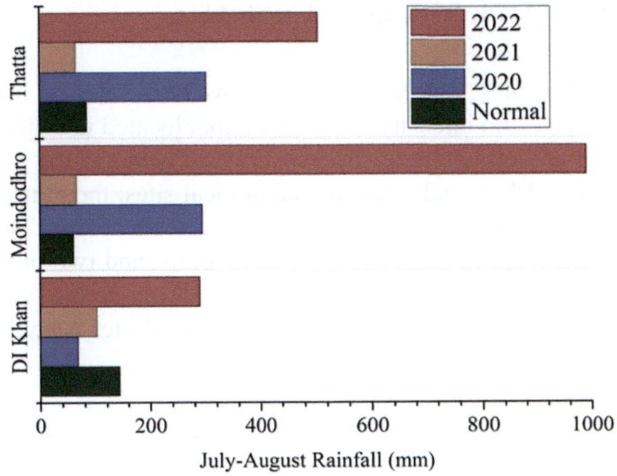


**Fig. 4.1** Comparison of rainfall data in July and August 2022 versus 2020, 2021, and the average historical values (own elaboration)

More recently, the catastrophic floods of summer in 2022, affected around 33 million people across the country, causing nearly 1500 fatalities, and extensive damage to infrastructure and livelihood, highlighting the vulnerability of the region to extreme events and floods (Qamer et al. 2023). In addition to these effects, record rainfall and associated floods also affected the heritage sites in various parts of Pakistan. The comparison of average precipitation at the metrological stations installed close to the selected cultural heritage sites (Mohenjo-Daro, Makli, Kafir kot, and Rehman Dheri) is shown in Fig. 4.1. All these heritage sites have received record rainfall. Amongst other sites, Mohenjo-Daro has received more than five times precipitation than normal and hence pose more threat to the site.

This dramatic trend stresses how the near real-time flood monitoring and post-disaster loss and damage assessment is crucial for effective planning for protection, recovery, and rehabilitation phases. It is imperative to develop evidence-based policies to mitigate disaster risks and minimize their impacts on various sectors (IPCC 2021). The pre-disaster assessment is extremely useful in planning and protecting heritage properties. Likewise, post-disaster assessments play a key role in preservation of cultural heritage sites that are often overlooked in such management plans.

## 4.3 Archaeological Context

In this study, four heritage sites have been selected in Pakistan to show the level of damage and intensity of precipitation, located in different zones from the geographical and climatological perspectives. Owing to the position of the World Heritage Sites (WHS) and other archaeological sites, the climatic characteristics are significantly different hence their proneness to the floods. The sites include the two WHSs of Mohenjo-Daro and Makli Necropolis, and two other important cultural heritage sites, Rehman Dheri and Kafir Kot fortress. In the following sections, the historical and archaeological context of the selected sites is provided for each site indicated in Fig. 4.2.

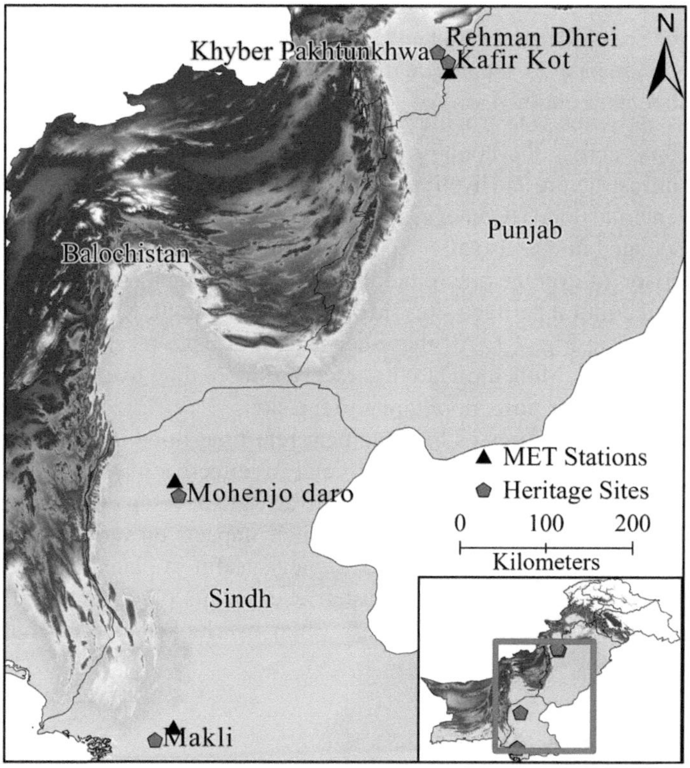


**Fig. 4.2** Locations of heritage sites and meteorological stations (modified after Khan et al. 2023a)

### 4.3.1 Mohenjo-Daro

Mohenjo-Daro is one of the most important ancient urban settlements along the Indus River in today's Sindh province of Pakistan (Fig. 4.3a). The site was discovered in 1922 and is considered a major center of the Harappan civilization dating between the 3rd millennium BCE and the first half of the 2nd millennium BCE (Possehl 2002; McIntosh 2008). It has a complex urban layout covering a 300 ha area and encompassing domestic, religious, and secular buildings like the *Great Bath*. The large flood defense platforms, multiple drainage systems, and wells for sewage at ancient Mohenjo-Daro confirm the complex interaction between the local people and the Indus River and provide a clue of an organized cultural setup during natural disasters such as floods.

Over the last decades, the site has been under threat by flood and heavy rains and recommendation for the improvement of the management and safeguarding system have been provided in UNESCO State of Conservation reports (UNESCO 2007b, 2011a).

**Fig. 4.3** Archeological Sites **a** The Mohenjo-Daro site (retrieved from UNESCO 2024a); **b** the Makli necropolis site (retrieved from UNESCO 2024b); **c** the Kafir Kot site; **d** the Rehman Dheri site

### 4.3.2 *Makli Necropolis*

The Makli necropolis located in the Sindh region, in southern Pakistan covers an area of approximately 10 $km^2$, with half a million tombs (Fig. 4.3b). It is considered one of the largest graveyards still in use across the globe. Since 1981, it has been recognized by UNESCO as a WHS. Given the important damage caused by the 2010 floods, a weather station was installed in 2011 for monitoring local weather patterns as per the recommendation of the State of Conservation report (UNESCO 2011b).

### 4.3.3 *Kafir Kot*

Kafir Kot complex is situated in the Khyber Pakhtunkhwa province of Pakistan and includes several forts and five Hindu temples dating back to the seventh century CE (Khan et al. 1995) (Fig. 4.3c). It is a national heritage site under the jurisdiction of the Directorate of Archaeology and Museum and the Government of Khyber Pakhtunkhwa, and the road along the Indus River provides the main access to the site.

### 4.3.4 *Rehman Dheri*

It is located in the southernmost district of the Khyber Pakhtunkhwa province of Pakistan (Fig. 6.3d). It is located in a flash flood zone because of the Sulaiman Range Mountains in the west, which is the area severely hit by flash floods in 2010 and 2022. Rehman Dheri was discovered in 1971 by Dr. Dani, when he was leading the Gumla excavations (Dani 1970–71). The site takes its name from the village Rehman located 3 km away. It is a well-designed city roughly rectangular in shape and the excavated structures indicate that mud, clay slabs, and clay blocks were used as construction material (Durrani 1988).

## 4.4 Satellite Remote Sensing for Built Heritage

Recently, space-borne satellite has increasingly been utilized for supporting cultural heritage management as a non-invasive tool in various parts of the world (Luo et al. 2019). This research uses the satellite data from the EU Copernicus Programme's satellite fleet. The Copernicus Programme is the European Union's flagship initiative for Earth observation,[4] designed to provide accurate and easily accessible information at high spatiotemporal scale, for managing environmental challenges and responding to crises. As one of the most advanced Earth observation systems in operation, it plays a vital role in monitoring and understanding global environmental dynamics.

Over the last two decades, archaeological cultural heritage studies have largely benefited from the applications of several space components within the Copernicus satellite fleet. In particular, Sentinel-1 and Sentinel-2 satellites designed and operated by ESA, provide a substantial enhancement in the research. Sentinel-1 is a key mission within the Copernicus Program, consisting of a constellation of radar imaging satellites. Equipped with synthetic aperture radar (SAR), Sentinel-1 operates day and night, regardless of weather conditions, providing high-resolution data. Sentinel-2 is another crucial component of the same program, comprising a constellation of optical imaging satellites, and provides multispectral imagery at high spatiotemporal resolution. Both missions deliver a wide range of applications, such as vegetation monitoring, land use mapping, hydrological changes, and disaster management, among others. The later one (Optical Sentinel-2A and Sentinel-2B sensors) have revisit time of five days at the equator whereas 2–3 days at mid-latitudes with a swath width of 290km. Several other freely available satellite Earth observation datasets, such as MODIS and Landsat, offer valuable data for a wide range of Earth's monitoring applications.

However, none of them provide the unique combination of high spatial, spectral, and temporal resolutions that the Copernicus satellite fleet delivers. The optical Sentinel-2 data was accessed from the Copernicus Open Access Hub (Sentinel Data Hub 2020). It utilizes wide-swath, high-resolution, multi-spectral imaging by sampling 13 spectral bands. It offers highest spatial resolution of 10m by sampling four spectral bands. The Sentinel-2 data was downloaded using Google Earth Engine (GEE), an open-source platform that enables users to download and process large-scale satellite imagery. For further processing of Sentinel-2 imagery, an open-source software Sentinel Application Platform (SNAP) was used. The SNAP is a user-friendly, tool free-of-charge tool provided by ESA to explore and analyze satellite measurements. It is widely used for different applications,[5] including flood and associated hazards.

---

[4] The programme (https://www.copernicus.eu/en) is managed by the European Commission in collaboration with the key partners, including the European Space Agency (ESA), European Organization for the Exploitation of Meteorological Satellites (EUMETSAT), and other entities. The broader objectives of the Copernicus program encompass monitoring Earth's Environment by providing comprehensive data on the atmosphere, oceans, and land; enhancing crisis management through improved emergency response to natural disasters, industrial accidents, and humanitarian crises; and supporting policymaking by delivering evidence-based information to governments, businesses, and international organizations.

[5] The critical role of these satellites in detecting and monitoring hydro-related damage to cultural heritage on a global scale has been widely demonstrated in numerous studies (Lasaponara and Masini 2020; Tapete and Cigna 2020; Cuca 2022).

## 4.5 Analysis of Impacts of the 2022 Floods on Built Heritage

Climate change induced extreme events have significant negative consequences not only for socioeconomic and food security but also endangered WHS of universal value across the world (Orr et al. 2021; Qamer et al. 2023). Addressing complex issues related to the management of prone-risk areas requires a paradigm shift involving multidisciplinary collaboration among professionals from various research disciplines, as no single field can adequately tackle them (Agapiou and Lysandrou 2015; Cunliffe et al. 2012). This is achieved by bringing together a range of technical skill sets, viewpoints, abilities, and approaches. Such multidisciplinary approach provides a platform for geologists, archaeologists, engineers, climate scientists, and remote sensing analysts from universities, research centers and intergovernmental institutions to work for seeking possible solutions. In the specific case of flood-related hazards to cultural heritage, the integrated approach is implemented in this work following a stepwise procedure, indicated in Fig. 4.4.

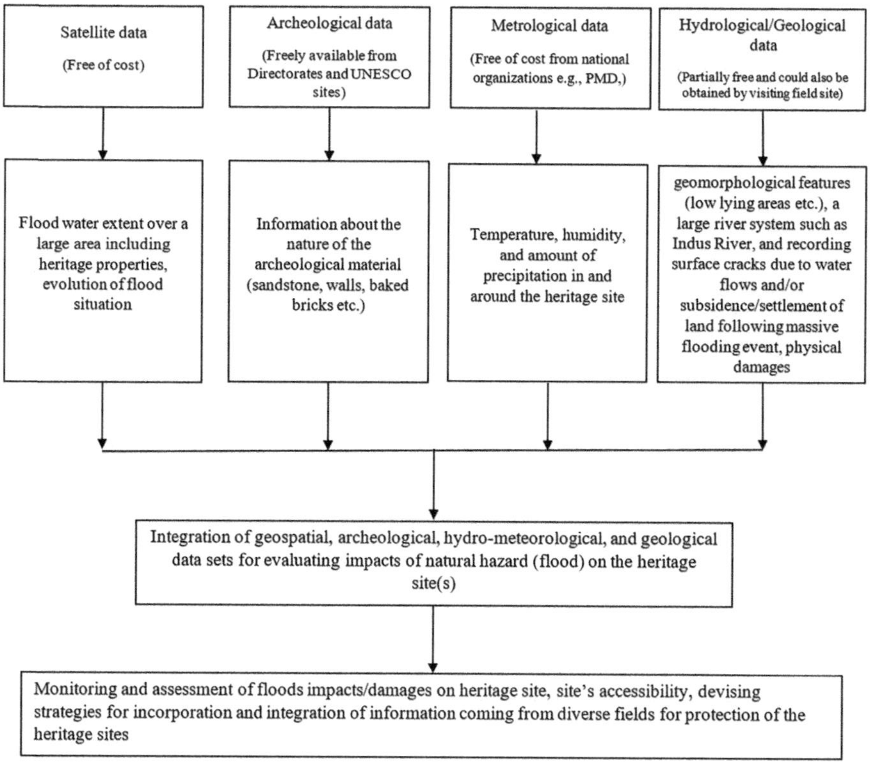


**Fig. 4.4** Flowchart showing stepwise procedure of the methodology proposed in this research (own elaboration)

First of all, satellite data (from Copernicus Sentinel-2 data sets in both pre- and post- flood situations) were collected and processed for assessment of flood damage over a large area covering the target sites. Then, archeological information of WHS and other heritage sites was obtained from in-field surveys, official documents (e.g., published on UNESCO website) keeping in mind that different archeological artifacts respond differently to climate change triggered extreme events and associated hazards. Hydro-meteorological parameters (e.g., groundwater table and precipitation data) was obtained from the locally installed weather stations to understand how the sites were influenced by the abnormal rainfall during July–August 2022 compared to previous years during the same months. A comprehensive fieldwork of the selected archeological sites located in different parts of the country were conducted to study the impact of key hydrological features (e.g., Indus River System) and man-made features (e.g., canals) coupled with topographical variations (e.g., depressions, high elevation), and surface expressions of water flows. The results derived obtained from in-field surveys were validated with the space-borne and few airborne remote sensing measurements. Finally, all data sets were integrated for evaluating the damage assessment of the heritage sites following the 2022 floods. In the following section, the impacts of 2022 floods on individual archeological sites in Pakistan have been discussed using multi-disciplinary data sets.

### *4.5.1 Mohenjo-Daro*

The pre-flood and post-flood situation at Mohenjo-Daro as captured by Sentinel-2 ascending image on 27 June and 31 August 2022 respectively is shown in Fig. 6. 5a–d. Figure 4.5a and b indicates absence of flooded water on 27 June 2022 whereas on 31 August 2022, the landscape around the site was completely flooded along the Indus River banks (Fig. 4.5c and d). The visual inspection of the image indicates that the site itself was not hit directly by the flood, but it restricted the access to the WHS (Khan et al. 2023a), contributed to the increased moisture content, and stagnation of water around the WHS (Fig. 4.5c and d). As suggested by Hegyi and Agapiou (2023), the enhanced moisture dynamics during record rainfall (> 900 mm, as indicated in Fig. 4.1) in the monsoon resulted in the physical damage (partial to complete collapse) of different parts at the WHS. It is noteworthy that visual inspection of high-resolution images is helpful in outlining the flood extent, flooded front routes/roads, whereas meteorological parameters such as abnormal amounts of precipitation in the context of changing climate provide evidence for the factors responsible to cause the damage at the site. This was followed by the field survey that confirmed the presence of standing water along the front walls of the site, which was drained later on, existence of standing water bodies for weeks in the immediate surrounding, and restoration activities at the WHS (Fig. 4.5). These results attest the integration of multiple measurements to assess the impact of the 2022 floods on the WHS and hence successful applicability of our proposed methodology that could be employed elsewhere with similar hydro-meteorological conditions around the heritage properties.

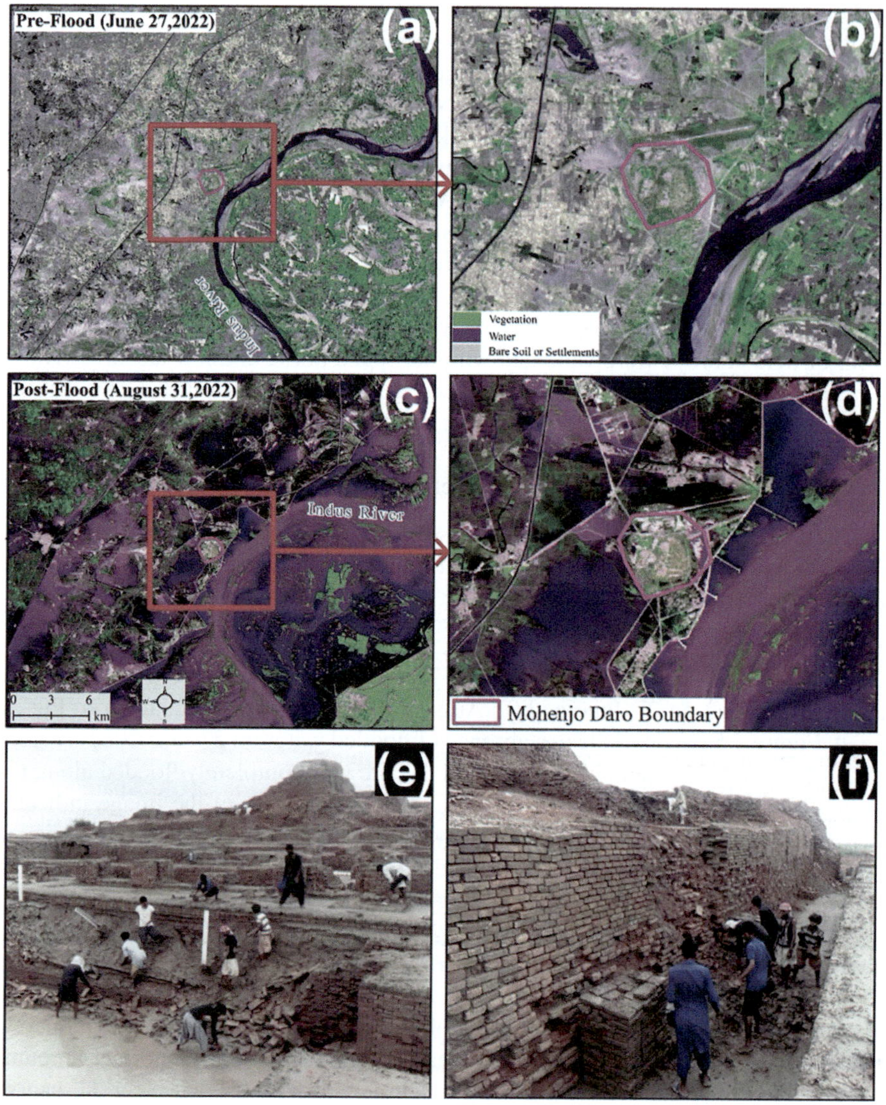


**Fig. 4.5** The Mohenjo-Daro site: Sentinel-2 images of the WHS; **a**, **b** pre-flood situation of the site and its surrounding and its zoomed-in view, respectively; **c**, **d** post-flood situation of the site and its surrounding and its zoomed-in view, respectively; **e**, **f** field observations showing the damaged walls due to heavy precipitation, and floods repair activities

### 4.5.2 *Makli Necropolis*

The satellite image in post-flood situation, which confirms that the site was safe and has not received any physical damage that could be attributed to a distance > 7.5 km from the river and located at relatively higher elevation than the surrounding area (Fig. 4.5b). However, the presence of water-filled topographic depressions beside the site may have contributed to the increased soil moisture and/or rising groundwater table and hence the water salinity on the monuments, walls, and related artifacts. The stagnant water around the site could be seen from the geospatial imagery as well as validated by field photographs, as shown in Fig. 4.6a–d.

### 4.5.3 *Kafir Kot*

The massive floods of 2022 affected the area around the Kafir Kot of Dera Ismail (DI) Khan. However, the site did not receive any damage primarily due to its location at higher elevation > 70 m than the surrounding areas (Khan et al. 2023a). The flooded waters accumulated around the fortress of Kafir Kot were captured by unmanned aerial vehicle (UAV) and Sentinel satellite images (Fig. 4.7). As inferred from the satellite measurements, fortunately, the flooded water could not submerge the road. Also, it could not make it to reach the archaeological remains of Kafir Kot. However, such record rainfall (twice than previous years), as shown in Fig. 4.7 could not cause damage to the site but resulting flood events may compromise the road access to the site in future (Fig. 4.7c).

### 4.5.4 *Rehman Dheri*

The pre- and post- flood scenarios at the Rehman Dheri site of D.I. Khan are indicated in Fig. 4.8a–d. The satellite image captured on 31 August 2022 indicates water accumulation near the site but no flood water inundation at the heritage site after the heavy rains. However, in-field observations indicate the fresh poetry material and recent erosion, as a result of the heavy rainfall (two times to that of previous years in the same months (Figs. 4.1 and 4.8e, and f) causing flash floods without leading to widespread inundation at the heritage site.

An attempt has been made to quantify the impact of the 2022 floods in the nearby areas around selected heritage sites through Normalized Difference Water Index (NDWI). The sum of the values of NDWI > 0.3 are plotted against different buffer zones to understand the flood severity around the selected sites (Fig. 4.9). An empirical threshold of NDWI > 0.30 indicates the presence of substantial amount of water. NDWI is a remote sensing Index used to detect and monitor water bodies in satellite imagery. It is particularly useful in identifying the presence of water in both

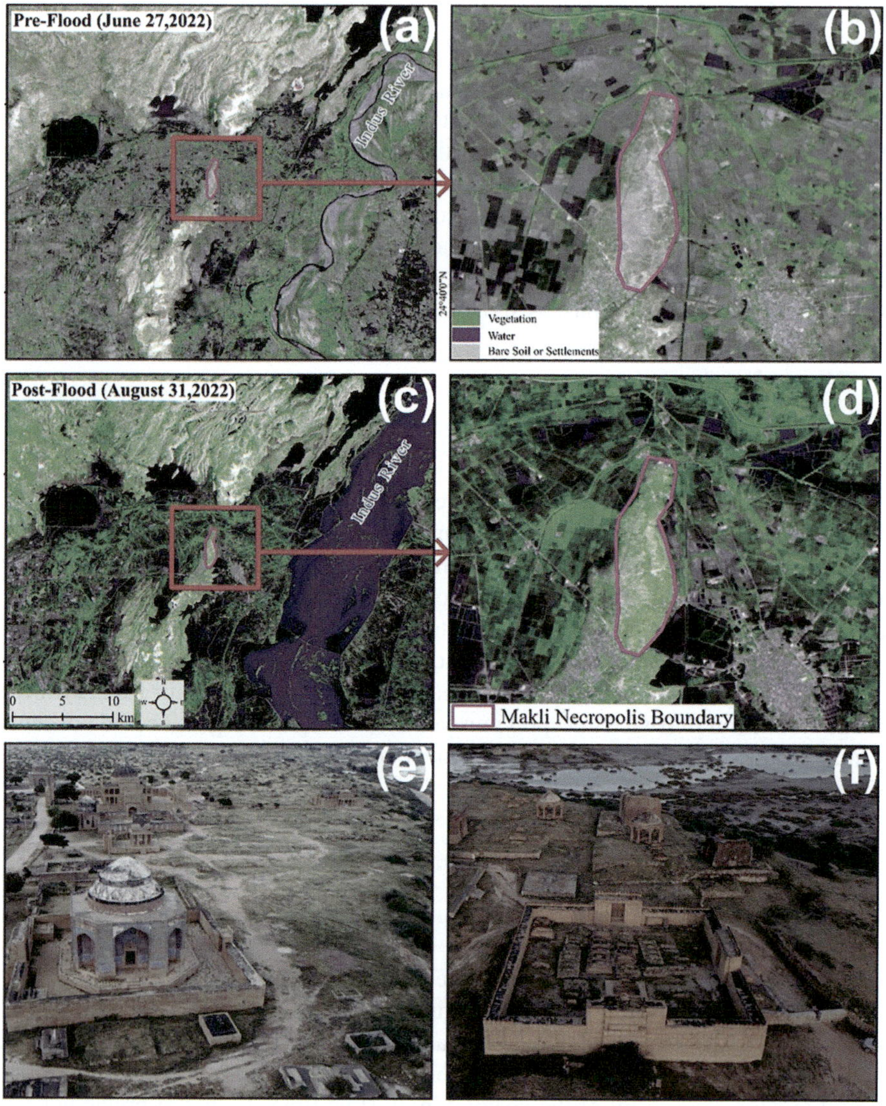


**Fig. 4.6** The Makli necropolis site: the Sentinel-2 images of the WHS; **a**, **b** pre-flood situation of the site and its surrounding and its zoomed-in view, respectively; **c**, **d** post-flood situation of the site and its surrounding and its zoomed-in view, respectively; **e**, **f** field observations showing the flood topographic lows near the site

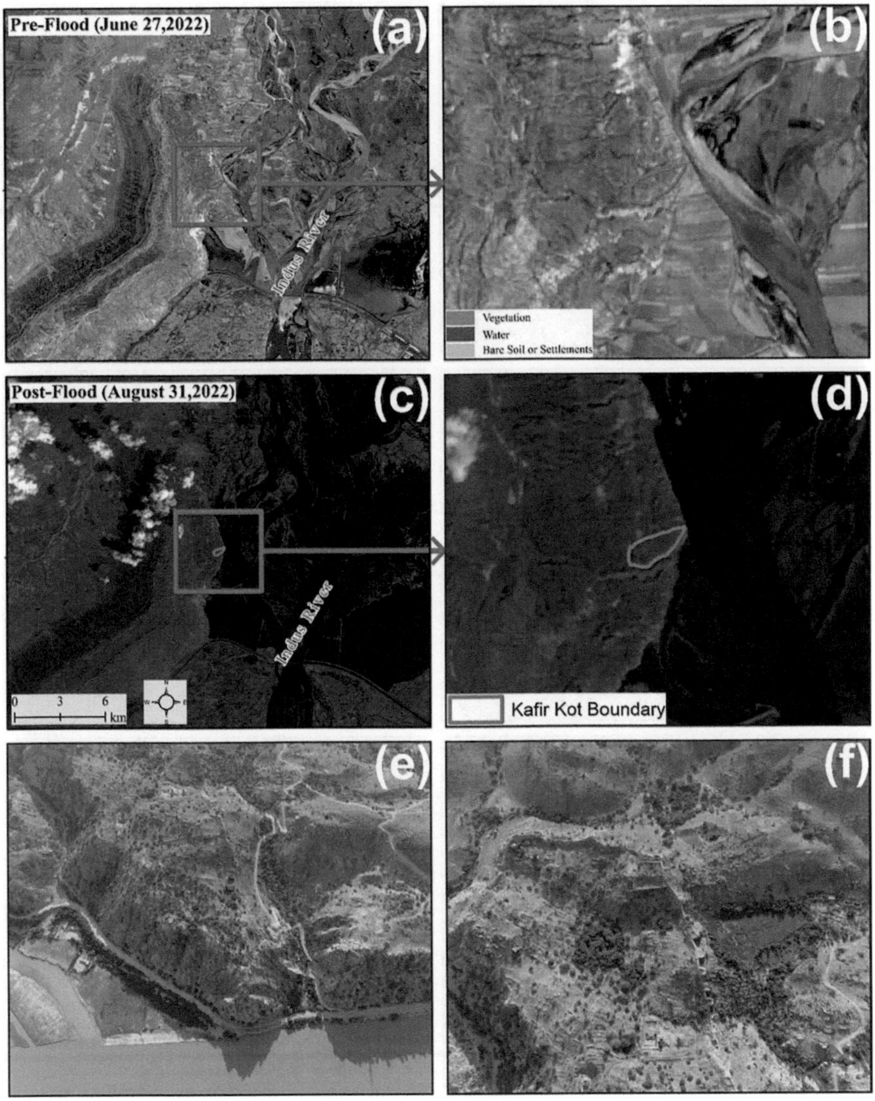


**Fig. 4.7** The Kafir Kot site: the Sentinel-2 images of the WHS; **a**, **b** pre-flood situation of the site and its surrounding and its zoomed-in view, respectively; **c**, **d** post-flood situation of the site and its surrounding and its zoomed-in view, respectively; **e**, **f** UAV based images showing the flooded topographic lows underneath the site

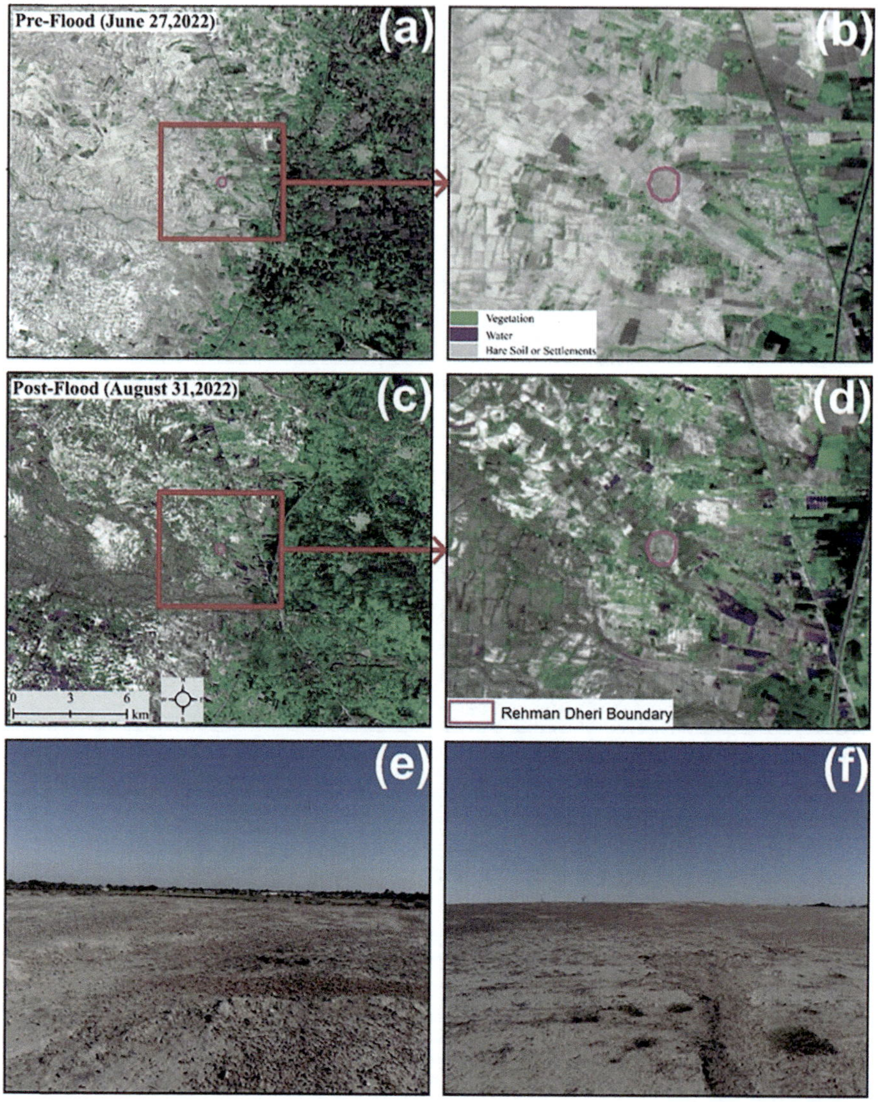


**Fig. 4.8** The Rehman Dheri site: the Sentinel-2 images of the WHS; **a**, **b** pre-flood situation of the site and its surrounding and its zoomed-in view, respectively; **c**, **d** post-flood situation of the site and its surrounding and its zoomed-in view, respectively; **e**, **f** fresh poetry material exposed after the heavy rainfall and recent soil erosion at the heritage site, respectively

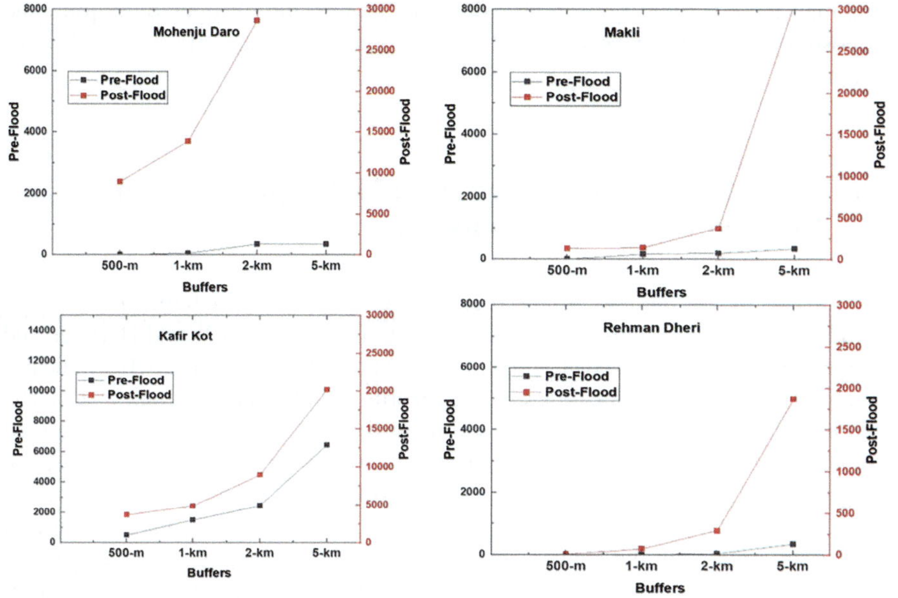


**Fig. 4.9** Pre- and post-flood variations in flood severity in different buffer zones (0–0.5, 0.5–1.0, 1–2, and 2–5 km) around the target sites

land-based and aquatic environments. It was calculated using the band ratio of green band (band-3) and Near Infrared (NIR) band (band-8a) of Sentinel-3 imagery. The formula is given below:

$$\text{NDWI} = \frac{\text{Green} - \text{NIR}}{\text{Green} + \text{NIR}}$$

The spatial statistics comparing pre- and post-flood conditions reveal a significant increase in water coverage in the post-flood scenarios across all buffer zones (0–500 m, 500–1000 m, 1000–2000 m, and 2000–5000 m). Notably, the areas in close proximity to the Indus River, such as Mohenjo-Daro, Makli, and Kafir Kot, show a marked rise in water levels, particularly around the site boundaries, within the 0–0.5 km buffer zone. Unlike other sites, Rehman Dheri site does not have monuments and walls on the surface and hence relatively less vulnerable. This suggests that floodwaters not only expanded across the general vicinity but also concentrated near the walls of these archaeological sites, highlighting the vulnerability of heritage sites to flooding. The increase in water presence in these buffer zones reflects the broader impact of flooding on the surrounding landscape and raises concerns about the preservation of these culturally significant locations.

The connection to mitigation measures for preservation could be further clarified by exploring how Copernicus and other geospatial datasets can be integrated into decision-making frameworks for the development of targeted mitigation strategies.

This may include identifying high-risk areas, monitoring changes over time, and proposing actionable measures for the protection of heritage sites in flood-prone regions.

## 4.6 Projected Climate Scenarios on Mohenjo-Daro, Kafir Kot, and Other Sites in Pakistan

The extreme events damage fragile rock structures, particularly heritage structures including mudbricks and/or sandstone in which monuments of World Heritage and other cultural sites are carved at Mohenjo-Daro and Kafir Kot. Figure 4.10a indicates the zonal map displaying historic climate records of Pakistan (Ali et al. 2021). The map is divided into five homogeneous climate zones, clustered based on observed climate data acquired at the meteorological stations operated by the Pakistan meteorological department (PMD). Makli and Mohenjo-Daro are located in zone 4 whereas Kafir Kot and Rehman Dheri are located in zone 5. Zone 4 includes the southeastern and coastal regions in the southern part of the country whereas zone 5 covers the central-eastern area and is regarded as the country's food basket due to its fertile agricultural landscape. Figure 4.10b shows the projected climate scenarios: two scenarios RCP8.5 and RC99p denote the concentration of carbon that delivers global warming at an average of 8.5 watts per square meter across the planet and the annual total precipitation above 99th percentile, respectively. A significant increase in precipitation occurred in the southeastern and coastal areas. There is a maximum decrease of 38% and an increase of up to 238.40%. During the future periods, R99p results indicate an increase in F1, and a maximum increase in F3. The southeastern region where WHS (Mohenjo-Daro and Makli) are located observe the most substantial increase in the form of precipitation changes. These changes suggest flash flooding that may damage the WHS, infrastructure damage, crop losses, and casualties in future. Massive flooding events such as the 2022 Pakistan floods, have substantial implications for the cultural heritage sites, severely affecting the sites in close proximity of the river system and/or in areas with limited financial resources and insufficient protective strategies. In this context, the site situated on the right bank of the Indus River i.e., integrity of Mohenjo-Daro sites was jeopardized by the catastrophic floods. This is evident from the inundated landscape around WHS along the Indus River (Khan et al. 2023a). The floods significantly damaged Mohenjo-Daro by extensive flooding visible around the site due to record heavy rains in July and August 2022. This monsoon precipitation led to a substantial amount of standing water outside the Mohenjo-Daro and Makli sites, impending accessibility, as shown in Figs. 4.5 and 4.6. Additionally, standing water within the site's premises likely contributed to increased soil moisture dynamics and subsequent wall collapses as indicated in Fig. 4.5. Similarly, the flooding restricted the accessibility of the Kafir Kot site (Fig. 4.7), illustrating the impacts of extreme events on heritage sites in such areas.

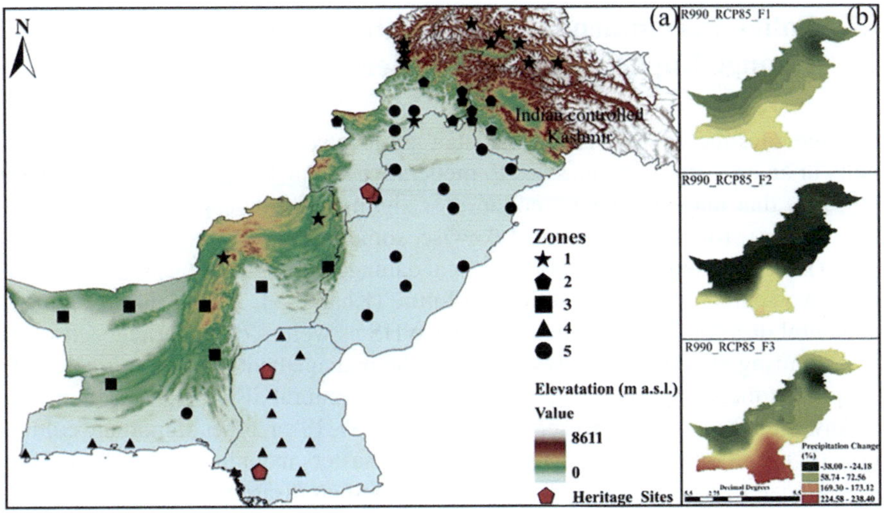


**Fig. 4.10** **a** Climate zonal map of Pakistan with heritage sites overlayed (on the left), and **b** spatial–temporal distribution of percent changes in RCP85 over Pakistan in future periods (F1: 2011–2040, F2: 2041–2070, and F3: 2071–2100) (on the right). The maps are adapted by the authors from Khan et al. (2023b)

In the light of the above climate related issues during the 2022 Pakistan floods, there is a great need for revising the policies by incorporating the mitigation measures needed to cope with the major challenge of climate change, the cultural heritage is facing and expected to recurrently hit the region in future as well. During the monsoon period in Pakistan, national (e.g., Directorate General of Archaeology and Museums) and local organizations (e.g., Directorate General of Archaeology and Museums Government of Khyber Pakhtunkhwa) responsible for cultural heritage management should remain vigilant and in contact with the metrological agencies such as the Pakistan Meteorological Department. The adverse effects on the heritage sites during the floods provide an opportunity for key stakeholders to train their personnel and use open access geospatial imagery and analysis tools to plan prior to the hazard and thereby reduce future damage. If not all, a limited number of technical staff at the national level institutions responsible for the management of cultural heritage in the country should be trained on the open-source satellite imagery as well as tools. This would not require substantial financial resources or the hiring of new employees. In addition to the routine visits of site managers, well-informed feedback relying on the open access imagery from the national/federal organizations would certainly be helpful to save the endangered heritage by minimizing damage.

## 4.7 Policy Recommendations for Mitigating Climate Change Impacts on Cultural Heritage Sites in Pakistan

Heritage sites including WHS in Pakistan are located very close to the geological faults in an area struck by massive to moderate earthquakes (as seismicity patterns indicate), that may completely collapse or significantly damage the cultural sites (e.g., Taxila) (Khan et al. 2023a). Likewise, some of the sites (e.g., Mohenjo-Daro WHS) may experience irreparable physical damage during the monsoon season due to the worsening climatic conditions in future (Khan et al. 2023a). In this context, all natural disasters can potentially impact WHS as well as other heritage sites, and thus requiring effective measures as part of the management plans to mitigate risks and protect these important cultural assets against natural disasters.

Any management and preservation plan for WHS or other important cultural property preservation should consider natural disasters including floods. To prevent or minimize disaster risks, it is critical to strengthen disaster risk governance and enhance preparedness. In this regard, over the last decade we observed a substantial increase of management plans for WHS to provide the appropriate responses based on modern theoretical based, such as the UNESCO Disaster Risk Management Cycle[6] and integrated approaches including remote sensing and ground truthing in the pre-disaster phase, followed by emergency response, assessment and recovery during and after the disaster event (UNESCO 2010). To go beyond the typical restoration measures in the post-disaster phase, there is a strong need to utilize freely available satellite data with near real-time coverage and open-source tools. The satellite measurements provide critical information in the pre- and post-flood conditions.

This research highlights the importance of open-access satellite data and open-source tools provided by the Copernicus Programme, coupled with metrological information, and field observations to cope with major disasters like the 2022 floods that affected an extensive area including WHS located in different provinces of Pakistan. There is a strong need to utilize multidisciplinary expertise by involving archeologists, remote sensing experts, climatologists, geologists, and hydrologists, among others. Archeologists or geologists without a multidisciplinary team may not be able to effectively contribute to the mitigation measures aimed at protection of the heritage sites. Therefore, an integrated approach with different fields (archeology, remote sensing, climatology, and hydrology) is needed to assess the impact of floods on heritage. In order to make these processes smoother and more systematic, key issues that Pakistani authorities should take into consideration are indicated below:

(i) *Human Resource Gaps:* Most personnel in national and local institutions are engineers and archaeologists. These organizations lack adequately trained team members with the expertise needed to conduct the necessary studies and analysis. A more diversified and highly skilled workforce is particularly recommended for addressing climate change-related challenges.

[6] https://whc.unesco.org/en/managing-disaster-risks/.

(ii) *Inadequate Computational Infrastructure:* Basic computational facilities and laboratories for processing satellite remote sensing data during disaster events are required.

(iii) *Limited Financial Resources:* Limited financial resources do not allow field-based observations for validation of remote sensing measurements

(iv) *Limited Collaborative Efforts:* Unlike other countries, Pakistan has experienced minimal

(v) Collaboration with national and international organizations through funded projects aimed at understanding the adverse effects of climate change and associated catastrophic floods.

(vi) *Absence of Management Plans:* The unavailability of climate change-related expertise is the main issue in realizing the potential impact of hazards on the heritage sites. Relevant authorities must prioritize the development of management plans that integrate modern methodologies for detecting, monitoring, and mitigating climate change-related hazards.

(vii) *Fostering academic Research:* The lack of interest at academic institutions to understand the impact of natural hazards in general and floods in particular on the cultural heritage. There is an increasing body of research devoted to climate change and heritage individually at academic and non-academic institutions but very little has been disseminated on how cultural heritage is affected by the climate-induced hazards. This could be addressed by providing grants to universities to conduct focused research on these lines.

(viii) *Media Involvement:* Media (both electronic and print) has played a minimal role in highlighting the impacts of climate change on cultural heritage. National authorities and academic institutions should foster closer relationships with the media to enhance

(ix) *Communication and public awareness:* Media (electronic and print) have played little role in outlining the impact of climate change on cultural heritage.

(x) *Buffer Zone Laws:* Existing laws concerning buffer zones around heritage properties are not effectively implemented, leaving sites inadequately protected. Local authorities and policymakers should address this issue.

(xi) *Coordination Deficiencies:* There is inadequate coordination among provincial and federal archaeological directorates and other relevant governmental bodies, such as public sector universities, the Ministry of Climate Change (MoCC), the National Centre of Excellence in Geology (NCEG), the Pakistan Meteorological Department (PMD), disaster management authorities (PDMAs and NDMA), and the Geological Survey of Pakistan (GSP).

Addressing such issues may potentially improve heritage site protection in pre- and post-natural disaster scenarios. This requires, fully effective, a cohesive framework should be established involving key organizations (e.g., academic institutions, and others mentioned in xi). This framework should focus on minimizing damage to cultural heritage sites, thus preserving their integrity. Capacity-building initiatives, such as training workshops on utilizing satellite imagery for studying extreme events, should be introduced for employees in archaeological directorates. Additionally, national-level directorates with basic computational infrastructure should be empowered to conduct comprehensive studies using freely available data and tools, including the ones described in this paper. No prioritizations should be made between UNESCO and non-UNESCO site, but a comprehensive approach that would consider the different necessities and regulations is welcomed.

## 4.8 Conclusion

Globally, heritage sites are located in environmentally sensitive areas, such as riverbanks, or mountainous terrain with depressions in the surroundings of the sites making them vulnerable to climate change. Abnormal rainfall may lead to devastating flooding that in turn cause erosion and shifts in these landscapes, putting heritage sites at serious risk.

Massive flooding that submerged large areas around the heritage sites (e.g., Makli and Kafir Kot), and unusual precipitation caused irreparable damage to heritage sites, such as the ancient city of Mohenjo-Daro. Similarly, global heritage sites in flood-prone regions in other parts of the world face the threat of being washed away or severely deteriorated due to rising sea levels, intense rainfall, and flooding caused by climate change. On a global scale, many countries with rich cultural histories face similar risks, where climate-induced extreme events threaten to erase priceless cultural heritage that may never be recovered.

Beyond the physical destruction of heritage sites, climate change also indirectly impacts such sites by displacing millions of people, and resulting in the destruction of homes, and infrastructure. This makes the heritage conservation a secondary concern in the face of immediate human needs. Therefore, extreme events like the 2022 floods in Pakistan highlight the need for global cooperation and shared solutions in preserving cultural heritage worldwide. These challenges necessitate enhanced climate adaptation strategies that prioritize heritage protection as a core component. Such strategies should adopt multidisciplinary approaches, leveraging ready-to-use open-source Copernicus datasets and analytical tools. The findings highlight a strong need for collaboration among governments, local communities, academic research institutions, and international organizations to develop sustainable solutions for safeguarding heritage from the escalating risks of climate change.

**Acknowledgements** The authors are thankful to Tahir Saeed from the Directorate of Archaeology and Museums for his cooperation and assistance regarding the fieldwork and Muhammad Suliman who is working at the Directorate of Archaeology and Museums, Peshawar, for providing data of Kafir Kot site. The authors also thank Zahid Latif, Khalid Latif, for their useful suggestions and assistance during this work. This work was also supported by the International Centre for Integrated Mountain Development (ICIMOD).

## References

Agapiou A, Lysandrou V (2015) Remote sensing archaeology: tracking and mapping evolution in European scientific literature from 1999 to 2015. J Archaeol Sci Rep 4:192–200

Alexakis D, Sarris A, Astaras T, Albanakis K (2009) Detection of Neolithic settlements in Thessaly (Greece) through multispectral and hyperspectral satellite imagery. Sensors 9(02):1167–1187

Ali S, Saeed A, Kiani RS, Muhammad S, Khan F, Babar R, Fahad S (2021) Future climatic changes, extreme events, related uncertainties, and policy recommendations in the Hindu Kush sub-regions of Pakistan. Theoret Appl Climatol 143:193–209

Blaikie P, Cannon T, Davis I, Wisner B (2014) At risk: natural hazards, people's vulnerability and disasters. Routledge

Bubeck P, Otto A, Weichselgartner J (2017) Societal impacts of flood hazards. In: Oxford research encyclopedia of natural Hazard science. Asters. Routledge

Canada CI, RB of Pakistan (2011) The impact of the 2010 and 2011 floods, including on mobility, reconstruction, housing and shelter, employment and access to food

Copernicus (2020) https://www.copernicus.eu/en. Accessed 30 Nov 2024

Cuca B (2022) Copernicus Sentinel imagery for more risk-resilient historic cities in coastal zones: contribution to the monitoring of Albenga archaeological site and delta of river Centa. Appl Geomat 14(Suppl 1):67–78

Cunliffe E, de Gruchy M, Stammitti E (2012) Project Development—Dam(Ned) Archaeology. Int Water Power Dam Constr 64:9

Douben KJ (2006) Characteristics of river floods and flooding: a global overview, 1985–2003. Irrig Drain 55:9–21

Durrani FA (1988) Excavations in the Gomal Valley: Rehman Dheri excavations, report no. 1. Ancient Pakistan 6:1–232

Fairclough G (2006) A new landscape for cultural heritage management: characterization as a management tool. In: Landscapes under pressure: theory and practice of cultural heritage research and preservation. Springer US, Boston, MA, pp 55–74

Haq M, Akhtar M, Muhammad S, Paras S, Rahmatullah J (2012) Techniques of remote sensing and GIS for flood monitoring and damage assessment: a case study of Sindh province, Pakistan. Egypt J Remote Sens Space Sci 15(2):135–141

Haq M, Rahman S, Rahmatullah J, Muhammad S (2010) Pakistan 2010 floods monitoring using MODIS data. CTWF Beijing, China

Hoegh-Guldberg O, Jacob D, Taylor M, Bindi M, Brown S, Camilloni I et al (2018) Impacts of 1.5°C global warming on natural and human systems. In: Global warming of 1.5°C. An IPCC special report on the impacts of global warming of 1.5°C above pre-industrial levels and related global greenhouse gas emission pathways

Hussain A, Cao J, Ali S, Muhammad S, Ullah W, Hussain I, Akhtar M, Wu X, Guan Y, Zhou J (2022) Observed trends and variability of seasonal and annual precipitation in Pakistan during 1960–2016. Int J Climatol 42(16):8313–8332

IPCC (2021) Climate change 2021: the physical science basis. Contribution of Working Group I to the Sixth Assessment Report of the Intergovernmental Panel on Climate Change. Cambridge University Press

Khan AN, Nisar A, Olivieri LM, Vitali M (1995) The recent discovery of cave paintings in Swat a preliminary note. East West 45:333–353

Khan F, Ali S, Ullah H, Muhammad S (2023b) Twenty-first century climate extremes' projections and their spatio-temporal trend analysis over Pakistan. J Hydrol Reg Stud 45:101295

Khan MY, Zaina F, ul Abedin Z, Tariq S, Khan MJ (2022) Evaluation of risks to UNESCO World Heritage (WH) sites in Taxila, Pakistan using ground-based and satellite remote sensing techniques. J Cult Herit 55:195–209

Khan MY, Zaina F, Muhammad S, Tapete D (2023a) Integrating Copernicus satellite products and ground-truthing for documenting and monitoring the impact of the 2022 extreme floods in Pakistan on cultural heritage. Remote Sens 15(10):2518 (p. 7)

Kiani RS, Ali S, Ashfaq M, Khan F, Muhammad S, Reboita MS, Farooqi A (2021) Hydrological projections over the Upper Indus Basin at 1.5 C and 2.0 C temperature increase. Sci Total Environ 788:147759

Lasaponara R, Masini N (2020) Big earth data for cultural heritage in the Copernicus era. In: Hadjimistis D et al (eds) Remote sensing for archaeology and cultural landscapes: best practices and perspectives across Europe and the Middle East, Springer, pp 31–46

Luo L, Wang X, Guo H, Lasaponara R, Zong X, Masini N et al (2019) Airborne and spaceborne remote sensing for archaeological and cultural heritage applications: a review of the century (1907–2017). Remote Sens Environ 232:111280

McCallum S, Fellendorf A, Khan B, Shah GM, Shrestha F, Muhammad S, Adler C, Thornton J, Llambi LD, Zwahlen J, Witton R, Sinisalo A (2023) Adaptation gap report-case study, mountains in silent thaw: losses and damages from the disappearing "frozen heartbeat" of Earth. https://doi.org/10.59117/20.500.11822/43796

McIntosh J (2008) The Ancient Indus Valley: new perspectives; ABC-CLIO: Santa Barbara

Memon AA, Muhammad S, Rahman S, Haq M (2015) Flood monitoring and damage assessment using water indices: a case study of Pakistan flood-2012. Egypt. J. Remote Sens. Space Sci. 18(1):99–106

Muhammad S, Tian L (2020) Mass balance and a glacier surge of Guliya ice cap in the western Kunlun Shan between 2005 and 2015. Remote Sens Environ 244:111832

Muhammad S, Tian L, Khan A (2019a) Early twenty-first century glacier mass losses in the Indus Basin constrained by density assumptions. J Hydrol 574:467–475

Muhammad S, Tian L, Nüsser M (2019b) No significant mass loss in the glaciers of Astore Basin (North-Western Himalaya), between 1999 and 2016. J Glaciol 65(250):270–278

Muhammad S, Li J, Steiner JF, Shrestha F, Shah GM, Berthier E, Guo L, Wu LX, Tian L (2021) A holistic view of Shisper Glacier surge and outburst floods: from physical processes to downstream impacts. Geomat Nat Haz Risk 12(1):2755–2775

Munich Re (2015) Topics geo. Natural catastrophes 2015: Analyses, assessments, positions. Munich Reinsurance, Munich

NDMA (2013) Annual flood report 2013. National Disaster Management Authority, Pakistan

Nguyen KN, Baker S (2023) Climate change and UNESCO world heritage-listed cultural properties: a systematic review, 2008–2021. Heritage 6(3):2394–2420

Nilson T, Thorell K (2018) Cultural heritage preservation: the past, the present and the future

Opitz R, Herrmann J (2018) Recent trends and long-standing problems in archaeological remote sensing. J Comput Appl Archaeol 1(1):19–41

Orr SA, Richards J, Fatorić S (2021) Climate change and cultural heritage: a systematic literature review (2016–2020). Hist Environ Policy Pract 12(3–4):434–477

Pachauri RK, Meyer LA (eds) (2014) Climate change 2014: synthesis report. Contribution of working groups I, II and III to the fifth assessment report of the intergovernmental panel on climate change. IPCC

Philip SY, Kew SF, van Oldenborgh GJ, Aalbers EE, Otto FE (2023) The role of climate change in extreme flooding in Pakistan. World Weather Attribution. https://www.worldweatherattribution.org

Possehl GL (2002) The Indus civilization: a contemporary perspective. Altamira Press, Walnut Creek

Qamer FM, Abbas S, Ahmad B, Hussain A, Salman A, Muhammad S, Nawaz M, Shrestha S, Iqbal B, Thapa S (2023) A framework for multi-sensor satellite data to evaluate crop production losses: the case study of 2022 Pakistan floods. Sci Rep 13(1):4240

Rahman A (2010) Disaster risk management: flood perspective. VDM Verlag Publishing, Saarbrücken, 192 pp. ISBN 978-3-639-29891-8

Sentinel Data Hub (2020) https://scihub.copernicus.eu. Accessed 30 Nov 2024

Tapete D, Cigna F (2020) Poorly known 2018 floods in Bosra UNESCO site and Sergiopolis in Syria unveiled from space using Sentinel-1/2 and COSMO-SkyMed. Sci Rep 10(1):12307

Terrill G (2008) Climate change: how should the World Heritage Convention respond? Int J Herit Stud 14(5):388–404
UNESCO (2010) Managing disaster risk for wold heritage sites. UNESCO, Paris
UNESCO (2021) World heritage review 100: climate change. UNESCO, Paris
UNESCO Enhancing our Heritage Toolkit (2024) Assessing management effectiveness of natural. https://whc.unesco.org/en/series/23/. Accessed 23 May 2024
UNESCO Enhancing our Heritage Toolkit, Assessing management effectiveness of natural. https://whc.unesco.org/en/series/23/. Accessed 19 Feb 2023
UNESCO (2006) Development of policy document on impacts of climate change and world heritage. https://whc.unesco.org/en/CC-policy-document/36070721. Accessed 20 May 2024
UNESCO (2007a) UNESCO World Heritage Centre—State of Conservation (SOC) Archaeological Ruins at Moenjodaro (Pakistan). https://whc.unesco.org/en/soc/1028. Accessed 19 Feb 2023
UNESCO (2007b) Case studies on climate change and world heritage. UNESCO. https://whc.unesco.org/en/documents/115528.36070721. Accessed 20 May 2024
UNESCO (2011a) UNESCO World Heritage Centre—State of Conservation (SOC) Archaeological Ruins at Moenjodaro (Pakistan). https://whc.unesco.org/en/soc/403. Accessed 19 Feb 2023
UNESCO (2011b) UNESCO World Heritage Centre—State of Conservation (SOC 2011) Historical Monuments at Makli, Thatta (Pakistan). https://whc.unesco.org/en/soc/402. Accessed 19 May 2024
UNESCO (2024a) Archaeological ruins at Moenjodaro—Gallery—UNESCO World Heritage Centre. https://whc.unesco.org/en/list/138/gallery/. Accessed 10 May 2024
UNESCO (2024b) Historical Monuments at Makli, Thatta—Gallery—UNESCO World Heritage Centre. https://whc.unesco.org/en/list/143/gallery/. Accessed 10 May 2024
United Nations (2018) Goal 13: take urgent action to combat climate change and its impacts. http://www.un.org/sustainabledevelopment/climate-change-2/
World Bank (2016) Climate change action plan 2016–2020, World Bank group reports. World Bank
World Bank (2023) Pakistan 2022 floods: post-disaster needs assessment. https://www.worldbank.org

# Chapter 5
# Data-Driven Documentation: Techniques for Historic Buildings After Anthropogenic and Natural Hazards

**Daniele M. S. Paulino, Saanchi S. Kaushal, Joe Kallas, and Rebecca Napolitano**

**Abstract** This study examines the challenges and opportunities in digitizing historic buildings following two distinct disaster events: the 2020 Beirut Port Explosion and the 2021 Quad State Tornado. Through these case studies, this research explores the critical role of rapid digital documentation in preserving cultural heritage and informing structural resilience strategies. The process of extracting key structural, architectural, and urban attributes from 3D point cloud models is detailed, highlighting the potential for this data to inform predictive modeling and enhance disaster preparedness. By comparing the methodologies and outcomes from both case studies, lessons are derived for future structural engineering focused documentation efforts, emphasizing the need for systematic pre-disaster documentation, high-resolution capture of critical structural elements, and strategic accessibility planning. Ultimately, this research seeks to bridge the gap between digital documentation and structural engineering applications to develop more data-driven approaches for protecting and preserving cultural heritage sites against future disasters.

**Keyword** Structural resilience · Beirut Port Explosion · Quad State Tornado disaster preparedness · 3D point cloud modeling

---

D. M. S. Paulino (✉) · S. S. Kaushal · J. Kallas · R. Napolitano
BEAM Lab, Department of Architectural Engineering, The Pennsylvania State University, University Park, PA, USA
e-mail: dpaulino@psu.edu

S. S. Kaushal
e-mail: saanchi.kaushal@psu.edu

J. Kallas
e-mail: jkallas@psu.edu

R. Napolitano
e-mail: nap@psu.edu

 
S. Stellacci and S. Aydin (eds.), *Endangered Heritage Sites*, Springer Series on Cultural Computing, https://doi.org/10.1007/978-3-031-91949-7_5

## 5.1 Introduction

Preserving and recovering cultural heritage sites after disasters is a complex undertaking that requires integrating diverse data sources and modalities. From 3D laser scans and photogrammetry models to community oral histories and expert assessments, this multifaceted information holds invaluable insights for effective documentation and restoration efforts (Benchekroun 2022). However, harnessing the full potential of these heterogeneous datasets is hindered by the lack of standardized frameworks for consolidating and harmonizing cultural heritage big data (Ranjgar et al. 2020). Existing approaches often operate in disciplinary silos, failing to synthesize complementary sources into comprehensive digital representations. This fragmented data landscape impedes informed decision-making and impairs the ability to develop holistic strategies for safeguarding invaluable cultural assets (Khalil and Stravoravdis 2022). To address these challenges, it is imperative to establish methodologies that ensure data standardization, integrity, and provenance throughout the harmonization process (Sielker et al. 2019).

This study exemplifies these challenges and considerations around data harmonization for cultural heritage preservation through two recent disaster case studies that required rapidly documentation efforts: the 2020 Beirut Port Explosion, which devastated historic neighborhoods in Lebanon's capital, and the 2021 Quad State Tornado, which impacted the historic downtown of Mayfield, Kentucky (United States). The catastrophic Beirut blast in Lebanon prompted an urgent digitization initiative, where teams worked to 3D model highly vulnerable Ottoman-era and French Mandate structures using drones and cameras before any further collapse occurred (Kallas and Napolitano 2023). The need for immediate high-resolution digitization was paramount, with teams racing against the clock just days after the explosion to 3D model severely damaged heritage buildings at risk of imminent collapse through photogrammetry before any additional loss occurred. Across the Atlantic, in Mayfield, Kentucky, researchers had the opportunity to conduct a two-phase reconnaissance, first rapidly assessing tornado damage extent before returning months later to document the damage to over 30 historic masonry buildings after the powerful tornado using photogrammetry and LIDAR (Light Detection and Ranging), as discussed presented in the work of several studies (e.g., Kaushal et al. 2023).

In this context, documentation techniques, such as photogrammetry and laser scanning, have become crucial technologies for generating point clouds and 3D models, especially in heritage preservation (Ulvi 2021). These techniques capture detailed spatial information, allowing for the creation of highly accurate digital replicas of cultural heritage sites. These digital models are invaluable for preservation, providing a record that can be used for restoration efforts, educational purposes, and virtual tourism. In disaster scenarios, the ability to quickly document and create 3D models of damaged heritage sites ensures that even if the physical structures are lost, their digital counterparts remain. This digital preservation allows for detailed analysis, historical record-keeping, and future reconstruction, thus safeguarding cultural heritage against further deterioration or complete destruction.

In addition to the data collection efforts, the ultimate goal for both studies was to use a data-driven approach to investigate key attributes in historic buildings, especially unreinforced masonry structures, that contribute to their structural response in the event of a disaster. The data acquired through photogrammetry and laser scanning can be leveraged to generate datasets used to develop prediction models through machine learning techniques. By analyzing the detailed 3D models and point clouds, extracting information on the building's attributes such as geometric, material, and typology data, machine learning algorithms can be trained to predict the impact of future disasters on historic buildings. These predictive models can assess vulnerabilities and simulate various disaster scenarios, providing valuable insights for disaster preparedness and risk mitigation. This proactive approach allows for better planning and protection of heritage sites, enabling stakeholders to implement targeted preservation and structural strengthening strategies to minimize potential damage.

However, harmonizing data from these complex multi-modal efforts highlighted issues around data collection and synthesis that must be addressed to leverage big data's full potential for protecting irreplaceable cultural assets against future disasters. Rather than relying on data-driven insights, efforts are often guided by intuition and general practices. This approach, while well-intentioned, failed to capitalize on the specific vulnerabilities and critical structural elements unique to different building types and disaster scenarios. The challenge lies not just in collecting data, but in knowing precisely what to document and how to document it for maximum utility in structural analysis and future disaster mitigation. By leveraging existing knowledge of building vulnerabilities and past performance data, more effective tailored documentation strategies can be developed. Such approach ensures that efforts focus on the most critical structural elements and vulnerable areas, thereby maximizing the value of collected data for protecting irreplaceable cultural assets against future disasters.

This research will not detail the machine learning process for predicting structural vulnerabilities, which can be exemplified in the work of Kallas and Napolitano (2024). Instead, it will present insights into how to effectively document historic buildings in post-disaster scenarios, with a particular emphasis on structural engineering applications.

In line with the ISCARSAH (The International Scientific Committee on the Analysis and Restoration of Structures of Architectural Heritage) guidelines (ICOMOS 2003), this study emphasizes the importance of a multi-disciplinary approach to heritage conservation, integrating expertise from various fields such as engineering, architecture, history, and archaeology. The proposed documentation strategies aim to support the anamnesis phase outlined in the guidelines, providing comprehensive data for diagnosis, structural performance assessment, and intervention planning. By sharing these lessons, this work contributes to the development of useful and targeted documentation practices that can directly inform structural analysis, rehabilitation efforts, and future disaster mitigation strategies for cultural heritage sites. Furthermore, this research aligns with the principle of 'minimum intervention' level in heritage intervention first stated in the 1964 Venice Charter (ICOMOS 1964), and followed by other heritage guidelines, advocating for documentation methods that support informed decision-making while minimizing impact on the heritage authenticity and cultural value. The data harmonization approaches proposed in this study aim to facilitate a holistic understanding of the building's condition based on the integration of qualitative and quantitative evidence in the assessment and intervention processes.

## 5.2 Case Studies

On August 4th, 2020, an industrial explosion at the port of Beirut (Fig. 5.1), one of the largest non-nuclear explosions in history, dramatically altered the landscape of the Lebanese capital (Kallas and Napolitano 2023). Beirut's historic neighborhoods were transformed from lively cultural centers into zones of destruction, with buildings reduced to rubble, walls collapsed, and roofs severely damaged. The blast heavily impacted Beirut's built heritage, particularly affecting the historical masonry buildings located in the port-side quarters overlooking the Mediterranean Sea (Kallas and Napolitano 2023).

The Gemmayzeh and Mar Mikhael neighborhoods, which had an unobstructed view of the port, were among the hardest hit. These areas, dating back to the nineteenth century, feature architecture from the Ottoman and French mandate periods. They represent some of the earliest expansions beyond Beirut's original city walls, preserving a relatively intact historic urban fabric despite modern developments (Bondestein 2021a). The Ottoman-era architecture from the late nineteenth century is

**Fig. 5.1** Satellite image showing a damage proxy map after the Beirut explosion 2020. Courtesy of NASA Earth Observatory (NASA 2020)

characterized by residential buildings, palaces, and mansions with red-tiled roofs and central halls featuring the distinctive triple-arched bays typical of Beiruti architecture. The French mandate period brought three to four-story buildings with balconies adorned with decorative wrought-iron railings (Bondestein 2021b).

The Ottoman-era buildings are particularly fragile. Structurally, the ground floors are the most stable, made of thick sandstone walls and earth and lime-based mortar (Chahine 2021). The upper floors, divided by the central hall and triple-arched bays, are constructed with thin single-sandstone walls and marble columns for the bays, with Carrara marble slabs for balconies and timber structures for the ceilings. Some ceilings also incorporate steel beams or jack-arch slabs in more elaborate designs (Dagher 2021). The attic floors, with timber pitched roofs covered in red clay tiles from Marseille, are especially vulnerable to damage. The explosion's pressure caused significant structural issues, shifting marble columns and destabilizing walls, with many buildings experiencing collapsed bays and out-of-plane deformations (Chalhoub 2021a, b). The timber roofs were heavily damaged, further compromising the buildings' stability.

According to the Lebanese Ministry of Culture and the Directorate General of Antiquities, 640 heritage buildings were damaged in the explosion, with initial damage estimates reaching USD 300 million (UNESCO 2022a, b). The disaster, which resulted in the deaths of at least 220 people, injuries to more than 5000, and the displacement of around 300,000 people, was attributed to thousands of Tonnes of ammonium nitrate, as per the preliminary investigation by Lebanese authorities (Guglielmi 2020; Aouad et al. 2021).

Months later, on the other side of the Atlantic, a tornado outbreak occurred in the Midwest region of the United States on December 10th, 2021, and notable damages were documented across Arkansas, Missouri, Tennessee, and Kentucky (Pilkington et al. 2021). This off-season tornado outbreak was influenced by the higher-than-average temperatures, and covered a distance of over 250 miles (Pappas 2021) at a speed of 94 mph (Samenow 2021). Among the impacted states, Kentucky underwent devastating damage (Schreiner and Lovan 2021), classifying the tornado's intensity as an EF-4 (McDonald et al. 2010).

The town of Mayfield has a rich history, dating back to its establishment in 1821, serving as a central hub for governmental, social, and commercial activities, as documented by the National Register of Historic Places (1984). Its growth was facilitated by key developments, such as building the public square in 1824, introducing railroads in the mid-1800s, as noted in Munday (1925), and the flourishing textile and tobacco industries, leading to a notable expansion between 1875 and 1934 (Poliarnyi and Pasumansky 2020). Recognizing its historical significance and early town planning efforts, the downtown of Mayfield was added to the National Register of Historic Places in 1984 (National Register of Historic Places 1984). This was subsequently updated in 1996 to encompass additional nearby structures that contributed to the town's character and historical value, as recorded by the National Register of Historic Places (1996).

Figure 5.2 shows the region encompassing the historic buildings. Given that almost 82 structures were listed in both the 1984 and 1996 National Register listings, only

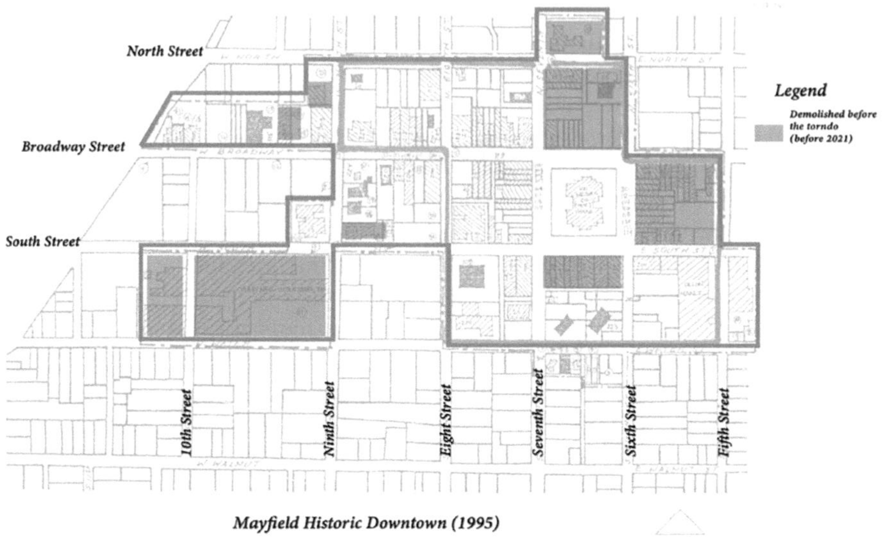


**Fig. 5.2** Mayfield Historic Downtown showing buildings demolished prior to the tornado in 2021 (Kaushal et al. 2023)

34 existed before the tornado occurred and could be broadly categorized into one-story structures, two-story structures, three or more storied structures, and unique structures (Kaushal et al. 2023). These historic structures were constructed in the early to mid-1900s, primarily as masonry buildings (National Register of Historic Places 1984).

## 5.3 Data Collection Efforts

### *5.3.1 2020 Beirut Explosion*

In the explosion's aftermath in Beirut, a comprehensive reconnaissance mission was launched to collect data on the destruction and understand the structural responses of historic masonry buildings (Kallas and Napolitano 2023). 40 architect-restorers formed the Beirut Built Heritage Rescue initiative (BBHR2020) under the Lebanese Ministry of Culture—the Directorate General of Antiquities. Their goal was to identify, assess, and preserve the built heritage affected by the blast. On August 6th, 2020, just two days after the explosion, an emergency 3D digitization mission was initiated by the author as part of the BBHR2020 initiative (Kallas et al. 2020; Kallas and Napolitano 2023). This marked the first extensive and systematic documentation and digitization of Beirut's historic buildings. The mission aimed to provide the

**Fig. 5.3** Point cloud models generated for two of the buildings hit by the 2020 Beirut explosion: (*left*) 3D model of a severely damaged building (*right*) 3D model of a moderately damaged building (Kallas et al. 2020)

Directorate General of Antiquities with detailed 3D models of the affected buildings, aiding in their assessment and making the data available for future research.

The documentation effort was divided into two main tasks: digitizing buildings at imminent risk of collapse and those moderately damaged (Fig. 5.3). One of the authors of this chapter documented 40 highly at-risk buildings and provided photogrammetry training for 12 architecture students, who then documented the moderately damaged buildings.

Photogrammetry technology was employed due to its speed, accuracy, and cost-effectiveness. Photogrammetry generates 3D point cloud models, offering a detailed representation of the structures. The data acquisition adhered to the 3 × 3 photogrammetric rules set by CIPA (International Committee of Architectural Photogrammetry) Heritage Documentation (Waldhausl et al. 2013). For aerial photogrammetry, a DJI Phantom 4 Pro drone was used (DJI 2024), while terrestrial photogrammetry utilized a Nikon D800 DSLR camera (NIKON 2024). The same camera was used for interior photogrammetry, both from the ground level and attached to a 5-m telescopic pole.

To streamline the data filtering and processing, smart photogrammetry techniques were applied (Eastwood et al. 2020). This method involves determining optimal camera positions to enhance the 3D model's quality and resolution while minimizing the number of images required. This approach was essential as personal equipment was used, and high-end processing workstations were unavailable. Ground sampling resolution (GSD) was set for each mission to determine camera locations and distances, which helped define how the cameras should move vertically and horizontally, both for the drone and DSLR, based on their sensor sizes and image resolutions.

### 5.3.2 2021 Quad State Tornado

Following the tornado, a comprehensive two-phase reconnaissance mission was coordinated to gather damage data from the impacted areas and understand the behavior of historic masonry building structures. The initial data collection occurred in collaboration with the Structural Extreme Events Network (StEER), concentrating on assessing the damage extent in Kentucky in December 2021. The second mission, conducted in March 2022 focused on digitally documenting the remaining historic building structures within the affected town. By that time, only 10 historic buildings listed by the NRHP and 2 buildings classified as religious typology could be documented, as the rest had already been demolished due to the damage. The efforts concentrated on documenting these structures using photogrammetry and LiDAR techniques.

For the first mission, The Virtual Assessment Structural Team (VAST) was activated on December 11, 2021. The team gathered information from online video-sharing websites (e.g., YouTube channels), social media sites (e.g., Twitter), newspaper articles (Kristin 2021; Finch 2021; Kobin 2021), and weather reports to determine the impacted towns, which included Mayfield, Cambridge Shores, Princeton, Dawson Springs, Bremen, and Bowling Green in Kentucky. From December 12 to 16, 2021, the Field Assessment Structural Team (FAST) was deployed to these towns to gather building-specific damage data. The authors (Kaushaul et al. 2023) and other volunteers participated in the on-site deployment. Team members were divided into smaller groups of 2–3, based on the assigned tasks. They used street-view cameras, unmanned aerial vehicles (UAVs), and door-to-door (D2D) assessment techniques to collect data and assess the extent of tornado damage. Each day concluded with teams backing up their data, updating one another on-site conditions, and drafting a written summary of their findings. The comprehensive report of the findings is available in Pilkington et al. (2021).

During the second mission, Unmanned Aerial Vehicles (UAVs) were employed to capture aerial imagery of each historic structure. The ability of UAVs to gather large-scale data along with high-resolution imagery has previously been leveraged for reconstruction (Zheng et al. 2018). The DJI Matrix (DJI X5S) was flown approximately 20–40 m above each structure to ensure comprehensive coverage. Moreover, flights were conducted using both a grid-like pattern and a circular pattern to collect images for the future construction of a point cloud. The Pix4DCapture flight app to design the drone flight and image captures in Mayfield (PIX4D 2022). The app uses mission settings such as flight altitude, overlap, camera type, camera angle, and drone speed to create the best image capture waypoints in a flight path, thus taking images over specific time intervals. These time intervals varied with each flight, but in general, the mission set included an oblique camera angle at 60 degrees, 80% overlap, and the normal drone speed. In addition to capturing aerial imagery, an extra measure was implemented to establish spatial connections among the images. Ground Control Points (GCPs) were specifically identified for this purpose. These GCPs serve as distinct and recognizable targets on the ground, facilitating the scaling and orientation of images concerning their global positions through GPS coordinates. In this project, the selection of GCPs was diverse, ranging from utilizing road markings to placing pre-printed markers near the structures. In total, 49 GCPs were employed for Mayfield, and coordinates were established for all four corners of the documented structure.

In addition to aerial photogrammetry, terrestrial photogrammetry was conducted using the Leica P50 and RTC360 Laeica scanners, along with a hand-held Canon camera. The Leica RTC360 scanner was utilized to capture the external facades of the majority of structures, while the Leica P50 was exclusively deployed for the courthouse and internal spaces. This decision was guided by the RTC360 scanner's capabilities, which include the accurate capture of image data at an impressive rate, the generation of a point cloud in under two minutes, and its convenient portability (Biasion et al. 2019). Conversely, the Leica P50 covers a larger distance of up to 1 km and provides high-quality 3D data and HDR imaging, with an exceptionally high-speed scan rate of 1 million points per second. Given its slower scanning pace compared to the RTC360, the P50 was selectively used in specific locations (Leica Geosystems 2022).

The scanners were strategically positioned at all the corners and mid-points of the structures, complemented by Canon camera imagery to overcome the limitations associated with UAVs, particularly their minimal coverage of building facades since they were not flown along the facades. This combined approach aimed to construct a comprehensive photogrammetry model. In addition to this, the Global Navigation Satellite Systems (GNSS) was enabled to identify the geospatial location for all the scans and help create a highly accurate point cloud.

In situations where it was safe to approach the buildings, coded targets were placed on the elevations and measured using a total station to scale and geo-reference the 3D models. If approaching the buildings was too dangerous, clear natural points around the structures were recorded and measured instead (Napolitano and Branko 2018). The number and accuracy of ground control points were determined according to the guidelines of the American Society for Photogrammetry and Remote Sensing (ASPRS) (ASPRS 2014).

All the collected data was processed using Agisoft Metashape Professional Edition, version 1.6.2 (Agisolft 2024). To expedite the processing and avoid system crashes, Python scripting was employed to process the models in chunks rather than as a single entity (Poliarnyi et al. 2020). This method significantly reduced the processing time and improved workflow efficiency.

The digitization mission provided invaluable data for preservation and restoration efforts. By creating detailed 3D models of the affected buildings (Fig. 5.4), the team could document the extent of the damage accurately and propose restoration strategies based on precise measurements. The geo-referenced and scaled 3D models generated from the digitization mission were instrumental in assisting engineers and experts with the emergency propping and sheltering efforts by providing accurate dimensions and detailed visualizations of the damaged areas, allowing for rapid implementation and structural stabilization. Additionally, these models facilitated preliminary structural analyses and the preparation of restoration files, enabling quicker assessment

**Fig. 5.4** Point cloud models generated for two of the buildings hit by the 2021 Midwest tornado: American Legion building (*left*) and The Clothing Mill building (*right*)

and intervention planning for the preservation and restoration of Beirut's damaged historic buildings. These efforts were crucial for preserving Beirut's architectural heritage, which holds significant historical and cultural value. This comprehensive documentation effort highlights the importance of modern technology in heritage preservation, providing a framework for similar initiatives in other regions facing threats to their cultural heritage.

## 5.4 Data Synthesis

While the 2021 Quad State Tornado and 2020 Beirut Port Explosion represented vastly different disaster types (a violent tornado outbreak versus a massive explosive blast), the urgency to rapidly document and digitize impacted cultural heritage sites was similar. Data acquisition strategies also diverged—Mayfield's effort utilized aerial drones, terrestrial LiDAR scanning, and architectural photography, while Beirut leveraged strategic smart photogrammetry techniques from drones and cameras to maximize model quality while minimizing processing requirements. Table 5.1 summarizes and compares the data collection process for both case studies.

In the aftermath of the Beirut explosion and the Mayfield tornado and collecting this data, the question remained about how to transform this wealth of data into actionable insights for structural engineering purposes. This question highlights a gap often present in post-disaster documentation efforts, where data collection and structural analysis are frequently disconnected. The proposed approach is aimed to bridge this gap, demonstrating how comprehensive 3D documentation can be leveraged beyond archival purposes to inform critical structural assessments and future resilience strategies. By integrating advanced data collection techniques with structural engineering principles, valuable information about building performance, damage patterns, and structural vulnerabilities can be extracted.

This process is based on two approaches: (i) data frame for understanding key attributes influencing damage patterns; and (ii) structural analysis using Finite

**Table 5.1** Data collected after Beirut Explosion (2020) and in Midwest Tornado (2021)

| | 2020 Beirut explosion | 2021 Midwest Tornado |
|---|---|---|
| Documentation equipment | DJI Phantom 4 Pro<br>Nikon D800 DSLR camera | Street-view cameras<br>DJI X5S and Canon EOS7D P50 and RTC360 Leica scanners<br>Door-to-Door (D2D) |
| Documentation techniques | Smart photogrammetry with Ground Sampling Resolution | Ground Control Points (GCPs) |
| Post-processing | Agisoft Metashape | Pix4D |
| Data collected | Point Cloud for 240 buildings (1st mission)<br>Urban model (2nd mission) | Survey into Fulcrum app (1st mission)<br>Point Cloud for 14 buildings (2nd mission) |
| No. of days of mission | 30 days (1st mission)<br>75 days (2nd mission) | 4 days (1st mission)<br>4 days (2nd mission) |

Element Modeling. This synthesis of documentation techniques and data and structural analyses showcases how digital documentation can be directly operationalized to enhance the understanding of historic structures under extreme loading conditions and inform more effective preservation strategies.

The following sections detail the methodologies and research findings, illustrating how the datasets were translated into practical structural engineering applications across both case studies.

### *5.4.1 Data Frame for Understanding Key Attributes Influencing Damage Patterns*

In both initiatives, the acquired data through documentation missions can be leveraged to generate datasets that can be used to develop prediction models through machine learning techniques (Kallas and Napolitano 2024). By analyzing the detailed 3D models and point clouds and extracting information on the building's attributes, such as geometric, material, and typology data, machine learning algorithms can be trained to predict the impact of future disasters on historic buildings (Kallas and Napolitano 2024).

A list of building attributes was defined aiming to understand the factors influencing the resiliency and vulnerability of unreinforced masonry buildings when subjected to disasters. At first, damage categorization was performed, classifying the observed damage into various levels ranging from 0 to 4, with 0 indicating minor damage and 4 indicating total collapse, as defined by the National Science Foundation-published Natural Hazard StEER VAST Handbook (Roueche 2020). This damage categorization serves as target variable for building predictive models, aiming to determine which attributes might influence the level of damage.

The first group of attributes encompasses spatial features related to the overall building shape and geometric information and can be extracted from the point cloud models. Primarily, spatial coordinates ($x$, $y$, $z$) for each point in the cloud were extracted, facilitating accurate mapping of the buildings' physical dimensions and geometry. This included metrics related to the overall building, such as footprint, height, volume, elevation, and number of stories, as well as to the building's elements, such as information on the facade openings' shape and height, wall thickness, and roof type.

Another relevant group concerns attributes related to architectural features, such as building typology type, the year the building was built, and occupancy type (e.g., residential, commercial). In addition, the presence and condition of decorative features like triple-arched bays and balconies, were included. Furthermore, the distance of each building from the explosion's epicenter in Beirut and the distance to the tornado path in Mayfield was calculated using the 3D Haversine formula.

Surface deformation metrics are another essential attribute, as they quantify displacement and deformation by comparing pre- and post-disaster point clouds, identifying areas with significant structural damage requiring immediate intervention. Unfortunately, in both case studies, there was no preexisting digitization of the historic buildings in Beirut's and Mayfield's affected areas. This lack of prior data highlights the critical importance of standardizing digitization practices for historic buildings. Standardizing digitization ensures that comprehensive and accurate digital records are available, enabling effective damage assessment and timely intervention in future disasters.

In sequence, information based on the structural assessment of the damaged historic buildings conducted onsite, several attributes were documented and compiled into the dataframe. This included information on the material composition of different structural elements. For masonry structures, this included the type of stone or brick, mortar, and plaster, along with any evidence of weathering or previous repairs. These details were crucial for evaluating the resilience of the buildings and planning appropriate restoration techniques.

Additionally, the foundation type for each building was recorded and entered as a specific attribute. Understanding the foundation type is essential for assessing the overall stability of the structures and identifying potential vulnerabilities. The roof type and the structural connections between different components were other key attributes. Assessments were made on how well walls, floors, and roofs were connected, as poor connectivity often leads to partial or complete collapse during a disaster. This included checking for proper anchoring and the condition of joints and connections, which are critical for maintaining structural integrity.

Although structural and architectural attributes are important for understanding the factors affecting the damaged state of buildings, the urban surrounding plays a significant role (Kallas and Napolitano 2024). Specifically, attribute such as the building's urban setting, its relationship to adjacent buildings, and its positioning on the street were included in the data frame. These factors, included in the data frame, can inform professionals about how a building and its components absorbs and disperses energy during a disaster, affecting its structural reliability. Furthermore, the potential impact of topography on the vulnerability of buildings is also investigated. Information about whether a building is situated on flat terrain, a hillside, or a foothill was recorded and incorporated into the data frame. This data allows to assess whether the building's location within the topographical landscape contributes to its vulnerability or resilience during such catastrophic events.

These recorded attributes were systematically compiled into the data frame, providing a dataset for analysis. This structured data facilitates the application of advanced analytical techniques, enabling a deeper understanding of the factors influencing structural resilience and informing more effective disaster mitigation and restoration strategies (Kallas and Napolitano 2024). By incorporating these diverse attributes into this study, a more holistic predictive model can be established based on structural factors as well as architectural, urban, and topographical features. This comprehensive approach enhanced the ability to predict damage levels and develop more effective mitigation and restoration strategies.

### *5.4.2 Structural Analysis Using Finite Element Modeling*

Once point cloud models are generated using digital documentation techniques such as terrestrial laser scanning or photogrammetry, they can serve as a foundation for creating finite element models for structural evaluation of buildings (Castellazzi et al. 2022; Cuadros-Rojas et al. 2024). Finite element models are crucial in structural analysis, allowing for detailed simulation and assessment of structural behavior under various loads and conditions (Roca et al. 2010). These models are also valuable in post-disaster recovery, enabling precise evaluation and reconstruction planning by assessing structural integrity and identifying critical areas needing repair.

The use of point clouds to generate numerical models is an increasingly popular research area, enabling the creation of highly detailed 3D models (Castellazzi et al. 2017). These models can be employed for structural analysis (Pepe and Costantino 2021), damage assessment (Cavalagli et al. 2020), and the preservation of historic buildings (Li et al. 2023). However, an intermediate step typically involves using computer-aided design (CAD) to create a geometric replica of the point cloud before it can be used as a numerical model, which is a time-consuming process. To reduce the time and effort required to produce CAD models, researchers have proposed methods to bypass this step and directly convert point clouds into numerical models (Hinks et al. 2013; Barsanti and Guidi 2018; Castellazzi et al. 2022).

Cloud2FEM, an open-source software developed by Castellazzi et al. (2022), can be employed to convert point clouds into finite element meshes. This software has been validated for various structures (Kassotakis et al. 2020; D'Altri et al. 2023). In Cloud2FEM, the point cloud is first vertically sliced into a user-defined number of slices. For each slice, a closed polygon is created by connecting all the points within it, typically representing internal and external walls. These closed polygons for all slices are then stacked together to generate a 3D voxelized object, where each voxel is converted into an 8-node hexahedral element to form a 3D solid mesh. More details about this process and the software can be found in the work carried out by Castellazzi et al. (2017, 2022).

This process allowed modeling of various structural systems, from unreinforced masonry to early twentieth-century constructions, with high fidelity (Kaushal et al. 2024). The models included detailed representations of key structural elements such as load-bearing walls, floor systems, and roof structures. These accurate digital twins enabled performing sophisticated structural analyses, including simulations of wind loads and assessments of structural integrity post-tornado.

### *5.4.3 Challenges During Data Synthesis*

One of the main challenges during data harmonization was dealing with the varied nature of the collected attributes. To address this, uniform protocols were established for data entry and formatting, ensuring all entries adhered to consistent criteria and measurement units. This standardization was essential for maintaining data integrity and facilitating reliable comparative analysis across different attributes.

Integrating spatial data from the 3D point cloud models with the on-site assessments posed another significant challenge. Precise georeferencing and validation processes were necessary to align these datasets accurately. Ensuring that spatial coordinates matched the physical locations of the buildings required serious attention to detail and validation techniques.

Data integrity and provenance were critical considerations throughout the consolidation process. Given the diverse sources and methods of data collection, ensuring the accuracy and reliability of historical and pre-existing data was a priority. Data from multiple sources were cross-referenced and employed field verification and expert reviews to validate the information. This helped mitigate potential issues related to outdated or incomplete data.

Despite these challenges, the consolidated data frame provided a robust and comprehensive dataset. Data integrity was ensured by addressing issues of consistency, accuracy, and validation, enabling reliable analysis and informed decision-making for disaster mitigation and restoration strategies. This approach to data consolidation highlights the importance of standardized digitization practices, which are important for future heritage preservation and effective disaster management.

## 5.5 Summary of Operationalizing Data

The research processes and steps for operationalizing the data collected in post-disaster missions is shown in Fig. 5.5. Actionable structural engineering insights were generated by operationalizing the collected data in these detailed ways. This approach not only informed post-disaster response strategies but also contributed significantly to understanding of how historic structures perform under extreme loading conditions. The knowledge gained from these case studies enhances the ability to develop effective, context-sensitive strategies for preserving and protecting cultural heritage in disaster-prone areas.

Damage assessment was conducted following the documentation process on-site conducted during the missions. For Beirut, Kallas and Napolitano (2024) conducted a comprehensive mapping of damage patterns across the affected buildings. This involved detailed documentation of cracks, out-of-plane deformations, and partial collapses on building facades. These features were correlated with the distance from the blast epicenter, revealing how the blast waves propagated and affected different structural elements. This analysis was particularly insightful for understanding the vulnerability of specific architectural features, such as the triple-arched bays common in Beirut's historic architecture.

In Mayfield, Kaushal et al. (2023), the damage pattern analysis focused on the effects of extreme wind loads. Scholars systematically documented and categorized damage to building envelopes, roof structures, and lateral force-resisting systems. This analysis revealed vulnerable areas in different building typologies, such as weak connections between load-bearing components of roofs and walls, or inadequate lateral bracing in unreinforced masonry structures. The patterns observed provided crucial insights into how tornado forces interacted with historic building forms and construction methods.

In both locations, vulnerability indices were developed based on the collected attribute data. For Beirut, assessment considered factors such as wall thickness, quality of floor-to-wall connections, presence and condition of tie rods, and overall building configuration. The study evaluated how these factors influenced the buildings' resilience to blast loads, creating a ranking system to prioritize structures for intervention. For Mayfield, the vulnerability assessment focused on tornado-specific factors. The study evaluated attributes like roof geometry, quality of roof-to-wall connections, presence of lateral bracing, and overall building shape. This assessment helped identify which structural characteristics contributed to better performance during the tornado, informing recommendations for enhancing resilience in similar historic structures.

The data from both disasters provided valuable insights for performance-based design approaches. In Beirut, the findings informed recommendations for blast-resistant design features that could be sensitively incorporated into historic structures, such as the need for i) strengthening wall-to-floor connections; ii) enhancing the ductility of masonry walls; and iii) improving the overall structural redundancy of buildings while preserving their historic character (Kallas and Napolitano 2024). For Mayfield (Kaushal et al. 2023), the analysis led to guidelines for tornado-resilient construction that respected the architectural heritage of the historic downtown, such as the need for (i) improving roof-to-wall structural connections; (ii) enhancing lateral bracing system; and (iii) developing more robust building envelopes. Importantly, while addressing these recommendations, strategies must be compatible with historic preservation principles, ensuring that resilience could be improved without compromising the architectural integrity of historic structures.

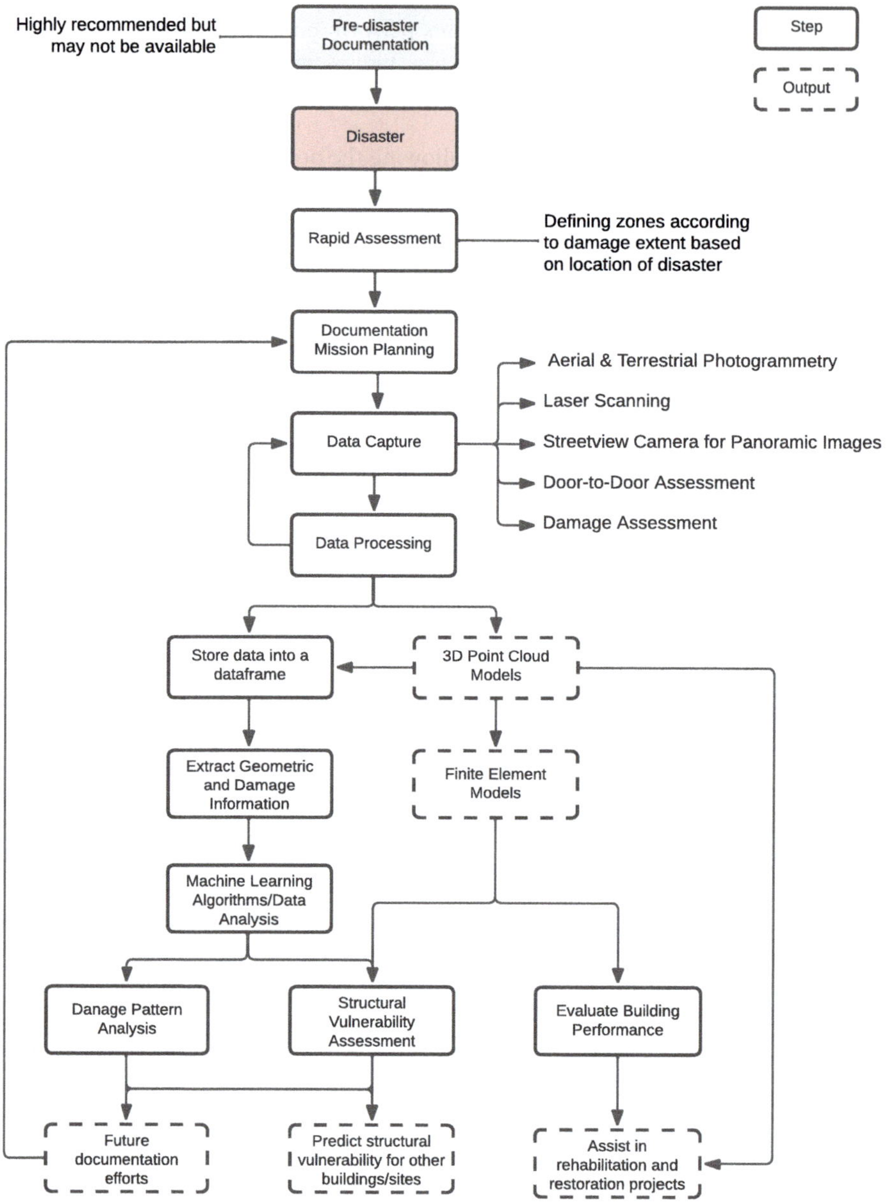


**Fig. 5.5** Flowchart summarizing the process of operationalizing disaster mission data (own elaboration)

## 5.6 Lessons Learned and Conclusions

Areas for improvement in data collection practices specifically tailored for architectural and structural engineering applications in post-disaster contexts were identified based on the experiences in Beirut and Mayfield. These lessons learned highlight the importance of strategically collecting data that can be directly operationalized for structural analysis and future resilience planning. The utility of post-disaster documentation for assessing building performance, understanding failure mechanisms, and developing targeted strengthening strategies was enhanced by refining data collection methods to capture key structural details. These insights are particularly valuable for future documentation missions in historic areas, where the goal extends beyond preservation to include improving the structural resilience of cultural heritage in the face of potential disasters. The following lessons are designed as a reflection for those documented in the future to ensure that the data gathered can directly inform critical decisions about structural integrity, rehabilitation, and risk mitigation in historic built environments.

### *5.6.1 Systematic Pre-disaster Documentation*

The lack of pre-disaster data severely limited the ability to quantify structural changes in both Beirut and Mayfield. In Beirut, the absence of baseline 3D models of the historic Ottoman-era and French Mandate buildings made it challenging to accurately assess the full extent of damage caused by the port explosion. Similarly, in Mayfield, the lack of pre-tornado documentation of the historic downtown structures hampered the ability to precisely measure the deformation and displacement of building elements. To address this, periodic 3D scanning of historic structures is recommended to prepare in the case of a disaster, focusing on mapping key architectural and structural components. This proactive approach would provide a crucial baseline for comparison, allowing engineers to quantify changes with a high degree of accuracy. For instance, regular scans of Beirut's triple-arched bays or Mayfield's historic masonry facades would enable precise measurement of blast-induced or wind-induced deformations in future similar events.

Building on the importance of systematic pre-disaster documentation, it is crucial to recognize that comprehensive documentation of every historic structure is often impractical due to resource constraints. Therefore, a strategic approach to pre-disaster documentation, informed by vulnerability assessments and risk analyses specific to each community, is necessary. By conducting thorough studies on the vulnerabilities of historic structures in different regions, studies can identify which building types, architectural features, or structural elements are most at risk from various disaster scenarios. For instance, in coastal areas prone to hurricanes, the focus might be on roof structures and roof-to-wall connections. In seismic zones, priority might be given to load-bearing walls and floor-to-wall connections. This targeted approach allows for more efficient use of limited resources. In Beirut, knowing the vulnerability of Ottoman-era buildings to blast effects could have prioritized the documentation of their characteristic configurations. In Mayfield, understanding the susceptibility of historic masonry structures to tornados might have led to focused documentation of roof-to-wall connections and unreinforced masonry walls.

### 5.6.2 Documentation on Connections of Load-Bearing Components

In both Beirut and Mayfield, standard resolution scans often missed fine details crucial for structural analysis, particularly in structural connections. In Beirut, the behavior of connections between walls and floors, critical in understanding the buildings' response to the blast, was poorly captured. Similarly, in Mayfield, the intricate joinery in some of the older timber-framed structures was not adequately documented, limiting the understanding of their performance during the tornado. To improve this, it is recommended using higher- resolution scans or close-range photogrammetry for critical structural elements like connections, load-bearing walls, and foundation interfaces.

Additionally, developing specific protocols for detailed documentation of structural connections, including close-up imagery and precise measurements, is crucial. This could involve using handheld scanners to capture detailed geometry of the structural connections for the masonry buildings in Beirut or employing macro photography to document the condition of nailed connections for the wooden structures post-tornado in Mayfield.

Building upon the importance of detailed structural connection documentation, it is essential to recognize that not all connections in a building are equally critical or vulnerable to disaster-induced loads. Therefore, a targeted approach to high-resolution documentation of structural connections is necessary, informed by engineering analysis and historical performance data. By conducting detailed structural analyses and reviewing past disaster performance of similar building types, studies can identify which connections are most crucial for overall structural integrity and most susceptible to failure under various loading conditions.

In unreinforced masonry buildings in seismic zones, the connections between walls and floor diaphragms might be prioritized. In timber-framed structures in hurricane-prone areas, the roof-to-wall connections might be of particular interest. This focused approach allows for more efficient use of advanced documentation techniques like high-resolution scanning or close- range photogrammetry. In Beirut, understanding the critical role of wall-to-floor connections in blast resistance could have prioritized these areas for detailed documentation.

In Mayfield, knowing the vulnerability of certain timber joints to wind-induced loads might have led to focused high-resolution scanning of these specific connection types. This targeted approach can inform the development of standardized protocols for connection documentation. These protocols could specify the required resolution and necessary contextual information for different connection types across various building typologies. Advanced documentation techniques can be effectively applied by aligning detailed structural connection documentation with engineering insights and historical performance data. This approach not only enhances the ability to accurately assess post-disaster damage and failure mechanisms but also contributes to more informed retrofit strategies and improved design guidelines for disaster-resilient connections in historic structures.

#### 5.6.2.1 Internal Structural Element Capture

Focusing on external scans in both case studies often resulted in missing critical internal structural elements. In Beirut, the internal configuration of load-bearing walls and the condition of floor diaphragms were often poorly documented due to safety concerns in entering damaged buildings. In Mayfield, the internal bracing systems of some structures, crucial in understanding their tornado resistance, were not adequately captured. While the interior of a building holds key structural knowledge for understanding performance and failure mechanisms, the difficulty and danger of accessing these areas post-disaster necessitates innovative target approaches to documentation. By leveraging advances in robotics and nondestructive evaluation, studies can develop strategies for safely documenting internal structural elements without risking human lives. However, it can be unfeasible to conduct internal material and geometry capture for every single wall in a town.

The development of such systems should be informed by the specific structural elements most critical for different building typologies and disaster scenarios. For instance, in masonry buildings prone to earthquakes, the focus might be on capturing the condition of internal load-bearing walls and floor diaphragms. In timber-framed structures in hurricane-prone areas, the emphasis might be on documenting internal bracing systems and connection details.

#### 5.6.2.2 Accessibility Planning

In both Beirut and Mayfield, inaccessible areas led to significant data gaps in the structural models. In Beirut, the upper floors and roofs of many damaged buildings were too dangerous to access, leading to incomplete documentation of these critical areas. In Mayfield, debris fields and unstable structures sometimes prevented approaching closer to certain buildings. It is crucial to recognize that effective documentation strategies for hard-to-reach areas should be informed by a comprehensive understanding of structural vulnerabilities specific to different building types and disaster scenarios. This proactive approach to accessibility planning can significantly enhance the efficiency and effectiveness of post-disaster documentation efforts. By conducting vulnerability assessments and analyzing historical disaster performance data, critical building components can be identified, as well as their damage vulnerability and post-disaster accessibility level of difficulty. For instance, in seismic zones, upper floor connections and roof structures might be prioritized for documentation planning. In flood-prone areas, foundation elements and lower floor structures could be the focus. This targeted approach allows for more strategic deployment of advanced documentation technologies, allowing to conduct tailored planning for different building types or structural components, rather than attempting to use drones or long-range scanners indiscriminately. For example, in Beirut, knowing the vulnerability of upper floor connections in blast scenarios could have led to pre-planned drone flight paths focused on these areas. In Mayfield, understanding the critical role of roof-to-wall connections in tornado resistance might have informed the development of specialized long-range scanning protocols for these elements.

## 5.7 Looking Ahead

The case studies of Beirut and Mayfield demonstrate both the value and significant challenges of rapidly documenting and digitizing cultural heritage sites in the aftermath of disasters. While the specific disaster types differed, many of the fundamental issues around data collection, integration, and operationalization were similar across both contexts. These experiences align closely with heritage guidelines (ICOMOS 1964, 2003), which emphasize the importance of comprehensive documentation in the anamnesis phase to support structural analysis and intervention planning. Structural engineers engaged in both documentation and analysis can refine documentation practices based on the specific data needs identified during structural assessments. These insights highlight opportunities to refine post-disaster documentation practices to better serve structural engineering applications. The utility of cultural heritage digitization for assessing building performance, understanding failure mechanisms, and developing targeted strengthening approaches can be enhanced by strategically capturing key structural details. This iterative process of documentation and analysis creates a valuable feedback loop, allowing to continually improve data collection methods to provide more relevant and detailed structural information for future assessments. More robust, evidence-based strategies for preserving historic urban fabric in the face of increasing climate and disaster risks can be developed by refining approaches to collect and synthesize data in ways that directly inform structural assessments. The lessons learned from these case studies provide a foundation for enhancing the resilience of cultural heritage worldwide through strategic digitization and data-driven decision-making.

## References


Agisoft Metashape Professional Edition (Version 1.6.2) (2020). https://www.agisoft.com. Accessed May 2024

Aouad CJ, Chemissany W, Mazzali P et al (2021) Beirut explosion: TNT equivalence from the fireball evolution in the first 170 milliseconds. Shock Waves 31:813–827. https://doi.org/10.1007/s00193-021-01031-9

ASPRS (2014) ASPRS positional accuracy standards for digital geospatial data 1st edn, version 1. https://www.asprs.org/a/society/committees/standards/Positional_Accuracy_Standards.pdf. Accessed May 2024

Barsanti SG, Guidi G (2018) A new methodology for the structural analysis of 3D digitized cultural heritage through FEA. In: IOP conference series: materials science and engineering, vol 364. IOP Publishing, p 012005. https://doi.org/10.1088/1757-899X/364/1/012005

Benchekroun S (2022) Preserving the past for an uncertain future: low-cost, open-source methods for 3-D digital documentation in applied cultural heritage preservation. Master's Thesis. https://doi.org/10.1145/3485444.3507684

Biasion A, Moerwald T, Walser B, Walsh G (2019) A new approach to the terrestrial laser scanner workflow: the RTC360 solution. In: FIG working week 2019: geospatial information for a smarter life and environmental resilience. https://www.fig.net/resources/proceedings/fig_proceedings/fig2019/papers/ts05f/TS05F_biasion_et_al_9968_abs.pdf. Accessed May 2024

Bondestein R (2021a) Historical and social background. In: Chahine N, Dagher F (eds) Houses of Beirut: 1860–1925, restoration manual. Al-Ayn, pp 16–19

Bondestein R (2021b) Typology of the Beiruti house. In: Chahine N, Dagher F (eds) Houses of Beirut: 1860–1925, restoration manual. Al-Ayn, pp 20–25

Castellazzi G, D'Altri AM, de Miranda S, Ubertini F (2017) An innovative numerical modeling strategy for the structural analysis of historical monumental buildings. Eng Struct 132:229–248. https://doi.org/10.1016/j.engstruct.2016.11.032

Castellazzi G, Lo Presti N, D'Altri AM, de Miranda S (2022) Cloud2FEM: a finite element mesh generator based on point clouds of existing/historical structures. SoftwareX 18:101099. https://doi.org/10.1016/j.softx.2022.101099

Cavalagli N, Gioffrè M, Grassi S, Gusella V, Pepi C, Volpi GM (2020) On the accuracy of UAV photogrammetric survey for the evaluation of historic masonry structural damages. Proc Struct Integr 29:165–174. https://doi.org/10.1016/j.prostr.2020.11.153

Chahine N (2021) Earth-lime mortar. In: Chahine N, Dagher F (eds) Houses of Beirut: 1860–1925, restoration manual. Al-Ayn, pp 56–58

Chalhoub M (2021a) Columns and arches. In: Chahine N, Dagher F (eds) Houses of Beirut: 1860–1925, restoration manual. Al-Ayn, pp 54–55

Chalhoub M (2021b) Walls. In: Chahine N, Dagher F (eds) Houses of Beirut: 1860–1925, restoration manual. Al-Ayn, pp 40–51

Cuadros-Rojas E, Saloustros S, Tarque N, Pelà L (2024) Photogrammetry-aided numerical seismic assessment of historical structures composed of adobe, stone, and brick masonry. Application to the San Juan Bautista Church built on the Inca Temple of Huaytará, Peru. Eng Failure Anal 158:107984. https://doi.org/10.1016/j.engfailanal.2024.107984

D'Altri AM, de Miranda S, Castellazzi G, Glisic B (2023) Numerical modelling-based damage diagnostics in cultural heritage structures. J Cult Herit 61:1–12. https://doi.org/10.1016/j.culher.2023.02.004

Dagher F (2021) Jack arch slabs. In: Chahine N, Dagher F (eds) Houses of Beirut: 1860–1925, Restoration Manual. Al-Ayn, pp 68–70

Eastwood J, Zhang H, Isa M, Sims-Waterhouse D, Leach R, Piano S (2020) Smart photogrammetry for three-dimensional shape measurement. Opt Photon Adv Dimen Metrol. https://doi.org/10.1117/12.2556462

Finch A (2021) Death toll climbs from one of the costliest tornado events in history. AccuWeather. https://www.accuweather.com/en/severe-weather/search-for-the-missing-goes-on-in-kentucky-as-death-toll-rises/1061451. Accessed 10 Feb 2022

Guglielmi G (2020) Why Beirut's ammonium nitrate blast was so devastating. Nature. https://www.nature.com/articles/d41586-020-02361-x. Accessed May 2024

Hinks T, Carr H, Truong-Hong L, Laefer DF (2013) Point cloud data conversion into solid models via point-based voxelization. J Surv Eng 139(2):72–83. https://doi.org/10.1061/(ASCE)SU.1943-5428.0000097

International Council on Monuments and Sites (ICOMOS) (1964) The Venice charter: international charter for the conservation and restoration of monuments and sites

International Council on Monuments and Sites (ICOMOS) (2003) Guidelines for the analysis, conservation and structural restoration of architectural heritage. Guidelines, International Scientific Committee for Analysis and Restoration of Structures of Architectural Heritage

Kallas J, Silver M, Vileikis O (2020) Beirut's shattered heritage: an emergency documentation. https://www.cipaheritagedocumentation.org/documentingbeirut/

Kallas J, Napolitano R (2023) Image-based 3D modeling as a damage prioritization tool for historic buildings in post-disaster areas: the case of the 2020 Beirut blast. J Cult Herit 62:314–321. https://doi.org/10.1016/j.culher.2023.06.007

Kallas J, Napolitano R (2024) Understanding critical masonry building attributes shaping vulnerability to blast loads: data-driven insights from the 2020 Beirut explosion. Int J Disast Risk Reduct 110:104640. https://doi.org/10.1016/j.ijdrr.2024.104640

Kassotakis N, Sarhosis V, Riveiro B, Conde B, D'Altri AM, Mills J, Milani G, de Miranda S, Castellazzi G (2020) Three-dimensional discrete element modelling of rubble masonry structures from dense point clouds. Autom Constr 119:103365. https://doi.org/10.1016/j.autcon.2020.103365

Kaushal SS, Gutierrez Soto M, Napolitano R (2023) Understanding the performance of historic masonry structures in Mayfield, KY after the 2021 tornadoes. J Cult Herit 63:120–134. https://doi.org/10.1016/j.culher.2023.07.002

Kaushal SS, Gutierrez Soto M, Napolitano R (2024) Assessing the behavior of historic masonry buildings to tornadic events: a comparative study of code-based analysis and point cloud-based simulation. Eng Fail Anal 163:108539. https://doi.org/10.1016/j.engfailanal.2024.108539

Khalil A, Stravoravdis S (2022) Digital building data longevity and interoperability challenges in the documentation of heritage buildings. In: The international archives of the photogrammetry, remote sensing and spatial information sciences, XLVI-2-W1-2022, pp 283–289. https://doi.org/10.5194/isprs-archives-XLVI-2-W1-2022-283-2022

Kobin B (2021) EF3, or higher? Early estimates of the strength and size of the main Kentucky tornado. Yahoo-Courier J. https://www.yahoo.com/news/strength-size-main-kentucky-tornado-155535202.html. Accessed 15 Jan 2022

Kristin S (2021) Tornado hits corvette plant in bowling green, damage reported. The Drive. Accessed 15 Jan 2022

Leica Geosystems (2022) Leica RTC360 3D laser scanner. https://www.leica-geosystems.com

Li Y, Zhao L, Chen Y, Zhang N, Fan H, Zhang Z (2023) 3D LiDAR and multi-technology collaboration for preservation of built heritage in China: a review. Int J Appl Earth Obs Geoinf 116:103156. https://doi.org/10.1016/j.jag.2022.103156

McDonald JR, Mehta KC, Smith DA, Womble JA (2010) The enhanced Fujita scale: development and implementation. In: Forensic engineering 2009: pathology of the built environment, pp 719–728. https://doi.org/10.1061/41082(362)73

Munday J (1925) The railroads of Kentucky 1861–1865. Master's thesis. University of Louisville, Louisville, KY

Napolitano R, Glisic B (2018) Minimizing the adverse effects of bias and low repeatability precision in photogrammetry software through statistical analysis. J Cult Herit 31:46–52. https://doi.org/10.1016/j.culher.2017.11.005

NASA Earth Observatory (2020) Image by Joshua Stevens, using modified Copernicus Sentinel data processed by ESA, Landsat data from the U.S. Geological Survey, and data from OpenStreetMap. Story by Esprit Smith, NASA's Earth Science News Team, and Michael Carlowicz

National Register of Historic Places (1984) National register of historic places nomination form: mayfield downtown. Register Number 84001477

National Register of Historic Places (1996) National register of historic places nomination form: mayfield downtown commercial district expansion. Register Number 96000791

Nikon Corporation, Nikon D800 DSLR Camera (2012). Accessed May 2024https://www.nikon.com

Pappas S (2021) Quad-state tornado may be longest-lasting ever. https://www.scientificamerican.com/article/quad-state-tornado-may-be-longest-lasting-ever/

Pepe M, Costantino D (2021) UAV photogrammetry and 3D modelling of complex architecture for maintenance purposes: the case study of the masonry bridge on the Sele River, Italy. Period Polytech Civil Eng 65(1):191–203. https://doi.org/10.3311/PPci.16398

DJI Phantom 4 Pro Drone. (n.d.) https://www.dji.com/support/product/phantom-4-pro-v2. Accessed May 2024

Pilkington S, Roueche D, Gutierrez Soto M, Alam M, Napolitano R, Kijewski-Correa T, Prevatt S, Kaushal D, Nakayama J, Saleem M, Ibrahim H, Lyda A, Lester H, Caballero-Russi D, Gurley I, Robertson K, Lombardo F (2021) StEER: 10 December 2021 Midwest tornado outbreak joint preliminary virtual reconnaissance report and early access reconnaissance report (PVRR-EARR). In: StEER—10 December 2021 Midwest Tornado Outbreak. DesignSafe-CI, 1, 1–15. https://www.designsafe-ci.org/community/news/2022/january/steer-team-releases-report-december-2021-tornado-outbreak/

PIX4D (2022) PIX4D mapper: professional photogrammetry and drone mapping software. https://www.pix4d.com/product/pix4dmapper-photogrammetry-software/

Poliarnyi N, Pasumansky A, Morreale JR (2020) GitHub: metashape scripts. https://github.com/agisoft-llc/metashape-scripts

Ranjgar B, Sadeghi-Niaraki A, Shakeri M, Choi S-M, Rahimi F (2020) Cultural heritage information retrieval: data modelling and applications. https://doi.org/10.1109/ACCESS.2024.3374769

Roca P, Cervera M, Gariup G, Pela L (2010) Structural analysis of masonry historical constructions: classical and advanced approaches. Arch Comput Methods Eng 17(3):299–325. https://doi.org/10.1007/s11831-010-9046-1

Roueche D (2020) Virtual assessment structural team (VAST) handbook: data enrichment and quality control (DE/QC) for StEER earthquake rapid evaluation form. NSF, StEER Network. https://www.steer.network/challenge-page/cc17aae5-6fae-4a55-8ad9-0c55300071bf

Samenow J (2021) December tornadoes aren't rare, but Friday's outbreak was something totally different. The Washington Post. https://www.washingtonpost.com/weather/2021/12/12/december-tornadoes-quad-state-outbreak/

Schreiner B, Lovan D (2021) Kentucky tornado toll in dozens; less than feared at factory. AP News. https://apnews.com/article/tornadoes-kentucky-illinois-arkansas-tennessee-missouri-e1ae21e0b7521c28411f8c360b756700

Sielker F, Sichel A, Allmendinger P (2019) Future cities in the making: overcoming barriers to information modelling in socially responsible cities. CDBB. https://doi.org/10.17863/CAM.43318

Ulvi A (2021) Documentation, three-dimensional (3D) modelling, and visualization of cultural heritage by using unmanned aerial vehicle (UAV) photogrammetry and terrestrial laser scanners. Int J Remote Sens 42(6):1994–2021. https://doi.org/10.1080/01431161.2020.1834164

UNESCO (2022a) 60,000 images to save Beirut's architectural heritage. https://dataviz.unesco.org/en/articles/60000-images-save-beiruts-architectural-heritage

UNESCO (2022b) It is time for action to safeguard Beirut's cultural heritage. https://www.unesco.org/en/articles/unesco-rallies-international-community-safeguard-beiruts-cultural-life-and-heritage

Waldhäusl P, Ogleby CL, Lerma JL, Georgopoulos A (2013) Updated 3x3 rules for simple photogrammetric documentation of architecture. In: ISPRS commission V symposium "close range techniques and machine vision". Melbourne, Australia (1994). http://close-range.com/docs/3x3.pdf

Zheng X, Wang F, Li Z (2018) A multi-UAV cooperative route planning methodology for 3D fine-resolution building model reconstruction. ISPRS J Photogr Remote Sens 146:483–494. https://doi.org/10.1016/j.isprsjprs.2018.11.004

# Chapter 6
# Digitally Aided Documentation and Analysis of English Medieval Vaults

**Nicholas J. Webb and Alexandrina C. Buchanan**

**Abstract** The introduction of advanced digital surveying methods, notably laser scanning and photogrammetry, has revolutionized the documentation of architecture, especially for features that were previously difficult to survey without scaffolding. Medieval vaulted ceilings, often high up in church and cathedral interiors, are an example of such a scenario, and for the last ten years the Tracing the Past research team at the University of Liverpool have been investigating these fascinating architectural features across England to better understand their design and construction. Although all are in sites of known significance not generally considered 'at risk', devastating fires at York Minster in 1984 and Notre-Dame in Paris in 2019, as well as earthquakes in Italy in 1997 and 2012, have resulted in the loss of significant vaults in recent decades. This study highlights several methods, demonstrating how they have been used to enhance knowledge of vault design by visualizing them orthographically as laser scan outputs, understanding their underlying geometric principles using 2D vector and 3D wireframe drawings as well as generative design software, and interrogating hard to read medieval plastered surfaces using photogrammetry and reflectance transformation imaging. It also discusses the importance of the digital records in terms of dissemination and archiving.

**Keywords** Medieval vaulted ceilings · Chichester cathedral · Lincoln cathedral · Wells cathedral · Laser scanning · Generative design software · Reflectance transformation imaging

---

N. J. Webb (✉)
School of Architecture, University of Liverpool, Liverpool, UK
e-mail: njwebb@liverpool.ac.uk

A. C. Buchanan
Department of History, University of Liverpool, Liverpool, UK
e-mail: alexb@liverpool.ac.uk

 
S. Stellacci and S. Aydin (eds.), *Endangered Heritage Sites*, Springer Series on Cultural Computing, https://doi.org/10.1007/978-3-031-91949-7_6

## 6.1 Introduction

Vaulted ceilings, often located high up in buildings including churches, cathedrals, and abbeys, are enticingly out of reach in most cases. Their designs, from simple quadripartite through to lierne and fan vaults, are underpinned by geometric principles of varying complexity, and detailed survey data is required to decode these processes. Increasingly from the nineteenth century onwards, scholars across Europe have been intrigued by vault design and construction (Willis 1842; Viollet-le-Duc 1854–68; Choisy 1899). Robert Willis, an English academic and engineer, wrote in his 1842 essay for the Institute of British Architects, during a period of both Gothic revival and medieval gothic conservation, that 'unless we thoroughly understand these constructions, and the methods and resources which governed and limited them, we shall never succeed in obtaining the master key to their principles…' (Willis 1842, p. 2). Hence, Willis saw his investigations as an opportunity to educate architects in the design and construction of vaults using methods that he identified as those used by the original medieval masons, rather than their nineteenth century counterparts; an ethos which is adopted in this current study led by digital methods. Critically, Willis described his essay as a sketch of vault design processes in England and used it as a call to architects working on medieval vaulted buildings to provide him with additional data, to complete his investigations. However, Willis's call was largely unanswered, and much of his data therefore relied either on low level vaults, such as the cloisters at Norwich cathedral, and destroyed building elements, for example from the north-west tower of Canterbury cathedral, which was rebuilt in 1832–41.

Willis, like Viollet-le-Duc and Choisy, was writing in the context of significant restoration work which often amounted to reconstruction (as with the work of Viollet at Notre-Dame and Vezelay); actual reconstruction after disasters (such as two fires at York Minster in 1829 and 1840 and the collapse of the spire and adjoining bays at Chichester Cathedral in 1861), and 'completion' of medieval buildings left unfinished by their original occupants (as at Cologne Cathedral, finally completed in 1880 or Chester Cathedral, where new stone and wooden vaults were added to the choir and nave during the nineteenth century). In the twentieth century, scholarship on medieval vaulting was further advanced by the significant damage caused by the First World War, where vaults were demolished by bombardment at numerous sites including St Remi and the cathedral at Rheims, and the cathedrals of Noyon and Soissons. Throughout their history, medieval vaults have been damaged or destroyed through earthquakes, most recently in Italy at the basilica of San Francesco in Assisi (1997) and Santa Maria Maggiore in Mirandola (2012), and Zagreb Cathedral in Croatia in 2020, which has prompted research into the structural behavior of vaults during seismic events (D'Altri et al. 2017; Bianchini et al. 2023; Gidak et al. 2022).

Over 180 years since Willis's essay on medieval vaults, advanced digital surveying methods, offering detailed and accurate data, have provided opportunities to decode and analyze these significant heritage assets further (Fig. 6.1). Complicating the logistics, as many vaulted ceiling sites are places of worship, and most of them tourist attractions, getting close to these structures is almost impossible without interrupting

**Fig. 6.1** Laser scanning the vaults at Westminster Abbey (photograph by J. R. Peterson)

their day-to-day running. Therefore, the choice of method must ensure that accuracy can be provided from floor level, without interruption via scaffolding, or closure of areas to allow devices such as an elevating work platform to be used. Likewise, drones may require additional authorization and are high-risk inside historic buildings. The advent of digital surveying via laser scanning and photogrammetry, and to some extent total station surveying, have consequently transformed the study of vaulting, which forms the focus of this chapter, but also other hard to reach heritage sites and building components.

Since the introduction of advanced digital surveying, scholars globally have progressed research into gothic design, including vaults, with early adopters including Stephen Murray and Andrew Tallon as part of the Mapping Gothic France project[1] (Murray and Tallon 2015). The primary purpose of Tallon's laser scanning campaign, including Notre-Dame de Paris, was to improve understanding of medieval building construction processes (Sandron and Tallon 2013). However, in April 2019, the significance of the digital surveys shifted, when the roof space of Notre-Dame de Paris caught fire, causing extensive damage to the upper levels, including two bays of vaulting. Digital surveys, like Tallon's, ensured that an accurate record of the cathedral, taken before the fire damage, existed and could be used as a key reference point for the subsequent restoration work. This event, while thankfully rare, serves as a painful reminder of the dangers that have the capacity to damage or destroy heritage assets, and the necessity for accurate digital records. Referring to the reconstruction

[1] https://mcid.mcah.columbia.edu/collection/mapping-gothic. Accessed 1 Aug 2024.

of the damaged and destroyed vaults at Notre-Dame de Paris, the work of scholars internationally has been essential in contributing to the authenticity of this (Maira Vidal 2021; Wendland and Gielin 2022).

The fire at Notre-Dame de Paris, and more recently the fire in the spire of Rouen cathedral, act as important steers for the aims of the English medieval vaults project: firstly, that the digital survey data must be archived to act as a record of these historic structures should damage or destruction occur, and secondly, that the research conducted leads to a better understanding of vault design and construction, which could be used to ensure that reconstruction, if ever needed, could be carried out faithfully, as per Willis's aim.

This study therefore aims to explore a variety of digital surveying, modeling, and analysis methods that have aided understanding of English medieval vaults, undertaken by the *Tracing the Past* project team over the past ten years and to situate these within the context of comparable heritage-related projects across the world. The study begins by outlining the digital surveying methods used, followed by a discussion of their outputs and how these are interpreted using simple vector-based drawings and wireframe 3D modeling. Focus then turns to advanced digital tools such as generative design and Reflectance Transformation Imaging (RTI), followed by the importance of dissemination and archiving.

## 6.2 Digital Surveying Methods and Orthophotos

The project began in 2015, when Alex Buchanan, who had previously researched the work of Professor Robert Willis, including his call for data to help answer questions on medieval vault design (Buchanan 2013), approached Nick Webb, who was using digital tools to research historic works of architecture (Webb and Brown 2016). Initial questions focused on the geometry of the choir aisle vaults at Wells cathedral, and whether digital tools could help inform our understanding of their designs. One of the first tasks to be carried out by the whole project team was therefore to identify appropriate digital methods to capture the form of the vaults from floor level, based on two essential criteria for observation and analysis purposes. First, a high level of legibility to enable clear and readable graphics of vaults and their different components including materiality and color, and second, the accurate capture of 3D vault geometry from rib curvatures down to rib profiles. Three surveying methods were identified, based on the precedents set by other researchers working in the digital heritage field, and specifically vault design and construction internationally (Fig. 6.2).

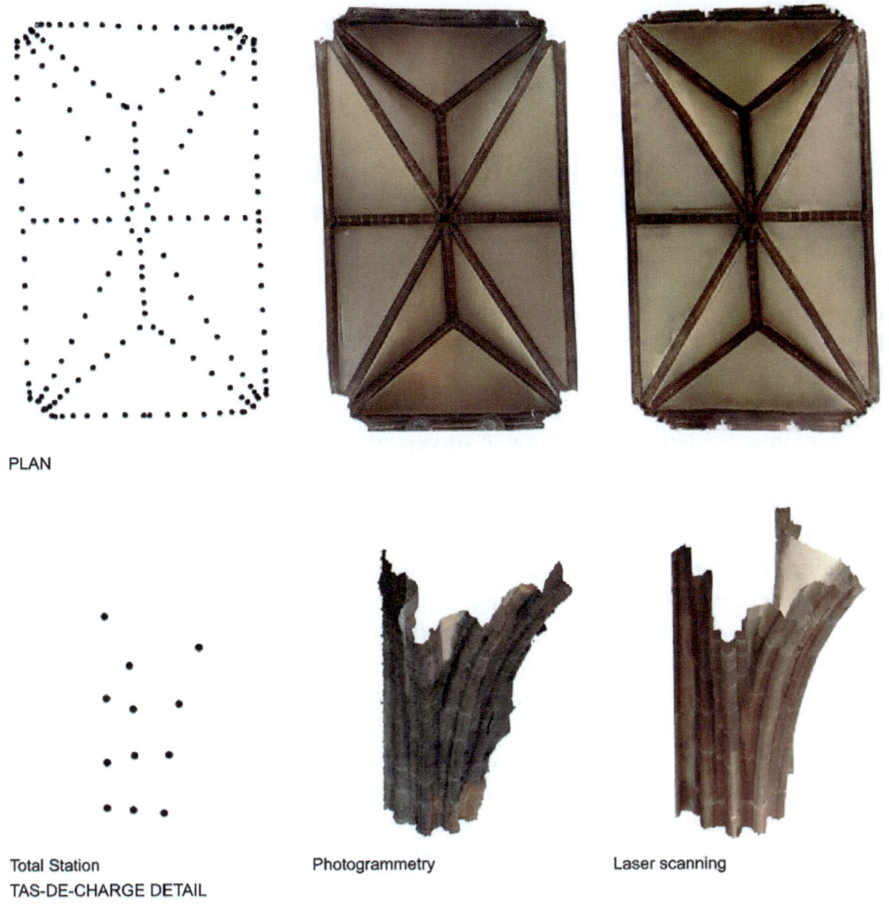


**Fig. 6.2** Comparison between digital surveying methods in the Chapter House at Chester cathedral (own elaboration)

The first of these methods[2] was total station surveying, which accurately records angle and distance measurements of individual points, allowing X, Y, and Z co-ordinates in 3D space to be identified. Once a point of interest is selected using the viewfinder and laser guide, this is recorded, then the next point of interest can be recorded, and so on, until all required geometry is documented (a process that is often painstaking and time-consuming). This data can then be imported into 2D drafting and/or 3D modeling software for observation and analysis purposes. Total station has been particularly useful, firstly, at the earlier stages of the project as an alternative dataset to test the reliability of other digital surveying methods, and secondly, in

[2] Maira Vidal (2017) used this method effectively to study record rib profiles as part of a wider study of sexpartite vaults, and Wendland (2019) has also used it to survey and analyze vaults in Germany and continental Europe.

**Table 6.1** Summary of digital surveying methods against key criteria for the project

| Survey method | Legibility | Accuracy | Survey time | Processing time |
|---|---|---|---|---|
| Total station | Low | High | Slow | Fast |
| Photogrammetry | High | Medium | Medium | Medium |
| Laser scanning | Medium–High | High | Medium | Medium |

recording targeted geometries to assist in with observation and analysis, such as rib profiles in the cloister at Norwich cathedral (Webb et al. 2023). While these examples demonstrate the advantages of total station surveying, they also expose the fact that this method, based on the one-by-one selection of individual points, does not enable the capture of dense point cloud models, which offer color, material, and full 3D form to be observed and analyzed. Terrestrial laser scanning and photogrammetry were therefore investigated as more suitable surveying methods for the project (Fig. 6.2).

Terrestrial laser scanning enables the fast and accurate creation of dense point cloud models for observation and analysis purposes. Likewise, photogrammetry facilitates the creation of such models, but instead relies on 'the art, science and technology of determining the size, shape and identification of objects by analyzing terrestrial or aerial imagery' (Boardman and Bryan 2018, p. 99). This process also results in a dense point cloud model as an initial output. However, the quality and accuracy of these two methods vary. Circling back to one of the main reasons why many aspects of medieval vault design are still underexplored, the fact that these ceiling structures are usually based several meters above floor level has previously made them very difficult to survey accurately. The project team therefore investigated the advantages and disadvantages of both photogrammetry and laser scanning surveys and concluded that the latter would be the primary digital surveying method based on its superior level of accuracy, given that scans were taken from the cathedral floor, often ten meters or more below the vaults above. While photogrammetry gave excellent results for visual analysis of texture and color, it was less reliable when it came to the accuracy of the point cloud data at close range (Fig. 6.2) given that photographs for photogrammetry were also taken from the cathedral floor, and the accuracy of the 3D photogrammetry outputs tend to be reduced as distances increase. Nonetheless, this method has produced reliable results in vault research, particularly that produced by the 'Docogothic' research group in Spain.[3] Table 6.1 summarizes the three surveying methods in terms of the two criteria of legibility and accuracy, as well as the time taken for surveying and processing of data, resulting in laser scanning being chosen as the primary method for the project.

One of the first outputs from the laser scanning process are images derived from the point cloud models.[4] Rather than viewing the 3D point cloud data in perspective, it is instead viewed orthographically. Therefore, the architectural data can quickly be presented in a format like a 2D plan, section or elevation, known as an orthophoto.

[3] Trans_ Got. Available from http://transgot.vaultsconstruction.es/. Accessed 6 Oct 2020.

[4] The project uses a Faro s150 laser scanner, with the associated Faro Scene software used to register, process and export point cloud and mesh models.

At Chichester cathedral, orthophotos obtained from a laser scan survey produced intriguing results that warranted further investigation (Fig. 6.3). Previous plan drawings of the cathedral suggested regular sized bays throughout, whereas Willis in his 1861 survey drawing demonstrates irregularities in bay sizes, including the fact that these were subtle quadrilaterals rather than strict rectangles, for example in bay C10 of the choir (Fig. 6.3). The orthophoto plan created of the vault bays was able to confirm this. Exploring Willis's survey data further, his internal elevation drawing depicts a regular ridge line for the vaulted ceiling of the choir. On the other hand, the new orthophoto internal elevation revealed many subtle variations along the ridge line of the high vaults, notably revealing an uplift at the east end of the choir in C6 and C7. The differences between Willis's hand-drawn survey and those produced using laser scanning are perhaps expected; in the plan versions, where Willis could easily take measurements from ground level, he was able to identify the subtle variations in bay plan dimensions, whereas in elevation, accurate measurements of the vaults above would have been difficult, thus the subtleties of ridge line changes noticed in the laser scan orthophotos are unlikely to have been identifiable.

These two irregularities, non-rectangular bays and varying ridge line heights, were an important acknowledgement. In 1861, the spire of Chichester cathedral collapsed

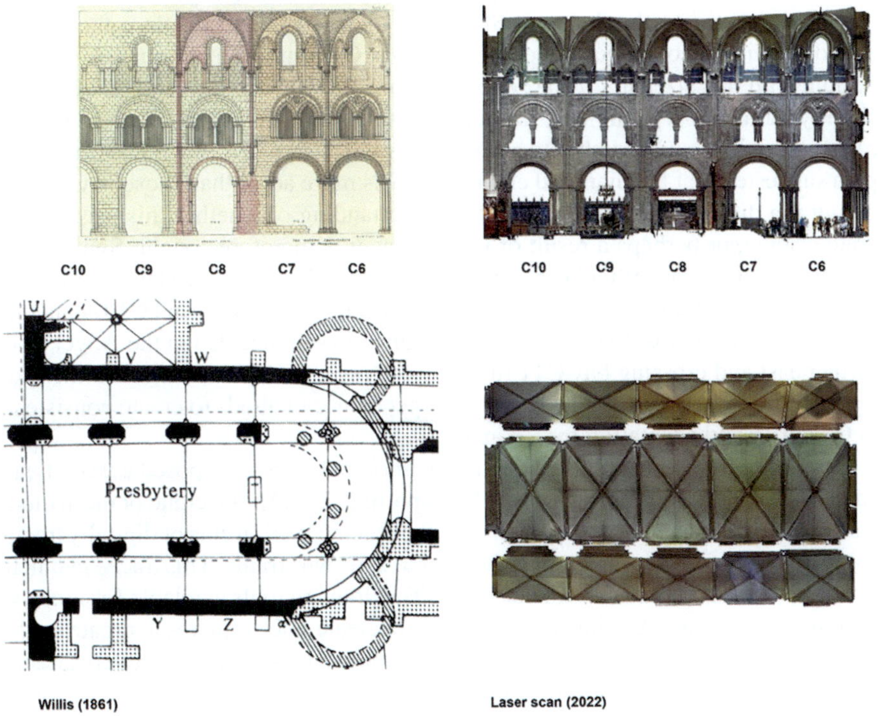


**Fig. 6.3** Chichester cathedral choir plans (*bottom*) and internal elevations (*top*) comparing Willis (1861) with laser scan data (2022) (own elaboration)

in on itself, damaging adjacent bays in the process. Willis's survey data, completed prior to this, formed a vital asset in the rebuilding works (Willis 1861; Buttress 2001). However, as the laser scan orthophotos suggested that irregularities exist to the vault ridge lines, and bay C10, reconstructed after 1861 appears to have a very regular ridgeline, this suggested that the vault may not have been constructed to the same design principles as its predecessor.

## 6.3 2D Vector Drawings and Wireframe 3D Modeling

The previous section has demonstrated how orthophotos are a key asset in visually examining vault geometry. However, they usually act as a starting point for further investigation, rather than providing the answers to research questions on their own. Focus, therefore, turns to the 3D geometry of the vaults, which can be better understood through analysis of point cloud or mesh models. To continue the discussion in this chapter, St Hugh's Choir at Lincoln cathedral is used as a case study. The choir includes the so-called 'crazy vault', an idiosyncratic asymmetrical design. Soon after its completion, the crossing tower between the choir and the nave collapsed in 1235 or 1237, necessitating extensive repairs to the surrounding bays. Like Chichester cathedral, creating orthophotos of St Hugh's Choir vaults at Lincoln cathedral also raised questions. Looking at the plan, bays C6 to C9 contain an asymmetric diamond design, with bay sizes in C7 to C9 being regular sized rectangles and bay C6 being slightly larger, as it is the east transept crossing vault. At the other end, bay C10 reduces in width, and switches to a sexpartite vault design (Fig. 6.4). The orthophoto plan suggested that the diamond created in C9 is more acute than those in C6 to C8, giving it a different design in plan. An understanding of whether this was a deliberate change, or perhaps a result of inaccuracy, was therefore sought. Switching to the internal elevation orthophoto of St Hugh's Choir, this revealed a level apex height for bays C7 to C9, albeit with bulging ridge ribs, and that bays C6 and C10 adapt their heights (Fig. 6.4) most likely acting as bridging bays to meet C5 in the Angel Choir further east and crossing bay C11 further west, respectively. Investigation therefore turned to how the medieval designers used geometric methods to create consistency in C7 to C9, and adaptation for C6 and C10.

To explore these questions, the intrados lines, the interior exposed curve of each vault rib, were traced over. This works by importing the 3D point cloud or mesh model data of each vault bay into Rhinoceros 3D, then taking section cuts or digitally tracing along the vault ribs to reveal their curvatures as a 3D wireframe. This traced geometry was then viewed in plan as a line drawing. The drawing tools available for medieval designers were limited, using a straight edge to create lines, squares to create angles, and a set of dividers to create curves. Drawing onto a plaster surface called a tracing floor (although we have no pre-fourteenth-century evidence for the use of tracing floors in England), these tools allowed the designers to test their ideas, usually at 1:1 scale. The aim was therefore to use the digitally traced 2D plan of the vault bays

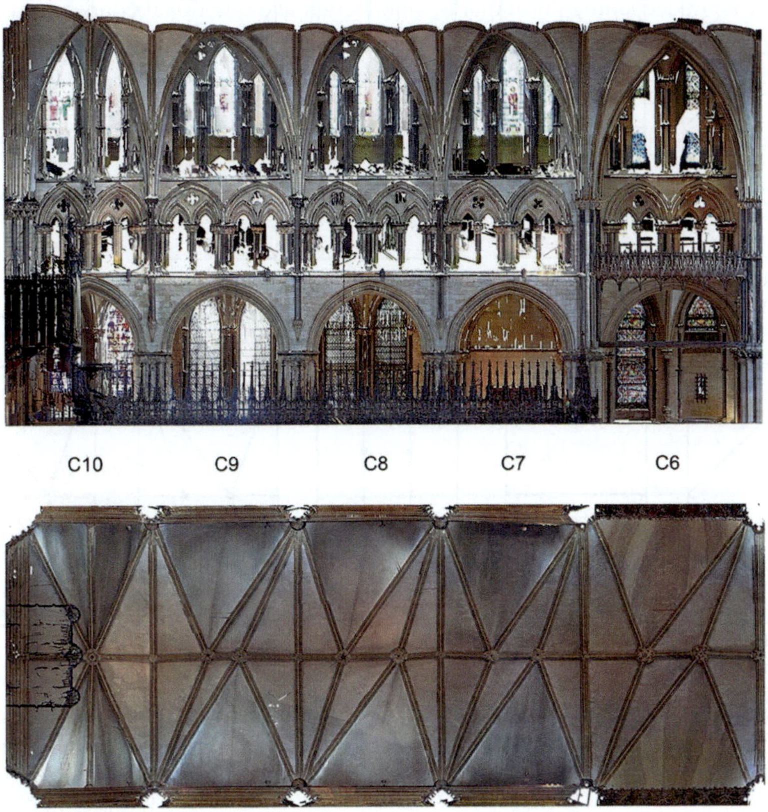


**Fig. 6.4** Orthophoto internal elevation (*top*) and plan (*bottom*) of the vaults in St Hugh's Choir at Lincoln Cathedral (own elaboration)

in St Hugh's Choir to reverse engineer how they may have been designed; for this process, 2D vector drawings were used, working in MicroStation (Fig. 6.5).

To start creating a bay design in plan, a geometric dividing diagram known as the starcut is often required (Stewart 2009). Here, a line is drawn from the corner of a bay edge to the opposite midpoint, then back from this midpoint to the other corner of the initial bay edge, to create a chevron. This is repeated for all four sides of the bay to create the starcut geometry. This is especially useful, as the various crossing points of the chevron lines can be used to divide the bay, for example into thirds or fifths (Fig. 6.5). This point was critical when comparing bays C6 to C8 with bay C9 in St Hugh's Choir. In both designs, a central ridge line is first drawn to divide the bay in two longitudinally. For C6 to C8, the starcut was then used to divide this central ridge line into thirds, whereas for C9 the starcut was used to find the central fifth of the ridge line. In both instances, bay corners could then be joined to the relevant central points to create the required bay plans (Fig. 6.5). Crucially for the research, the change in geometry in bay C9 appeared to be deliberate, considering how closely

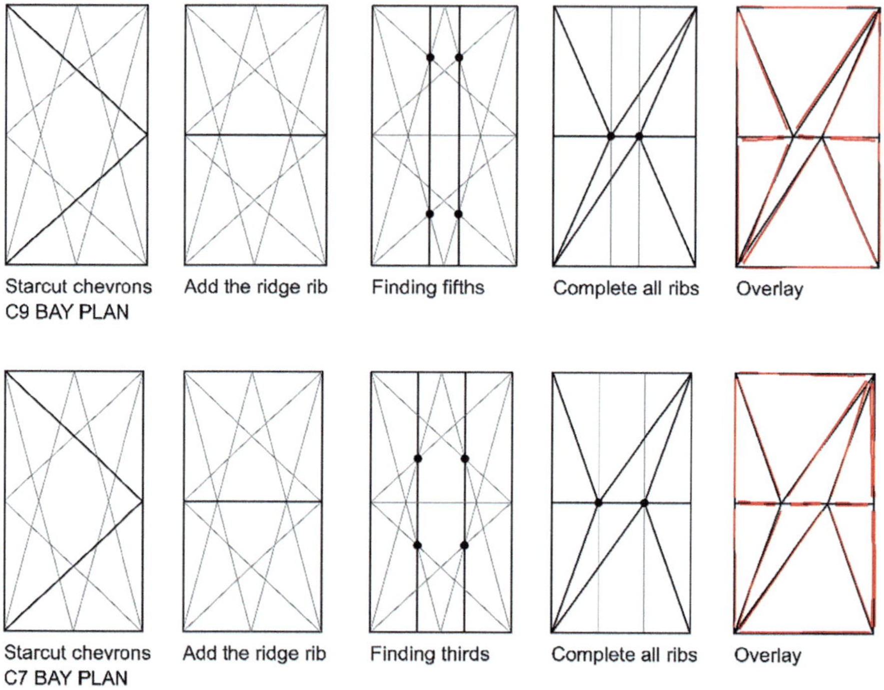


**Fig. 6.5** Hypotheses for the bay plan design in C9 as well as C6 to C6, demonstrated here by C8, including an overlay of lines traced from the laser scan data in red, to justify the result (own elaboration)

the hypothesized bay plan aligned with the data traced from the laser scan survey of the vaults. It is unclear why this change in geometry was decided upon; perhaps it acted as a transition, starting to close the diamond pattern before folding completely into the diagonal ribs of C10 (Fig. 6.4).

Continuing to the 3D design of St Hugh's Choir, the traced intrados lines derived from the point cloud data were again used. These wireframe curvatures were converted into best fit arcs in Rhinoceros, to enable geometric properties to be extrapolated, namely their radius, notional apex height, span, and arc center point in relation to the impost line, usually level with the springing of the rib (Fig. 6.6, *left*). Data for every rib in every relevant bay was then inputted into a table to enable trends to be identified, which is critical in understanding the geometry of the vaults (Table 6.2). The process of using the traced intrados lines derived from the point cloud data to create best fit arcs is not usually straightforward. For example, alignment between the two is never exact due to reasons such as fuzzy point cloud data, damaged vault ribs and possible structural subsidence. Likewise, rib arcs, whist often made of a single curvature, sometimes include more than one curvature, and the best fit process therefore includes the added complexity of identifying these. The tracing and best fit process consequently requires substantial time in terms of testing different proposals

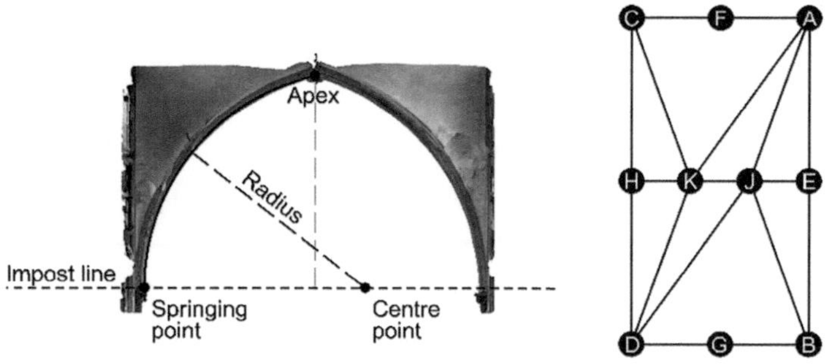


**Fig. 6.6** Orthophoto section through bay C8 at Lincoln cathedral demonstrating key vault geometry (*left*) and wireframe key plan (*right*) (own elaboration)

**Table 6.2** Average figures for key vault rib geometries in bays C7 and C8 of St Hugh's Choir at Lincoln cathedral

| Rib name (bays C7 and C8) | Av. apex from impost (m) | Av. center to impost (m) | Av. radius (m) |
|---|---|---|---|
| Transverse ribs AE, BE, CH, DH | 7.711 | 0.088 | 7.907 |
| Tri-radial ribs AJ, BJ, CK, DK | 7.631 | – 0.050 | 7.943 |
| Tri-radial ribs AK DJ | 7.631 | – 0.047 | 7.706 |

before a satisfactory outcome is proposed, and it is critical that these complexities are acknowledged when sharing the research.[5]

For the 3D design process, focus was on bay C7 and C8 as they share a similarly flat ridgeline, as identified in the orthophoto internal elevation (Fig. 6.4) and the same bay plan based on thirds. The average data for each rib type in these bays (except the wall ribs which have a freeform geometry) supports consistent apex heights above the impost line, with a difference of only 0.080m. The center points of each arc also appeared to be on the impost line, with average values close to 0m, with a maximum variation of 0.138m. Finally, there appeared to be some difference between the average radius of each rib, with tri-radial ribs AK and DJ having a slightly smaller curvature (Fig. 6.6, *right*, for key to ribs), and an overall difference between ribs of 0.201 m.

Using this data enabled a hypothesis to be formed in terms of how the vaults were projected into 3D, with the 2D plans already established acting as a starting point. Given that all ribs in C7 and C8 have a similar apex height, similar center point close to the impost line, and slightly different radii, the chord method of geometric construction is likely to have been used (Fig. 6.7). This is a common method in vault design, for example, it appears also to have been used for the vault ribs of the Chapter House at Chester cathedral, built in the 1250s. To use the chord method, a line is

[5] See Webb and Buchanan (2017) for further discussion of the challenges of the tracing process.

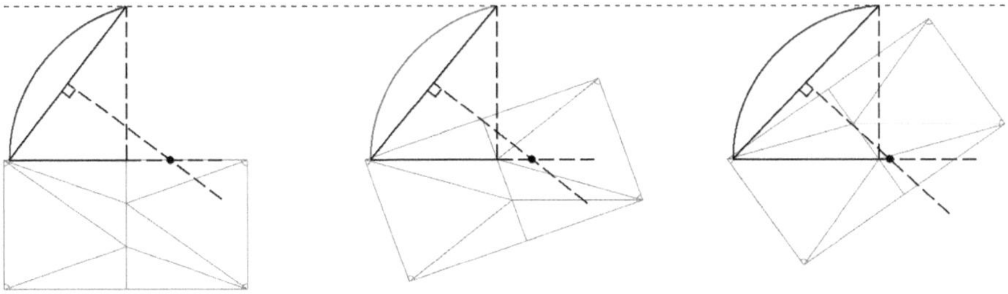


**Fig. 6.7** Demonstration of the chord method of geometric design, as applied to bays C7 and C8 at Lincoln cathedral (own elaboration)

first drawn between the springing point and known apex of each rib type. Next, a perpendicular bisector is created from this line, and where it crosses the impost line gives the location of the arc center point, which can then be used to complete the arc and determine its radius. Data from bay C9 also suggested that the chord method could have been used in the same way, despite working with a plan based on fifths rather than thirds.

Similarly, data from bay C6, which is based on thirds in plan, but is slightly bigger and bridges to different bays, appeared to use the chord method to create most ribs. Data for bay C10 was inconclusive based on a large variety of geometries recorded but may also use the same method. Based on the above investigations, if the medieval designers were using the chord method throughout St Hugh's Choir, this suggested an understanding of its ability to manipulate and control apex heights as required. This method was also found in the Angel Choir and nave of Lincoln cathedral, as well as at other sites of similar dates, which connects Lincoln to them in terms of shared design practices. It is also possible that other geometric processes, such as the three circles method, could have been used (Buchanan et al. 2021a, b). It is important to acknowledge that other processes were tested, as the nature of this research can easily result in paradigm blindless. Nonetheless, the geometry of St Hugh's Choir, particularly bays C7 and C8, is highly likely to be based on the chord method, especially when the original traced laser scan data is overlaid with the hypothesis in 3D (Fig. 6.8).

Again, returning to the focus of this study, the above processes are essential in better understanding vault design, and acknowledging their similarities and differences across bays. If reconstruction were ever required, this information would ensure that rib curvatures were completed using the likely methods of the original designers.

**Fig. 6.8** Isometric views of bay C7 at Lincoln, shown as the traced intrados lines from the laser data (*left*, red), hypothesis based on the chord method (*center*, black) and an overlay of the two to demonstrate a match (*right*) (own elaboration)

## 6.4 Generative Design

Investigations into the geometry of medieval vaults described in the previous section start to reveal the rule-based nature of these designs. For example, the research confirmed that bay C6 and C7 of St Hugh's Choir at Lincoln cathedral both used the same diamond design in plan based on thirds, yet their bay dimensions differ (Fig. 6.4). It would be possible to create a bay plan of this design to any dimensions yet retain the same diamond design principles. Given the prominence of generative and algorithm-led architectural design in recent years, focus therefore turned to software such as Grasshopper for Rhinoceros, and how this could assist in better understanding medieval design principles, a method successfully applied by Akahane-Bryen (2015), Vitali (2017), and Capone et al. (2022). To simplify the argument for this chapter, focus turns to quadripartite vault designs with semicircular diagonal ribs, their underlying rules, and how these can be better understood using generative design software.

Quadripartite vaults featuring semicircular diagonal ribs usually follow a simple process to complete their 3D design. First, the span of the diagonal rib is used as the radius to form the diagonal semicircular arch, with the bay center point, on the impost line, forming the arch center point. Drawing this arch in turn defines its apex height, therefore, this geometry is a generative process, working from a set bay plan to define the height of the vault (Fig. 6.9, *left*). English medieval vaults, unlike their continental counterparts, tend to work to a level ridge line. Therefore, the next step is to complete the 3D design of the bounding transverse and longitudinal ribs to the same apex height as the diagonal ribs. Because the spans of the bounding ribs are necessarily shorter than those of the diagonal ribs, designers working in the Gothic style usually used pointed arches (arches composed of two separate arcs), and the simplest way to generate the appropriate curvatures was to use the chord method, as previously discussed (Sect. 6.3, Fig. 6.7). If round arches were used (as in the earlier Romanesque style), the span of the arch would dictate its radius and it would need to be raised, or stilted, to reach the required height.

Generating the radius from the span sounds like a simple solution to quadripartite vaults with semicircular diagonal ribs and was used for several of the high vaults at

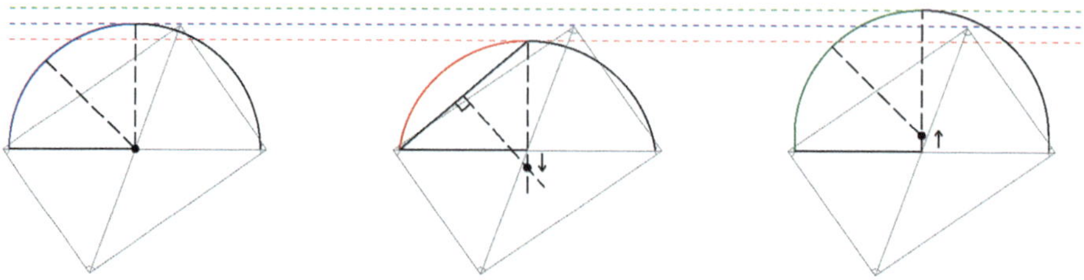


**Fig. 6.9** Generation of a true semicircular arch (*left*), a lower apex height resulting in a segmented semi-circular arch (*center*), and a higher apex height resulting in a stilted semi-circular arch (*right*) (own elaboration)

Chichester cathedral, as well as in the nave aisles at Malmesbury Abbey. However, data collected across several sites in England suggested that this method was not always so straightforward. For example, the quadripartite eastern bays of the north choir aisle at Ely cathedral (erected under Bishop Northwold, c. 1234–52) most likely worked to a pre-existing apex height based on the elevation of the Romanesque cathedral, which still remains in the nave. The side aisles of the Romanesque cathedral had groin (unribbed) vaults over roughly square bays, whose height was defined by the semicircles of the bounding arches and was therefore below the height that would be generated using a semicircular diagonal rib. In order to address this lower height, the semicircular diagonal arch was pushed down, or segmented (Fig. 6.9, *center*). This method uses a variation of the chord method, with the crossing point of the perpendicular bisector with the center line of the rib enabling the radius to be generated. Similarly, designers occasionally required a higher apex than the one generated from the semicircular diagonal, therefore the whole arch could simply be stilted, to accommodate this (Fig. 6.9, *right*).

The Grasshopper software plugin, based on visual scripting, allows rules to be input, which can then be visualized in Rhinoceros 3D. Here the rules to create a quadripartite vault, including methods to create a chord and variations on the semi-circular diagonal rib design, allowed different scenarios and their limitations to be visualized and analyzed quickly and accurately. This was valuable as it meant that less time was spent redrawing and testing different geometry, as these were already modeled and adaptable in Grasshopper, hence more time could be spent on scholarly enquiries. For *Tracing the Past*, using generative design software enabled many different variations of vault designs to be created, in this instance quadripartite vaults with semicircular diagonal ribs, and aligned with sites of investigation across England (Fig. 6.10). Not only did this process enabled a better understanding of the rule-based nature of medieval vault design, but it also helped to understand the subtleties in the process, for example by stilting or segmenting an arch, or by tweaking a design to increase or decrease the prominence of ribs, as investigated for the tierceron high vaults at Exeter cathedral, which increase in complexity compared to a quadripartite vault (Webb and Buchanan 2019).

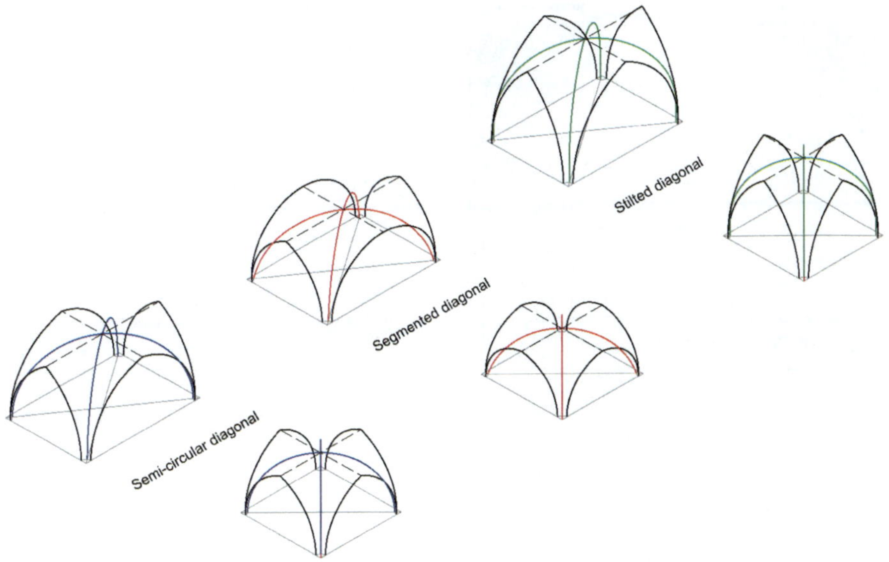


**Fig. 6.10** Results from Grasshopper showing two bay plans projected with different semi-circular diagonal rib types, and the effect on the bounding ribs (own elaboration)

This example of quadripartite vaults therefore serves as a simple demonstration of the use of generative design tools. The rule-based and processual nature of medieval design helped medieval masons to address the realities of medieval construction, where they were often working with pre-existing buildings which provided fixed elements, such as bay sizes and elevation heights. For example, at Ely cathedral in Cambridgeshire, the height of the Romanesque elevation not only determined the heights of Bishop Northwold's choir in the thirteenth century but also the work that partially replaced it a century later after the Romanesque crossing tower collapsed in 1322, necessitating reconstruction of the adjoining bays to the east.

## 6.5 Photogrammetry and Reflectance Transformation Imaging

When medieval designers tested their ideas prior to construction, the tracing floor was a key tool in which lines and arcs were inscribed onto a surface, typically plaster floors, and usually at 1:1 scale. Overlapping and overlaid drawings would often exist on the same floor, creating a complex array of geometry. In England, such working drawings rarely survive; for example, there is one at Wells cathedral, another at York Minster and also at Christchurch Priory. Based on prior research investigating the vaults at Wells cathedral, the project team wanted to explore potential links between these and the tracing floor geometry. The plaster tracing floor at Wells is in the roof

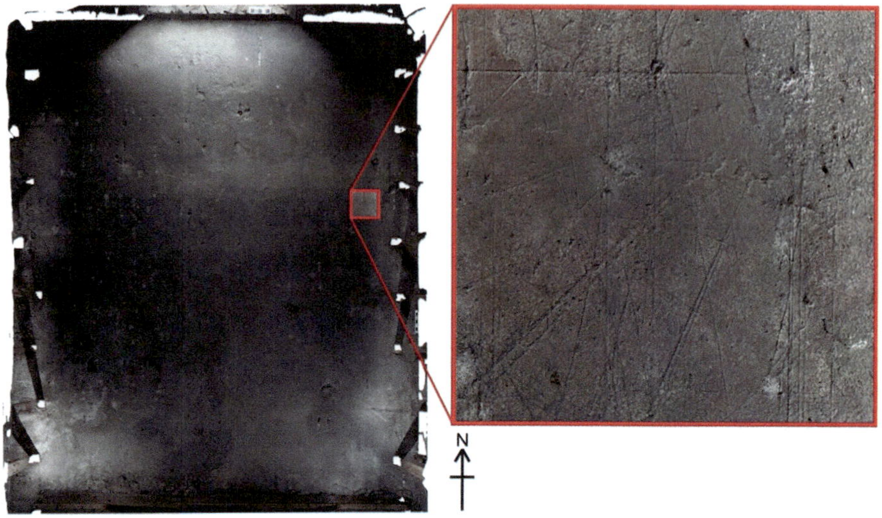


**Fig. 6.11** Photogrammetry orthomosaic of the tracing floor at Wells cathedral (*left*) including large-scale sample (*right*) (own elaboration)

space above the north porch, and measures 5.5 by 6.5m. Not only is this design device a rare example; it is also endangered based on several known factors including age, leaving it prone to cracks, weathering, including leaks from the roof, and wear and tear, particularly as the space was used for a period by schoolchildren. Colchester and Harvey (1974) were able to produce a drawing of the tracing floor based on a series of photographs taken for the National Monuments Record. Nearly 50 years later, the project team aimed to produce an accurate digitized version of the tracing floor, followed by 2D vector drawings traced from these outputs.

Photogrammetry became a key method to digitize the medieval tracing floor.[6] Encountered issues included photographing around the roof joists, which restricted the positioning of the camera tripod, as well as uneven natural lighting, which was corrected by adding two flash guns to the south, away from the single north window. The photographs were processed using the photogrammetry software Agisoft Metashape, producing a 3D point cloud model of the floor, which was then exported as a 2D orthomosaic plan, with a resolution of 0.25mm per pixel. This image (over 500MB) gave a detailed and accurate digital record of the tracing floor as shown in Fig. 6.11.

To do this, it was imported into MicroStation, and each line and arc painstakingly traced over to form a 2D vector drawing, aided by a grid system to search individual squares for any relevant geometry, then moving on to the next one (Fig. 6.12). This was very much a manual process, where lines and arcs had to be distinguished from

[6] A Sony A7 Mk3 camera was used to take hundreds of photographs, pointing straight down at the surface and obliquely, as well as using wide and narrow focal lengths to capture different levels of detail.

cracks and scrapes; a difficult procedure that often-involved judgement calls being made to determine relevant geometries.

To further interrogate this geometry, particularly as faint lines and arcs were very difficult to identify, experimentation turned to Reflectance Transformation Imaging (RTI). This process has the potential to reveal details that are difficult to see by eye, by taking multiple images from a static location that are lit from a systematic series of positions around a target area in plan (Duffy 2018). These images are processed using RTIBuilder software, which is used to simulate raking light and highlight very fine

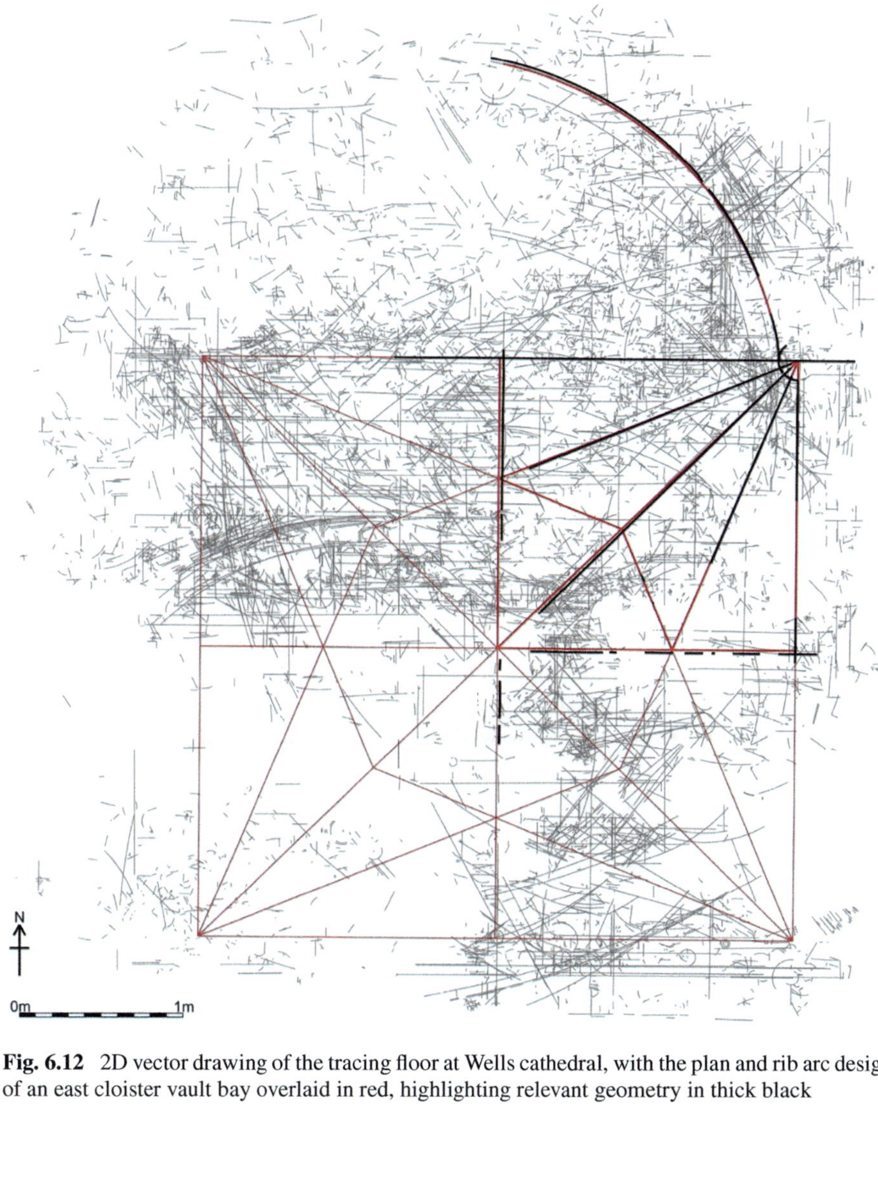


**Fig. 6.12** 2D vector drawing of the tracing floor at Wells cathedral, with the plan and rib arc design of an east cloister vault bay overlaid in red, highlighting relevant geometry in thick black

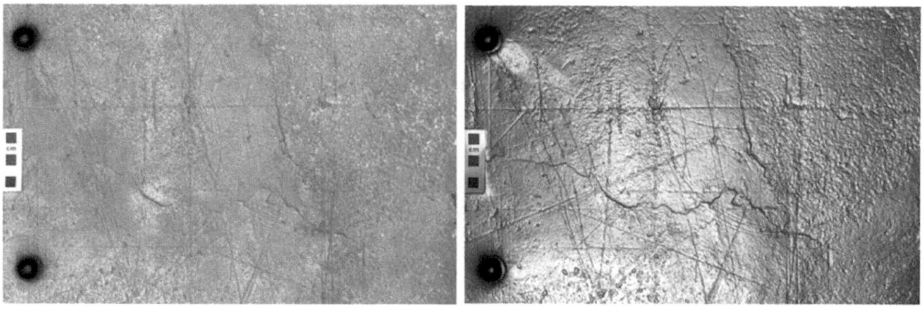

**Fig. 6.13** Tracing floor at Wells cathedral viewed using RTI in default (*left*) and aided by specular enhancement (*right*)

surface textures and marks. Over a small case study area of 0.3 by 0.2 m, this method demonstrated that an increased number of lines and arcs were identifiable when retracing the floor as a vector-based 2D drawing (Fig. 6.13), offering the potential for enhanced analysis, for example if these previously hard to see lines and arcs formed part of a significant medieval drawing.

Pacey (2007) previously attempted to analyze the same tracing floor, aided by the drawings of Colchester and Harvey (1974), as well as additional tracings of selected areas. Pacey identified two drawings of designs within Wells cathedral, with one of them being the vaults of the east walk in the cloister. In recognizing this connection between the cloister and tracing floor drawing, Pacey also stated that testing his theory would require more accurate surveys of both the tracing floor and built vaults. Hence, the new digital 2D vector drawing derived from the photogrammetry and RTI surveys of the tracing floor, as well as a 3D laser scan of the east cloister vault, formed valuable assets to further explore Pacey's theory.

Using the 3D laser scan data, vault rib curvatures in the east cloister were traced over, then viewed in plan, which enabled the identification of their 2D geometric design. This was followed by analysis of 3D rib curvatures to understand their geometric properties, using the same methods described in Sect. 6.3. This information was then exported to MicroStation as vector drawings and overlaid with the tracing floor drawing (Fig. 6.12) which showed a very close alignment, as suggested by Pacey (2007). The project data was therefore able to strongly support his hypothesis.

Future plans are to continue by documenting further English tracing surfaces, such as those at York Minster and Christchurch Priory. In doing this, pattern recognition and machine learning will be investigated as methods to automate and speed up the tracing process of the image-based orthomosaic outputs, given that this was a particularly laborious task, also made difficult in trying to distinguish between intentional marks and regular cracks. Nonetheless, this process enabled an up-to-date photogrammetric orthomosaic to be produced, as well as a vector-based line drawing, both serving as key digital assets in documenting and analyzing the tracing floor. The data is also important in terms of accessibility; the tracing floor sits above the north porch at triforium level and is reached by stairs only. Therefore, this data

**Fig. 6.14** North transept at St Mary's Nantwich (*left*) and point cloud data of the same space (*right*) (own elaboration)

allows greater access to those who cannot visit the tracing floor in person. A further plan is to continue to use this data to link the tracing floor survey with that of the cloister vault it was likely used to design, for example by using augmented reality methods to overlay the data.

## 6.6 Dissemination and Archiving

The above sections outline some of the methods used to document and analyze English medieval vaults, and the *Tracing the Past* website (Buchanan et al. 2021a, b) forms a key asset in sharing project information digitally, particularly as 3D models can be embedded from Sketchfab, which contains a catalogue of key vaults analyzed for the project (Sketchfab 2024). Other researchers have used online information too, such as the Mixtec Stonecutting Artistry website.[7] Each site in England have produced findings based on analysis of the vaults, and digitally aided techniques have helped to further disseminate these, as demonstrated at St Mary's Church in Nantwich (Fig. 6.14).

St Mary's features an ambitious run of three bays of vaulting from the fourteenth century, which became a key case study for the project, particularly given possible design links to sites such as the choir aisle vaults at Wells cathedral. However, the site was also intriguing as it contains either an incomplete or partially destroyed vault in the north transept, which became another focus of investigation (Fig. 6.14). Here, the remaining springer stones, which are the starting point of the vaulting, as well as the wall ribs, were traced over using the 3D survey models, as per the methodology discussed in Sect. 6.3. Analysis then turned to best fit arcs, which were projected out from the springer stones, to ascertain how the vault may have looked

[7] Mixtec Stonecutting Artistry. Available at www.mixtecstonecutting.com. Accessed 2 Aug 2024.

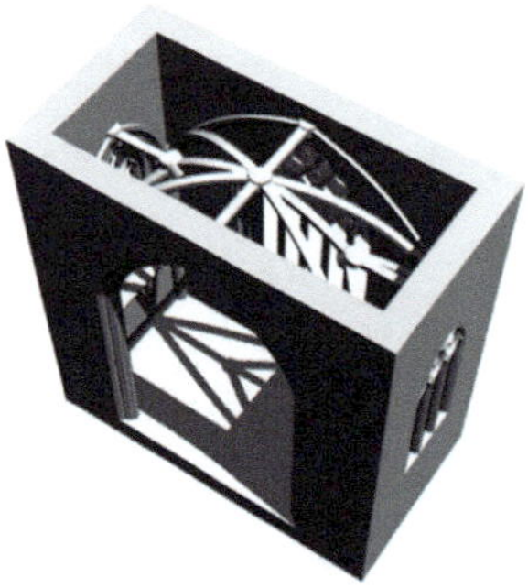

**Fig. 6.15** Dissemination methods in the north transept at St Mary's Nantwich: 3D digital model of option 3 uploaded to Sketchfab (*left*) and 3D prints of all three options (*right*) (own elaboration)

if completed. Three options were proposed, with focus on how similar designs can be found at other sites, and the likelihood of each option based on how they related to the existing fabric. In disseminating the results of this study, 3D digital models were hosted online via Sketchfab and 3D prints of all three options were also created, which could be slotted in and out of a base model to demonstrate the different options to complete the vault (Fig. 6.15). This method was particularly useful during talks and lectures, acting as a tactile example to help explain our results. The north transept vault, if it was destroyed rather than incomplete, serves as a reminder that sites of medieval vaulting are not immune to damage, and that dissemination of what is lost is also critical. A future investigation will turn to Malmesbury Abbey, partially destroyed during the English reformation. The boss stones from the lost vaults are currently stored on site, which could be pieced back together digitally based on a photogrammetry survey of these, as well as a laser scan survey of the remaining building. Bereczki (2022) used a similar technique, basing a digital analysis and reconstruction of a lost vault partially on physical fragments.

The *Tracing the Past* project has produced a wealth of survey data, including registered point cloud models, which not only include the medieval vaults as the focus of the research, but also the surrounding interior context of these spaces (Fig. 6.3). In addition, 3D meshes and point cloud models of individual vaults formed the key sources for the project, as well as orthophoto plans and sections. Unfortunately, however, appropriate archiving of such potentially huge datasets is costly and is often an overlooked element of project design. Individual site custodians rarely have the infrastructure for long-term digital preservation and universities rarely have the resources to preserve research data far beyond the life of the project. Digital data requires active preservation to remain usable and the creation of accessible archives of architectural heritage data needs to be a priority for the heritage community, if the work involved in documenting sites is not to be wasted. The project data was therefore archived internally at the University of Liverpool, but crucially, it was also archived via the Archaeology Data Service (Webb et al. 2021). The data is available online via standard file types and under Creative Commons licensing. This ensured that a permanent and publicly accessible record of the data was available in perpetuity, as per the ICOMOS Principles for the Recording of Monuments, Groups of Buildings and Sites (1996), the London Charter (2009) and internationally agreed FAIR (Findable, Accessible, Interoperable, and Reusable) principles. Again, this was a critical element of the project, as it meant that site custodians, professionals such as architects and archaeologists, researchers as well as the public could use the data, particularly should future damage or destruction occur as well as to assess gradual changes over time. Nonetheless, such archiving of data can be expensive, and it therefore this was fully costed as part of the project in order to ensure it was not an afterthought. For projects without funding, however, the cost of archiving is therefore problematic.

## 6.7 Conclusions and Future Plans

This study has outlined methods used to digitally document medieval vaults in England, primarily using laser scanning, but also total station and photography-based methods including photogrammetry and RTI. This data has helped to answer previously underexplored questions relating to vault design and construction, such as how vaults were designed in plan, and how these were projected as rib arcs into 3D. Likewise, the data has confirmed that medieval vaults often springs from structures that are not based on regular geometry, for example bay designs are often subtle quadrilaterals rather than strict rectangles, which further complicates the subsequent geometric design of the vaults. The data assisted in understanding the rules involved in vault design, for example the use of the chord method, and how this can be applied to vault bays that change dimensions, yet keep the same design principles, as aided by generative design software. Understanding the design principles of single bays, and how these relate to other bays in the same run has proved insightful, for example the adaptability of the design used in St Hugh's Choir at Lincoln cathedral. Likewise, this understanding can be compared to vaults at the same site for comparison, and to other sites in England and internationally. Photogrammetry provided a detailed and accurate record of a medieval tracing floor at Wells cathedral, which could be used to verify the relationship between this drawing and the built vaults of the cloister, based on laser scan data also collected. Similarly, RTI proved a useful tool to further interrogate the lines and arcs of the tracing floor.

Dissemination is essential to the project, focusing on site custodians, architects, archaeologists and stonemasons, researchers investigating vault design and construction internationally, as well as site interest groups. Dissemination has utilized digital methods such as 3D printing, online 3D digital model platforms, as well as websites. Likewise, archiving of data is critical, and ten years of laser scan data of church, cathedral and abbey interiors have been publicly archived online via the Archaeology Data Service, for others to use. Looking to future plans, extended reality (XR) is being investigated as a method to further disseminate results, particularly in cases of damaged or destroyed vaults, where augmented reality could be used to visualize what the vaults may have looked like, focusing on sites such as the north transept at Nantwich St Mary's, the porch at Norton Priory, and several areas of Furness Abbey.

The methodologies discussed in this study rely heavily on tracing rib curvatures 'manually' in 3D modeling software (such as Rhinoceros), then extracting data for individual ribs into a data table, both of which are time-consuming processes. Next steps therefore include investigating the use of machine learning and artificial intelligence to assist with this task; first to use edge detection methods to trace vault rib intrados lines automatically, and second, to use software such as Galapagos for Grasshopper to investigate if rib geometries such as radii and arc center points can be automatically extracted from the traced intrados lines. Crucial to these investigations will be the accuracy of such methods in comparison to existing ones used for the project. Likewise, structural analysis methods, such as those used by D'Altri et al. (2019) offer opportunities to greater understand vault structure and construction. Such methods will enable the team to continue to draw on new and innovative methods to better understand and share knowledge of medieval vaulting design in England. The *Tracing the Past* data, as well as other digital surveying campaigns, serve as vital assets should the worst ever happen, enabling faithful restoration and reconstruction work to take place, in line with Robert Willis's original aim in the 1840s. While there are no known immediate risks to sites of vaulting in England, their histories tell a story of collapse and rebuilding.

**Acknowledgements** Thank you to the Arts and Humanities Research Council in the UK for their funding between 2018 and 2021, and Dr. James Hillson and Dr. Sarah Duffy who both contributed a wealth of time and knowledge to the project as part of this grant. Thank you also to J.R. Peterson for his technical expertise, and the custodians of all case study sites for allowing access.

## References

Akahane-Bryen S (2015) South German Late Gothic design and building Praxis. NSW Architects Registration Board. https://www.architects.nsw.gov.au/download/BHTS/Akahane-Bryen_Sean-South_German_Late_Gothic_Design_Building_Praxis_BHTS.pdf. Accessed 5 Aug 2024

Bereczki Z (2022) Order, procedure, and configuration in gothic architecture: a case study of the Avas Church, Miskolc, Hungary. Architecture 2(4):671–689. https://doi.org/10.3390/architecture2040036

Bianchini N, Nuno Mendes C, Lourenço P (2023) Effects of earthquakes with different nature on the seismic performance of masonry vaults. Proc Struct Integr 44:1244–1251

Boardman C, Bryan P (2018) 3D laser scanning for heritage: advice and guidance on the use of laser scanning in archaeology and architecture. Historic England

Buchanan A (2013) Robert Willis (1800–1875) and the foundation of architectural history. Boydell Press, Woodbridge

Buchanan A, Hillson J, Webb N (2021a) Digital analysis of vaults in English medieval architecture. Routledge, London

Buchanan A, Hillson J, Webb N (2021) Tracing the past. www.tracingthepast.org.uk. Accessed 2 Aug 2024

Buttress D (ed) (2001) Chichester Cathedral spire. The collapse (1861). Otter Memorial Papers 13. University College Chichester

Capone M, Lanzara E, Palomba D (2022) From geometric rules to ribbed vaults procedural modeling parametric tools to study star vaults geometry in St-Eustache. Estado del arte. En: XIX Congreso Internacional de Expresión Gráfica Arquitectónica: 2–4 de junio de 2022. Universidad Politécnica de Cartagena, Cartagena, pp 391–394

Choisy A (1899) L'histoire de l'architecture, 2 vols. Gauthier- Villars, Paris

Colchester L, Harvey J (1974) Wells Cathedral. Archaeol J 131

D'Altri AM, De Miranda S, Castellazzi G, Sarhosis V, Hudson J, Theodossopoulos D (2019) Historic Barrel vaults undergoing differential settlements. Int J Arch Herit 14(8):1196–1209. https://doi.org/10.1080/15583058.2019.1596332

D'Altri AM, Castellazzi G, De Miranda S, Tralli A (2017) Seismic-induced damage in historical masonry vaults: a case-study in the 2012 Emilia earthquake-stricken area. J Build Eng 13:224–243

Duffy S (2018) Highlight-reflectance transformation imaging (H-RTI) for cultural heritage. Historic England

Gidak P et al (2022) Geometry generation and modelling of non-standard cross vaults. In: Proceedings of the IASS 2022 symposium affiliated with APCS 2022 conference innovation sustainability legacy, pp 1–9

ICOMOS (1996) Principles for the recording of monuments, groups of buildings and sites. https://www.icomos.org/en/charters-and-texts/179-articles-en-francais/ressources/charters-and-standards/387-principles-for-the-recording-of-monuments-groups-of-buildings-and-sites-1996. Accessed 2 Aug 2024

Maira Vidal R (2017) The evolution of the knowledge of geometry in early gothic construction: the development of the sexpartite vault in Europe. Int J Arch Herit 11(7):1005–1025. https://doi.org/10.1080/15583058.2017.1332254

Maira Vidal R (2021) Geometry and construction of the severies of the vaults in the Cathedral of Notre Dame de Paris. In: History of construction cultures. CRC Press, pp 341–348. https://doi.org/10.1201/9781003173434-156

Murray S, Tallon A (2015) Mapping gothic. https://mcid.mcah.columbia.edu/art-atlas/mapping-gothic/about. Accessed 8 July 2024

Pacey A (2007) Medieval architectural drawing: English craftsmen's methods and their later persistence (c.1200–1700) Tempus, Stroud

Sandron D, Tallon A (2013) Notre-Dame de Paris: Neuf siècles d'histoire. Parigramme, Paris

Sketchfab (2024) Liverpool school of architecture medieval vaults collection. https://skfb.ly/po6NO. Accessed 2 Aug 2024

Stewart M (2009) Patterns of eternity: sacred geometry and the Starcut diagram. Floris Books, Stourbridge

Trans_ Got (2020) Trans_Got. http://transgot.vaultsconstruction.es/. Accessed 6 Oct 2020

Viollet-le-Duc E-E (1854–68) Dictionnaire raisonné de l'architecture française du XIe au XVIe siècle, 10 vols. B. Bance and A. Morel, Paris

Vitali M (2017) 3D parametric models for 'Planterian' vaults in Turin. Nexus Netw J 19:301–321

Webb N, Buchanan A (2017) Tracing the past: establishing tolerances when investigating medieval Vault Rib geometries using digital tools. In: Envisioning architecture: space/time/meaning, vol 1. Glasgow School of Art, , pp 30–37

Webb N, Buchanan A (2019) Digitally aided analysis of medieval vaults in an English cathedral, using generative design tools. Int J Arch Comput 17(3):241–259. https://doi.org/10.1177/1478077119866126

Webb N, Brown A (2016) Digital re-analysis of lost architecture and the particular case of Lutyens' Liverpool Metropolitan Cathedral. Front Arch Res 5(2):265–275

Webb N, Buchanan A, Duffy S et al (2021) Tracing the past: analysing the design and construction of English medieval vaults using digital techniques. https://doi.org/10.5284/1084971. Accessed 2 Aug 2024

Webb NJ, Buchanan AC, Hillson JE (2023) Digitally aided analysis: a new reading of the cloister Vaults at Norwich Cathedral. Int J Arch Herit 1–24. https://doi.org/10.1080/15583058.2023.2247379

Wendland D (2019) Steinerne Ranken, wunderbare Maschinen: Entwurf und Planung spätgotischer Gewölbe und ihrer Einzelteile. Imhof Verlag, Petersberg

Wendland D, Gielin M (2022) The design and construction of the vaults in Notre-Dame in Paris and the development of medieval vaulting and stereotomy: surveys, analyses and experiments. In: Campbell J et al (eds) Proceedings of the ninth annual conference of the construction history society. Queens' College, Cambridge

Willis R (1842) On the construction of the vaults of the middle ages. Trans R Inst Brit Arch 1(2):1–69

# Part III
# Interactive Participation in Virtual Heritage

# Chapter 7
# Amplifying the Future of Industrial Heritage Through Digital Representation and Communication

**Anetta Kepczynska-Walczak**

**Abstract** In light of the challenges posed by climate change, there is a pressing need for the building industry to embrace sustainable practices. This objective can be attained through the implementation of circularity principles in the design and construction of building materials and structures. It is therefore recommended that adaptive reuse should be given a high priority. One of the most endangered categories of heritage is that of post-industrial buildings and sites. Therefore, they are frequently included on lists of heritage at risk. The reversal of this process and the promotion of adaptive reuse may only be successful if there is a societal recognition of the industrial legacy. It is therefore not surprising that this topic is of pivotal importance for architectural research, practice and education. The arguments discussed in the chapter are illustrated by selected projects and case studies that involve enhanced representation techniques for raising awareness of heritage value and its appreciation by local communities as well as wider audience. In this regard, special focus is on the work presented at the international exhibition—Łódź Design Festival, showing results of the use of digital photogrammetry and 3D printing for the increased heritage awareness and accessibility.

**Keywords** Adaptive reuse · Industrial heritage · Digital imaging · Social awareness · Architectural storytelling · Łódź Design Festival · Circular economy

## 7.1 Introduction

This study addresses the application of digital technologies in the field of heritage conservation. In particular, it examines the experiments with digital photogrammetry in the context of the industrial heritage of Łódź, Poland. The utilization of digital imaging as a tool to raise awareness among the local community of the value of neglected cultural heritage is also of pivotal importance in this context.

A. Kepczynska-Walczak (✉)
Institute of Architecture and Urban Planning, Lodz University of Technology, Łódź, Poland
e-mail: anetta.kepczynska-walczak@p.lodz.pl

 
S. Stellacci and S. Aydin (eds.), *Endangered Heritage Sites*, Springer Series on Cultural Computing, https://doi.org/10.1007/978-3-031-91949-7_7

The background for the aforementioned activities constitutes the issue of adaptive reuse as a means of reducing the carbon footprint of the Architecture, Engineering, and Construction (AEC) sector and social awareness of these processes. Based on recent educational projects carried out with architecture students at the Lodz University of Technology (TUL), observations were made and conclusions were formulated that can inform future research and pedagogy in the field of digital technologies in architecture and urban planning.

## 7.2 Project Background

### *7.2.1 Climate Change, Circular Economy, and Adaptive Reuse of Cultural Heritage*

Centuries of human activity are contributing to changes on our planet, particularly in terms of climate, which is primarily influenced by greenhouse gas emissions. The built environment plays a special role—globally, cities already account for 60–80% of greenhouse gas emissions, 75% of natural resource use, and 50 percent of global waste production (Ellen MacArthur Foundation 2017). Meanwhile, the building sector is responsible for 33% of greenhouse gas emissions, 40% of resource consumption, and 40% of waste production (Ness and Xing 2017). In addition, only 20–30% of building resources are recycled or reused at the end of their life (Ellen MacArthur Foundation 2014). Buildings are the single largest source of energy consumption in the European Union (EU), accounting for around 40% of energy consumption and a percentage of energy-related greenhouse gas emissions (European Commission, n.d.), and around 30 percent of waste in EU countries is generated by the building sector (Acharya et al. 2018).

The adoption of circular economy principles in the built environment is therefore of great importance and of growing interest to practitioners and researchers (Cheshire 2016; Zimmann et al. 2016). However, the majority of interest has focused on the minimization and recycling of construction waste (Tebbatt Adams et al. 2017). Less attention has been paid to the recycling of whole structures through their adaptive reuse, which is in line with the circular economy as it facilitates certain R-strategies (Refuse, Rethink, Reduce, Reuse, Repair, Refurbish, Remanufacture, Repurpose, Recycle, Recover) and is crucial to enable the built environment to withstand future changes, respond to contextual dynamics, eliminate waste generation and maximize the use of embodied energy—the energy input that went into the building process. This is calculated as the carbon dioxide avoided by reusing the existing building (or the carbon dioxide equivalent resulting from energy and material consumption). After all, what could be more in keeping with the trend toward material recycling than the reuse of an entire existing building? (Foster 2020).

Taking these arguments into account, the adaptation of existing buildings seems to be the most ecological approach. In line with this idea, Carl Elefante formulated a slogan that sums up environmental and historic preservation efforts and emphasizes the importance of existing buildings and their adaptive reuse: 'the greenest building is the one that has already been built' (Elefante 2007).

There are many more reasons to reuse existing buildings: it is considered a valuable approach to reactivate disused or abandoned buildings, sites, or areas, giving them a new purpose that is useful to society. Adaptive reuse of buildings has a positive impact on urban sprawl and land consumption. In this sense, its key role in the concept of circular economy within the construction sector is evident (Gaballo et al. 2021).

The concept of sustainability reached a milestone with the 2030 Agenda and its 17 Sustainable Development Goals (SDGs) (United Nations 2015). In 2020, the European Commission also launched the New European Bauhaus (NEB), which forms part of a Renovation Wave (European Parliament 2020) and complements the EU Green Deal—a commitment to tackling climate and environment related challenges by 'decoupling' economic growth from resource use, while leading to a 'fair and prosperous' society. The NEB initiative emphasizes sustainability as a central element, and beauty and inclusion to rethink cities, making them more liveable, functional, and accessible to all. Within this framework, built heritage is a key asset. It is therefore worth noting that the contribution of cultural heritage to the implementation of the EU Green Deal has been highlighted by ICOMOS and Europa Nostra to build an internationally agreed green policy agenda for cultural heritage through the 'European Cultural Heritage Green Paper'. The focus of the document is that cultural heritage should be seen more as a resource and less as an obstacle (Potts 2021). In addition, the complexities associated with sustainable technologies make built heritage the most challenging experimental laboratory ever to test new technologies and approaches and their scalability, and this also requires continuous upskilling of the professionals and stakeholders involved (Gigliarelli et al. 2023). However, when the adaptive reuse approach is applied to cultural heritage, the expected outcome is not only the protection of the building, but also the preservation of its historical and cultural significance, and the trade-off between the preservation of symbolic values and the adaptation to new alternative (economically profitable) uses becomes paramount. In particular, industrial sites are often left to deteriorate as their conservation is not considered as important as other types of heritage. Nevertheless, they are characterized by specific architectural and technical features, as well as by large spaces that are suitable for redevelopment for new uses (Bottero et al. 2019). Furthermore, adaptive reuse is of great importance for the urban regeneration of post-industrial regions, such as the Ruhr in Germany and the Manchester basin in the UK, which is in line with the 'just transformation' advocated by the EU Green Deal and the NEB (Rybski 2023).

### 7.2.2 *Adaptive Reuse and Social Awareness of Industrial Heritage in Łódź*

The processes described above took place in post-industrial centers in Poland, of which Łódź comes to the fore. Over the past 30 years, Łódź, one of Poland's largest cities, has struggled with the effects of industrial decline. Historic post-industrial buildings have been both a problem and a challenge. In the absence of other determinants of identity, the adaptation of former textile factories has become a key element in shaping the historic urban landscape of Łódź. Several hundred sites have changed function due to the typological characteristics of the buildings and their location in the urban structure. Recent research has confirmed the effectiveness of adaptive reuse in the process of industrial heritage conservation. Moreover, the scale of this phenomenon makes Łódź a leading center of post-industrial regeneration. The local experience can be a source of lessons for similar processes in other cities in Central and Eastern Europe (Kepczynska-Walczak and Walczak 2024).

Despite the success of many projects on historic industrial sites, this type of heritage still has to contend with the perception that they are 'second-class' sites. This perception of factories dates back to the nineteenth century. An excellent illustration of this phenomenon can be found in *Contrasts*, published by A. W. Pugin in 1836. The publication contains comparative illustrations that contrast the aesthetic appeal of medieval architecture with the perceived ugliness of new developments. One illustration shows a traditional European merchant town with its historic silhouette, spatial and social structure distorted by the proliferation of industrial buildings and chimneys (Pugin 1996). The main task is therefore to build social ties with the industrial legacy and to use it skillfully in the urban regeneration and adaptive reuse processes.

In this respect, it should be recalled that notion of sustainability encompasses not only the management of natural resources, but also the concept of quality of life (United Nations 2015). From this perspective, the harmonious development of the urban environment entails, in particular, the restoration of social equilibrium and the protection, conservation, and enhancement of the cultural heritage for the sustainable exploitation of its socio-economic potential. This implies integrating cultural heritage and its conservation in urban development. This interconnection presents potential avenues for addressing housing challenges while simultaneously fostering a sense of civic pride in the aesthetic appeal and quality of life in their cities. Consequently, the restoration and adaptive reuse of local heritage assets may become an integral aspect of the 'cultural sustainability' of the town and its community. Moreover, such a sustainable heritage restoration may offer tangible economic benefits (Cotterill et al. 2001).

In this context, it should be stressed that there is no doubt that post-industrial buildings are an important aspect of the heritage of Łódź. However, in the eyes of local residents, the dilapidated and neglected buildings of former industrial complexes can appear unattractive and unworthy of attention. Yet, thanks to several high-profile revitalization projects in the city of Łódź, the public has begun to recognize the value of historic factory buildings. This is an extremely important phenomenon, because it is only through social acceptance and awareness that the industrial heritage of Łódź can be protected (Daraz 2021).

In light of the growing influence of digital technologies on the functioning of contemporary society, these technologies can be leveraged as a valuable tool for raising public awareness of the significance of local heritage. When employed in an appropriate manner within the educational setting, they can also foster greater engagement and involvement of architecture students (who will be architects in the near future) in heritage adaptation projects.

### 7.2.3 Educational Challenges

The aforementioned issues present significant challenges to the architectural education process. This encompasses issues pertaining to the adaptation of historic buildings, the utilization of digital tools, and the impact of climate change on the AEC industry. For example, recent research has demonstrated that architecture students in Poland lack the requisite knowledge of the latest contemporary challenges, including the concept of the NEB. Furthermore, they exhibit a deficiency in interdisciplinary knowledge, which impairs their ability to effectively and comprehensively address design issues, resulting in the creation of contemporary architecture that aligns with the principles of sustainable development, while also demonstrating consideration for aesthetic appeal and social integration. The concepts of climate change, recycling, and biodiversity remain merely slogans for students, and they are unable to discern how to operationalize them (Taraszkiewicz and Taraszkiewicz 2024).

Similarly, students combine conservation design with architectural history, which they perceive as a subject that is unconnected to their professional skills and therefore of little relevance. In the same vein, the learning of computer-aided architectural design (CAAD) technology is perceived exclusively through the lens of the competencies required by employers.

One potential solution is to integrate threads that are dispersed throughout the curriculum into additional activities. This approach would facilitate the integration of fragmented knowledge and skills into a coherent and meaningful learning pipeline. The following section discusses examples of such activities undertaken in recent years at the Institute of Architecture and Urban Planning, Lodz University of Technology (TUL), with a particular focus on imaging/envisioning and digital photogrammetry for built heritage.

## 7.3 Project Description

### *7.3.1 Image of Industrial Heritage—Digital Representation and Architectural Storytelling*

The experience of architectural envisioning gained through teaching and research conducted at TUL and presentation of the results at international conferences have facilitated the formation of contacts with academics engaged in similar research. Subsequently, significant conferences such as European Architectural Envisioning Association (EAEA 2015) and Education and research in Computer-Aided Architectural Design (eCAADe 2018) were organized in Łódź by the author of this study. The eCAADe conference featured a workshop dedicated to contextualized digital heritage (Di Mascio and Walczak 2018). During this workshop, digital photogrammetry was employed to document the site of Wojtowski Mlyn in Łódź. The photogrammetric capture of the building reflected its dramatic state of disrepair and semi-rural setting with an abundance of ubiquitous greenery (Fig. 7.1). Despite the intention of the workshop to concentrate on methodologies pertinent to digital heritage, this activity, along with some problems with the poor image of the site in question, inspired another project (Walczak 2023).

Wojtowski Mlyn is a site with a lengthy and intricate history in Łódź. Its origins can be traced back to the Middle Ages, when a grain mill was constructed on the premises. Following an expansion in the 1820s, the mill became the inaugural spinning mill in the region. Several decades later, when the site was incorporated into the Scheibler

**Fig. 7.1** Photogrammetric representation of the building at Wojtowski Mlyn. *Source* D. Di Mascio, B.M. Walczak, C.K. Cogima, E. Dezen-Kempter, M. Hadighi, A. Kreutzberg, Presentation of the outcomes of the Contextualized Digital Heritage Workshop at the eCAADe Conference, Łódź 2018

complex, which was one of Europe's largest textile companies, it served as the residence for the manager of the adjoining farmstead. Unfortunately, the building's rich historical and cultural heritage was not reflected in its poor condition, raising the question of how architectural design can preserve both the tangible and intangible aspects of industrial heritage. Therefore, in 2019, as part of a heritage conservation course at TUL, architecture students undertook a design exercise focused on preserving the memory of the historical buildings at Wojtowski Młyn. The principal objective was to deploy adaptive reuse of endangered heritage building, which would respond to the social and environmental context and enrich architectural forms in a manner that reflected the complexity of the historical development of the site. In other words, the students were required to investigate whether it was feasible to preserve the memory of lost heritage and integrate it into the existing space and its new function. Consequently, the exercise became a research endeavor to reinterpret the site by uniting the surviving remnants of the past and employing architecture as a narrative device. Additionally, students were expected to provide meaningful visual representation of the concept.

Key observations emerged from the project. First, adaptive reuse is crucial for fostering emotional connections with the space, as daily interaction helps people relate to its industrial past. Second, interpretation plays a pivotal role in rendering the heritage object comprehensible and appreciated by modern viewers. Third, effective architectural narration requires thoughtful choices of forms and materials, ensuring the story is clear and engaging for contemporary audiences. Finally, students participating in such projects often struggle focusing too much on the process of narration at the expense of the subject matter of the narrative itself.

The graphic representations of the project were also of interest. It should be stressed that students had freedom to choose their communication technique. As a result, there was an array of techniques deployed (Fig. 7.2): (i) sketches, which can be described as a foundation of architectural storytelling; (ii) conceptual diagrams; (iii) models; and (iv) renderings and visualizations.

It is, however, necessary to be aware that a visualization medium should be chosen in order to be understandable for the audience and transmit the idea in a clear and straightforward way (Archipreneur 2015). Therefore, in case of the site in question, not only shapes and dimensions were responsible for the proper understanding of places, but also an array of intangible values. Despite the adopted techniques, the most important seems not only to achieve a certain level of accuracy but also to reflect atmosphere (ambiance) of a represented site, which is often elusive but essential for an authentic design.

It is worthy of note that a more conceptual project was undertaken a few years earlier for another part of the aforementioned Scheibler factory complex, known as Ksiezy Mlyn. This represents one of the most impressive examples of *industrial paternalism* in Europe. In this instance, however, the objective was not to represent the authentic appearance of the site, but rather to evoke the lost atmosphere of the location, as experienced by the younger generation (in this case, architecture students). The result may be characterized as a sentimental journey through time. Rather than attempting to recreate the heritage buildings themselves, the objective

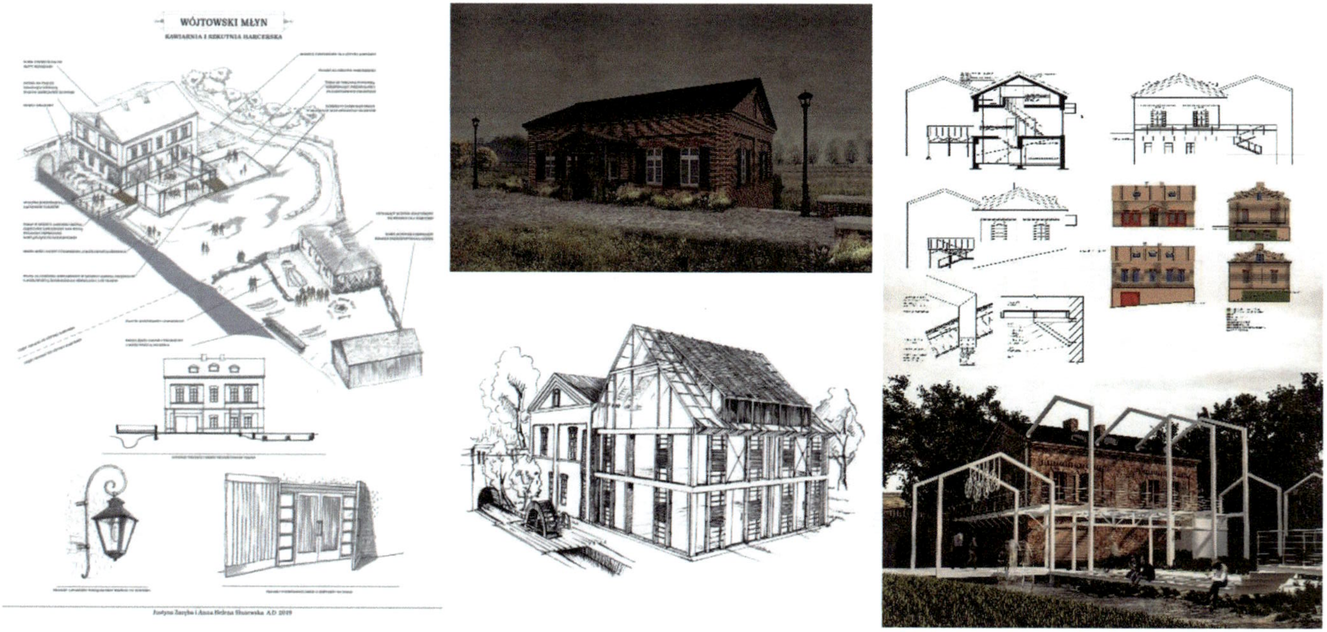


**Fig. 7.2** Variety of representations showing the adaptive reuse strategies and/or referring to the ambiance of the place. *Source* Archive of the Department of History of Architecture, Heritage Conservation and Urban Regeneration, TUL

**Fig. 7.3** Built heritage representation with focus on the bygone genius loci. *Source* Archive of the Department of Digital Technologies in Architecture and Urban Planning, TUL

was to evoke the lost 'spirit of place'. In other words, the reconstruction was not an accurate reproduction, but rather a critical reinterpretation. This was achieved through a series of views, based on previously created 3D models, in the style of old postcards from the turn of the nineteenth century and twentieth centuries (Fig. 7.3).

### *7.3.2 Heritage Awareness—Digital Photogrammetry and Local Community Outreach*

The concept of a distinctive atmosphere associated with a heritage site, as previously discussed, also served as the foundation for another project. During the period of industrial prosperity, Łódź attracted people of all nationalities and religions from all over Europe. As early as the mid-nineteenth century, a cemetery for people of different faiths was established. The cemetery is the final resting place of individuals from all social classes. The tombs and family mausoleums of industrialists are particularly noteworthy, although many former factory owners were forced to leave the city during and after World War II.

As a result, the tombstones were neglected and subsequently deteriorated. The largest object was the private burial chapel of the Scheibler family, located in the Lutheran section of the cemetery. It is noteworthy that the Scheibler chapel was identified by World Monument Watch as one of the most endangered sites in 2006. Since then, it has undergone a comprehensive restoration process, which is still ongoing. Concurrently, architectural students were tasked with creating a digital representation of the chapel, with the objective of focusing on its intrinsic features, particularly the distinctive lighting conditions and the 'worn-out' appearance of the interior (Fig. 7.4).

In the period between 2012 and 2014, other students were tasked with creating virtual models of a dozen smaller tombstones in the same cemetery. The selection of these tombstones was made in collaboration with a local foundation and the city museum. All of the tombstones were crafted by the same stone workshop, which was originally owned by the Urbanowski family. The history and achievements of

**Fig. 7.4** Built heritage representation with the objective of focusing on its 'worn-out' appearance. *Source* Archive of the Department of Digital Technologies in Architecture and Urban Planning, TUL

this firm were the subject of a museum project entitled 'Urbanowski's Workshop—Family, Work, Creators'. This comprised a series of activities, including research, the organization of exhibitions and conferences, and the publication of a commemorative volume. The exhibition comprised a variety of exhibits, including photographs, archival documents and memorabilia from the Urbanowski family collection, works of art from both private and museum collections, film miniatures, photographic panels as well as outcomes of architecture students' 3D modeling exercises, exhibited in the form of multimedia and presentation boards. Subsequently, the students presented a selection of virtual models and freehand drawings of tombstones at a dedicated museum event, entitled 'Digital and Analog Representation of Urbanowski's Workshop Works', which accompanied the exhibition (Fig. 7.5).

**Fig. 7.5** Various representations of one of the gravestones: a photograph; a measured drawing; wireframe and 3D models. *Source* Archive of the Department of Digital Technologies in Architecture and Urban Planning, TUL

The models were created as part of the 3D Digital Modeling Studio course using modeling software such as 3DStudioMax and ArchiCAD. The act of modeling tombstones proved to be an efficient pedagogical exercise. This task required students to focus on accurately reproducing architectural and sculptural forms from the late nineteenth and early twentieth centuries, as well as selecting appropriate textures to represent different types of stone. These approaches diverged from the conventional solutions and libraries embedded in 3D modeling computer programs. As a result, the students gained new skills, increased their competence, and acquired knowledge of architectural and art history. The experience was so positive that, after a few years, the idea was born to revisit the same tombstones using other, newer digital technologies and compare the results of the two projects (Kepczynska-Walczak et al. 2024).

The second project was conducted in collaboration with the New Jersey Institute of Technology (NJIT), USA, in 2023. In addition to the gravestones, the list of objects to be studied was expanded to encompass a further range of historical artifacts sourced from the Lapidarium of Architectural Elements, which is managed by the Łódź City Council. This latter example represents an intriguing case of the redefinition and reinterpretation of the concept of the lapidarium. The range of objects on display has been expanded to encompass all relics of historical construction, extending beyond stone to encompass stucco, ceramics, metal and even wood. These elements were retrieved from endangered historic buildings, with the idea that at least they would be preserved as a testament to the past, and perhaps even used as part of restoration work on other adaptively reused buildings in the city. What could also be interpreted as a tentative attempt to implement the principles of the circular economy (Fig. 7.6).

The project was centered on the concept of transforming digital data into interactive formats. The data was collected, and 3D models were created using photography and photogrammetry software. The project commenced with introductory lectures that contextualized photogrammetry within the conceptual frameworks of digital heritage and digital media arts, as well as outlining the practical applications, methods and tools. The students were introduced to a production pipeline that focused on six

**Fig. 7.6** The Lapidarium of Architectural Elements at the Łódź City Council: introductory exhibition (*left*); variety of object types (*center*); warehouse-style presentation of objects (*right*). *Source* Photo by A. Zarzycki, 2023

key areas, as follows: (i) maintaining data integrity; (ii) selecting appropriate environmental conditions (lighting); (iii) photo capture and 3D model creation strategies; (iv) 3D model and texture editing (v) photogrammetric model optimization; and (vi) visualization strategies.

The study employed a cross-platform application, KIRI Engine, which is compatible with both Android and iPhone Operating System (iOS). The application facilitated precise calibration of the photogrammetry process, enabling the addition or removal of photographs, trimming of geometry, and optimization of texture unwrap and geometry meshing parameters. The 3D models were exported and subsequently optimized and retopologized in accordance with the specifications of the intended visualization platform. The topologizing was conducted using the Blender software, which permitted the generation of models with varying degrees of detail while maintaining the original texture mapping alignments. The results included fully textured 3D models presented within WebGL interfaces (SketchFab), rendered images and narrative-based animations (SketchUp, 3D Studio Max), as well as interactive presentations based on Unity3D and Prezi.

The outputs can be categorized into three major groups:

i. The presentation of a scanned object in a 2D, 3D, or mixed format within a wider contextual framework, such as the façade of a building, is designed to guide the viewer's gaze and direct their attention toward specific components (Fig. 7.7).
ii. Interactive, Prezi and Web Graphics Library (WebGL)-based presentations that allowed users to control their own experience. The presentations were structured as a series of nested geometries (analogous to the concept of the nested matryoshka doll), commencing with an overview of the artifact and subsequently unpacking different scales, elements, and details through mouse clicks (Fig. 7.8).
iii. The Unity3D-based interactive game environment, which served as a spatial collage of individual objects that facilitated the conveyance of a specific narrative akin to the conventional nineteenth century 'analytique' drawing projected into 3D space (Fig. 7.8).

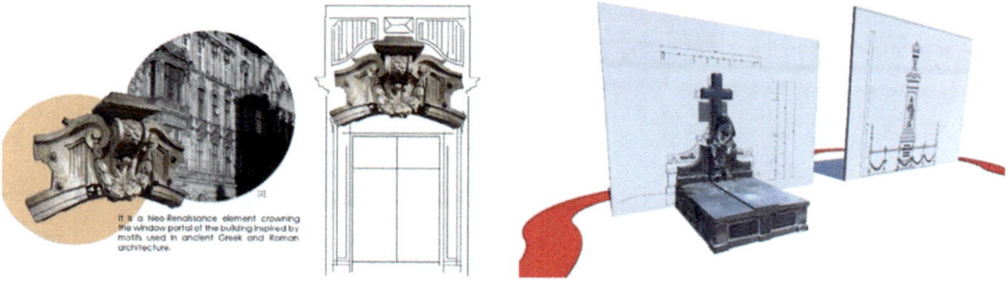


**Fig. 7.7** 2D collage of 3D-scanned objects from the lapidarium superimposed over a 2D drawing (*left*). A 3D representation of a monument presented alongside a 2D illustration of its dimensions (*right*). *Source* Archive of the Department of Digital Technologies in Architecture and Urban Planning, TUL

**Fig. 7.8** Hierarchically structured Prezi presentation showing the landing page (*left*). The game engine-based (Unity3D) interactive environment (*right*). *Source* Archive of the Department of Digital Technologies in Architecture and Urban Planning, TUL

The application of mobile photogrammetry generated considerable interest, prompting another cohort of architecture students to engage in experimentation with this technology. In this instance, the project was developed in collaboration with a museum located within the Scheibler Palace (Łódź), which serves as an exemplar of an industrialist's luxury residence from the latter half of the nineteenth century. It is pertinent to note that such edifices were erected by factory owners near their textile mills, thereby becoming an integral component of the local industrial heritage. Consequently, a number of architectural elements that constitute the interior of this residence were selected for scanning. The students utilized the KIRI software and employed the methodology that had been developed during the aforementioned workshop. However, this time the aim was not to provide virtual presentations but create 3D-printed replicas of scanned architectural objects. Accordingly, the resulting scans necessitated disparate post-production processes. It was essential to attain a level of quality and detail that would enable the accurate reproduction of the artifacts via 3D printing.

The results were presented to the public at the exhibition entitled 'R3DEFINE', which was held during the Łódź Design Festival (LDF) in May 2024. The Festival, which was established in 2007, is currently regarded as one of the most significant events dedicated to the broad field of design. This is evidenced, among other factors, by its long-standing membership of the World Design Weeks, an international network that brings together the most prominent design events from around the globe. The LDF presents projects that combine artistic and social activities, offering commentary on the most significant challenges of the contemporary world. Its expansive thematic scope encompasses a range of design disciplines, including graphics, crafts, industrial design, fashion, and architecture. In alignment with the core theme of this chapter, the Festival is held at the Art_Inkubator, situated within the repurposed warehouses of the former Scheibler factory complex.

The exhibition comprised a series of 3D-printed artifacts and associated presentation boards, which highlighted several potential applications of photogrammetry and 3D printing in heritage conservation and museology. These included the possibility

**Fig. 7.9** Exhibition at the Łódź Design Festival: overall view with 3D-scanned and 3D-printed historic objects (*left*); close-up of one of the exhibits (center); an object optimized for or tactile engagement and accompanied by a description in Braille (*right*). *Source* Photos by B.M. Walczak, 2024

of scanning objects and using the resulting models as a replacement for disassembled elements, as well as the redesigning of existing elements using 3D printing techniques. Another area of potential application was in making exhibits accessible for visually impaired members of society. In response to this issue, the exhibition included tactile exhibits and descriptions in Braille (Fig. 7.9).

## 7.4 Summary and Conclusion

The reorientation of the AEC sector from the construction of new structures to the adaptive reuse of existing buildings in accordance with the principles of the circular economy represents one of the most significant challenges in reducing the industry's carbon footprint. This transition offers the prospect of increased investment in historic buildings, yet simultaneously gives rise to concerns regarding the safeguarding of heritage and its associated cultural values, particularly in terms of authenticity. And it is heritage that determines the uniqueness of European cities, and the beauty of the built environment is precisely one of the pillars of the New European Bauhaus.

Among historic buildings, post-industrial structures, which have undergone an irreversible loss of their production function, are the most vulnerable. However, they also present the greatest potential for adaptation to new functions. Nevertheless, they also require innovative conversion in order to meet the challenges of climate change and the requirement to reduce energy consumption. It is therefore necessary to view this resource in terms of industrial heritage and to implement appropriate solutions.

The aforementioned green building transformation process can be supported by new digital technologies. These can provide both analytical tools and support for the investment process. Solutions such as Building Information Modeling (BIM) and, in the case of historic buildings, Historic Building Information Modeling (HBIM) are becoming increasingly prevalent. Nevertheless, the implementation of advanced digital tools is frequently associated with significant costs, which can act as a barrier to initiating the adaptation process. Consequently, the activities delineated in this chapter are devised to address the particular requirements of the moment and to target audiences in an appropriate manner. Furthermore, a cost-effective approach to digital technology selection allows for greater accessibility and dissemination of digitization developments.

From a pedagogical standpoint, it is crucial to equip prospective architects with the requisite skills to navigate the complexities of the digital and dynamic volatility, uncertainty, complexity, and ambiguity (VUCA) landscape. The aim should be comprehensive learning, oriented more toward problem solving than applying methods and procedures. The teaching of the graphic representation of heritage forms an essential part of an architect's training. However, the teaching of adaptive reuse, heritage conservation, and digital technologies is usually fragmented across multiple standalone courses, dispersed throughout the curriculum. The incorporation of workshops and supplementary activities facilitates the integration of knowledge and skills into a coherent and structured learning pathway.

The current promotion of photogrammetry in the teaching of architectural surveying and the subsequent digital representation of heritage is a consequence of the affordability of the requisite equipment. This can be observed not only in TUL but also in numerous other schools of architecture (Fernández-Morales 2020). Therefore, it is crucial to avoid focusing on a single technique or software tool. Instead, it is essential to convey to the student the potential offered by various existing technologies, enabling them to identify solutions for the effective digital representation of architecture and built heritage.

In conclusion, the emerging digital technologies afford novel opportunities for the presentation of heritage in innovative ways. In many instances, the original artifacts are too fragile, too valuable, or otherwise difficult to make widely available. This issue can now be addressed through the utilization of digital replicas and their 3D prints. Digital replicas can serve as the foundation for virtual collections that can be accessed via the Internet. Furthermore, digital products can be developed based on these models with the objective of engaging with different audiences in innovative ways and offering new avenues for the exploration of heritage. While 3D-printed replicas enhance accessibility and facilitate multisensory experiences of heritage, which is of paramount importance for individuals with diverse disabilities, as evidenced by the students' exhibition during the Łódź Design Festival. Notable examples of such endeavors already exist, including the immersive replica of Lasceaux in France (Mayer 2020). In this context, however, it is important to recall that, despite the advantages and disadvantages, open mobile technologies are much more accessible due to their cost. This enables the substitution of costly hardware and software with smartphones and mobile applications, which have become ubiquitous. Therefore, the promotion of such solutions facilitates the dissemination of digital technologies and their utilization for laudable objectives, including the documentation and promotion of cultural heritage.

Finally, it is important to recall the three major pillars of the New European Bauhaus: *sustainability* (including climate goals, circularity, zero pollution, and biodiversity), *aesthetics* (including the quality of experience and style beyond functionality), and *inclusion* (including valuing diversity and securing accessibility and affordability). From this perspective, the widespread use of digital technologies represents an additional benefit for public participation in the broadest sense. This is because the members of the public have the opportunity to lend their support to the rescue of endangered industrial heritage, in particular through their votes on local plans and civic budgets. However, in order to do so, it is necessary for them to understand the heritage in question, to view it from a specific perspective, and even to interact with it physically. These goals can undoubtedly be amplified with the support of digital technologies.

**Acknowledgements** The author would like to express her sincerest gratitude to all individuals and organizations whose involvement was instrumental in the completion and dissemination of this study. In particular, the author would like to acknowledge the assistance and resources provided by the Society for the Care of the Old Cemetery, the City Museum of the City of Łódź, the Film Museum in Łódź, and the Łódź Lapidarium of Architectural Elements throughout the course of this project. The author would like to extend her gratitude to Danilo Di Mascio and the participants of the Contextualized Digital Heritage Workshop, which was held in Łódź during the eCAADe Conference in 2018, for their contributions to this work. She would also like to acknowledge Professor Andrzej Zarzycki of the New Jersey Institute of Technology for his invaluable support. She would also like to acknowledge the contributions of Mateusz Grabowski, a PhD candidate and students from the Institute of Architecture and Urban Planning at TUL, who have demonstrated a commendable dedication to investigating and implementing digital techniques in the field of cultural heritage.

## References

Acharya D, Boyd R, Finch O (2018) From principles to practices: first steps towards a circular built environment. ARUP and Ellen MacArthur Foundation, London

Archipreneur (2015) Top 5 architectural storytelling tools to market your project. Retrieved from: https://archipreneur.com/top-5-architectural-storytelling-tools-to-market-your-project/

Bottero M, D'Alpaos C, Oppio A (2019) Ranking of adaptive reuse strategies for abandoned industrial heritage in vulnerable contexts: a multiple criteria decision aiding approach. Sustainability 11(3):785

Cheshire D (2016) Building revolutions: applying the circular economy to the built environment. RIBA Publishing, London

Cotterill D et al (2001) The economic benefits of heritage restoration. In: Heritage economics. Challenges for heritage conservation and sustainable development in the 21st Century. Australian Heritage Commission, Canberra, pp 120–130

Daraz A (2021) Adaptation of the area of former L. Domanowicz spinning mill at 100 Pomorska street in Lodz for service purposes. Lodz University of Technology (master dissertation supervised by Prof. A. Kepczynska-Walczak), Lodz

Di Mascio D, Walczak BM (2018) Contextualized digital heritage workshop—Lodz. In: Kepczynska-Walczak A, Bialkowski S (eds) Computing for a better tomorrow: proceedings of the 36th eCAADe Conference. eCAADe/Lodz University of Technology, Lodz, pp 49–52

Elefante C (2007) The greenest building is... One that is already built. Forum J 21(4):26–38

Ellen MacArthur Foundation (2014) Towards the circular economy: accelerating the scale-up across global supply chains. Retrieved from: https://ellenmacarthurfoundation.org/towards-the-circular-economy-vol-3-accelerating-the-scale-up-across-global

Ellen MacArthur Foundation (2017) Cities in the circular economy: an initial exploration. Retrieved from: https://www.ellenmacarthurfoundation.org/cities-in-the-circular-economy-an-initial-exploration

EAEA (2015) 12th conference of the European Architectura Envisioning Association. Retrieved from: http://www.eaea12-2015.p.lodz.pl/

eCAADe (2018) 36th conference of the education and research in computer aided architectural design in Europe: computing for a better tomorrow. Retrieved from: https://ecaade2018.p.lodz.pl/

European Commission (undated) Energy performance of buildings directive. Retrieved from: https://energy.ec.europa.eu/topics/energy-efficiency/energy-efficient-buildings/energy-performance-buildings-directive_en

European Parliament (2020) A renovation wave for Europe—greening our buildings, creating jobs, improving lives. Retrieved from: https://ec.europa.eu/commission/presscorner/detail/en/fs_20_40

Fernández-Morales A (2020) Considerations on the teaching of graphic representation of heritage. In: Agustín-Hernández L, Vallespín Muniesa A, Fernández-Morales A (eds) Graphical heritage. EGA 2020. Springer series in design and innovation, vol 7. Springer, Cham, pp 504–514

Foster G (2020) Circular economy strategies for adaptive reuse of cultural heritage buildings to reduce environmental impacts. Resour Conserv Recycl 152:104507

Gaballo M, Mecca B, Abastante F (2021) Adaptive reuse and sustainability protocols in Italy: relationship with circular economy. Sustainability 13(14):8077

Gigliarelli E, Martinelli L, Calcerano F (2023) An integrated approach for energy and environmental improvement of built heritage through Building Information Modeling (BIM). In: Ali Sayigh (ed) Mediterranean architecture and the green-digital transition. Springer, Heidelberg, pp 569–578

Kepczynska-Walczak A, Walczak BM (2024) Adaptive re-use of industrial heritage in Lodz, Poland. Int J Conservation Sci 15(2):955–966

Kepczynska-Walczak A, Walczak BM, Zarzycki A (2024) The use of photogrammetry in historic preservation curriculum: a comparative case study. In: Eurographics 2024: Education Papers

Mayer L (2020) Authenticity in 3D: immersive rock art replicas as cultural tourism and heritage. The University of Western Australia (Doctoral Thesis), Perth

Ness DA, Xing K (2017) Toward a resource-efficient built environment: a literature review and conceptual model. J Ind Ecol 21(3):572–592

Potts A (2021) European cultural heritage green paper. Europa Nostra – ICOMOS

Pugin AW (1996) Contrasts with an introduction by H. R. Hitchcock. Leicester University Press, Leicester

Rybski R (2023) New European Bauhaus as EU sustainability tool. In: Zajdler R (ed) Solutions for modern society of the future. The new European Bauhaus manual. Warsaw University of Technology, Warsaw, pp 38–52

Taraszkiewicz A, Taraszkiewicz K (2024) Ideas of the New European Bauhaus (NEB) in architectural education. World Trans Eng Technol Educ 22(1):12–17

Tebbatt Adams K, Osmani M, Thorpe A, Thornback J (2017) Circular economy in construction: current awareness, challenges and enablers. Waste Resource Manage 170:15–24

United Nations (2015) Transforming our world: the 2030 Agenda for sustainable development. A/RES/70/1

Walczak BM (2023) The role of architectural design in industrial heritage interpretation—the case of Wójtowski Młyn in Łódź. Architectus 73:75–83

Zimmann R, O'Brien H, Hargrave J, Morrell M (2016) The circular economy in the built environment. ARUP, London

# Chapter 8
# Enhanced Knowledge Transfer in Historical Site Interpretation: A Gamified Approach for Yedikule Fortress/Türkiye

**Derya Güleç Özer, Leman Figen Gül, Emirhan Coşkun, Elif Sezen Yağmur Kilimci, and Murat Gül**

**Abstract** This study explores the integration of wearable and portable devices in enhancing the interpretation and communication of Yedikule Fortress, a 1600-year-old historical site on the outskirts of the Istanbul's Historic Peninsula. This interpretation involves users taking of the site tour with augmented reality/mixed reality-enhanced using audio accompaniment and gamification. The designed route provides tailored information, enhanced by a digital layer and a storyline. This study examines the quality of the information, visitor route design, and the integration of game elements. The multi-modal guidance system fosters interaction between historical narratives and spatial context, with participants reporting increased interest and improved recall of historical details. Building on the refinement of the process through expert input and participant feedback, this study also highlights limitations related to device affordances that influenced user behavior and interaction. Future research should explore the adaptability of this framework to other heritage sites, ensuring its educational and experiential relevance.

D. G. Özer (✉) · L. F. Gül · E. S. Y. Kilimci · M. Gül
Istanbul Technical University, Istanbul, Türkiye
e-mail: dgulec@itu.edu.tr

L. F. Gül
e-mail: fgul@itu.edu.tr

E. S. Y. Kilimci
e-mail: esyagmurkilimci@itu.edu.tr

M. Gül
e-mail: mgul@itu.edu.tr

E. Coşkun
MEF University, Maslak, Türkiye
e-mail: emirhancoskun@gmail.com

 
S. Stellacci and S. Aydin (eds.), *Endangered Heritage Sites*, Springer Series on Cultural Computing, https://doi.org/10.1007/978-3-031-91949-7_8

**Keywords** Yedikule Fortress · Spatial computing · Expert-driven assessment · Visual storytelling · Game-based narratives · Immersive cultural heritage experiences · Diegetic elements

## 8.1 Introduction

The promotion and integration of multi-layered cultural heritage structures in the historical core of modern cities is essential for ensuring their long-term preservation. The concept of multi-layered heritage refers to the layers formed by the architectural imprints of different civilizations that have shaped the cities. The challenges of formulating and implementing public policies, combined with fast population growth, uncontrolled urbanization and tourism, and real-estate demands, impose significant development pressures on heritage assets (Panzera et al. 2021; Kaya 2020; Gül 2025).

In ever-changing cities like Istanbul, with an history spanning thousands of years, it is especially important to consider approaches to preserving multi-layered historical landscapes, considering horizontal and vertical protection of cultural assets, especially in the face of economic pressures within the neoliberal system. Istanbul, with a population of over 15 million (as per the 2020 census) and an economy that accounts for 31% of the national Gross Domestic Product (GDP),[1] is a megacity and home to numerous historical sites. A significant portion of its cultural heritage is located in the area known as the 'Historic Peninsula', which is particularly vulnerable to the above-mentioned pressures.

To fully protect cultural heritage sites, both facility managers and public authorities must fully understand and realize the heritage significance of these sites represent. Cultural significance is inherent in the place itself, including its fabric, setting, use, associations, meanings, historical records, and connections to related places and objects (ICOMOS 2013). Over the past decade, cultural heritage studies have seen significant growth in the use of spatial computing (SC) technologies, including augmented reality (AR), virtual reality (VR), and mixed reality (MR). The term 'spatial computing' is a comprehensive concept designating the fusion of the digital layer with the physical realm (Greenwold 2003; Xu et al. 2024). One of the key aspects of SC is the integration of immersive, natural, and intelligent multi-modal interactions in both physical and virtual spaces. This integration is employed in various studies for protecting cultural heritage, reconstructing cultural heritage in a virtual environment, creating virtual museums, educational areas, and enriching the cultural heritage, among others, as discussed by Ariza-Colpas et al. (2024). The advent of SC offers an opportunity to interpret the multi-layered structure and history of cultural assets. Heritage interpretation plays a vital role in understanding the significance of heritage sites, especially those with a multi-layered history such as Yedikule Fortress.

[1] www.ipa.istanbul (Accessed at 29.11.2024).

In this context, the use of SC and gamification to disseminate information and communicate the value of these places in a heritage site is becoming increasingly common. Gamification is the use of game design elements in non-game contexts with the objective of enhancing user engagement, motivation, and interaction (Deterding et al. 2011; Nicholson 2015). Several systematic reviews on gamification in cultural heritage practices highlight its potential to enhance visitor engagement and learning outcomes, thereby promoting the interpretation of cultural heritage (Marques et al. 2023, 2022; Khan et al. 2021). In heritage studies, gamification is the process of making the exploration of historic sites more interactive, engaging, and informative through a route experience that includes interpretive information and how the site should be presented, with game elements designed for this purpose (Gül et al. 2023). These elements use spatial and contextual data, often leveraging technologies like GPS and augmented reality, to create immersive and engaging experiences where users interact with their physical or virtual environment to explore, learn, or achieve specific objectives. In the Yedikule Fortress, the application of gamification and aural accompany presents a unique opportunity to enrich visitor experiences and ensure that the site's narratives are compellingly conveyed. The integration of narrative and storytelling elements facilitates the creation of an engaging and educational experience. The narrative provides historically significant and authentic information, tailored to each context, using a thematic and audience-centric approach. This approach draws inspiration from the guidelines by Tilden (2008) and the interpretive communication principles by Ham (2013). The narrative is brought to life by storytelling through *diegetic design*, which incorporates 3D visuals, animations, and layered information. By using interpretive principles, storytelling offers an interactive framework based on the integration of sensory elements and thematic contents. This allows users to explore at their own pace and fosters a meaningful connection with cultural heritage. Collectively, these elements create a cohesive and immersive journey through history. In this study, this auditory narrative is limited to providing factual information regarding the historical background of the visited sites and the development of their spatial features, explicitly excluding any elements of fictional storytelling.

This study investigates the influence of SC and gamification techniques on visitor's experiences of a heritage site through a case study of Yedikule Fortress.[2] As part of a broader research initiative, previous publications explored the modeling and optimization processes (Sancak et al. 2023) and the design of visitor routes (Gül et al. 2023). This study specifically focuses on the development of game-based narratives, highlighting the integration and impact of various technologies, Android tablets for augmented reality (AR) and Microsoft HoloLens 2 for mixed reality (MR).

[2] More information can be found at www.kumio.itu.edu.tr.

## 8.2 Historical Analysis of Yedikule Fortress

Situated on the edge of Istanbul's historic core, the Yedikule Fortress (meaning 'Fortress of the Seven Towers'), with its 1600 years of history, represent a cultural intersection spanning Roman, Byzantine, and the Ottoman eras. This historical structure has a pentagonal shape and is surrounded by seven towers. Of these towers, only six have survived to the present day. The castle has undergone various changes and conservation campaigns throughout its history.

The first historic layer of the Roman citadel begins with the construction of the Golden Gate (400 AD) which forms the two towers of the castle at the southern end of the land walls of Istanbul. The Golden Gate was the main entrance through which emperors entered the city upon their return from victory. The gate, featuring marble covered pylons on either side of three arches, takes its name from its gilded wings. It marked the start of triumphal processions and served as the point of intersection between the Mese (the principal thoroughfare of the ancient city) and the Egnatia Road (Eyice 1993; Mango 2000). The second layer of Yedikule dates to the fifteenth century, following the Ottoman conquest of Istanbul in 1453. In addition to the two pylons of the Golden Gate and the two Byzantine towers on the city walls, Mehmet the Conqueror ordered the construction of three new towers (Yılmaz 1994). At the same time, small building blocks were built in the courtyard, consisting of single-story houses built around a mosque (*masjid*) in the center of the fortress as the residences of the soldiers and shopkeepers (Çelebi 2008).

Only a few remains of the *masjid*, and a portion of the minaret have survived to the present day. The Yedikule Fortress also served as a prison until the nineteenth century, holding ambassadors of foreign states and Ottoman statesmen from its earliest years of construction until the reign of Mahmut II. Later, the castle was used for housing lions belonging to the palace and storing gunpowder and ammunition. In 1895, the fortress turned into the Museum-i Hümayun (Imperial Museum), where it remained largely unused for an extended period before being integrated into Istanbul Hisarlar Museum Directorate in 1968. Since the 2000s, Yedikule has been restored and has become the venue for a variety of activities, including concerts, film screenings, and serving as an open-air museum.

## 8.3 Theoretical Background

### *8.3.1 Heritage Interpretation and Technology-Driven Heritage Experiences*

Heritage interpretation encompasses a comprehensive array of activities aimed at raising public consciousness and enriching comprehension of cultural heritage sites, as stated in the ICOMOS Charter for the Interpretation and Presentation of

Cultural Heritage Sites (2008). Furthermore, this document underscores the importance of interpretation and presentation in enriching personal encounters, cultivating widespread respect and comprehension, and emphasizing the necessity of preserving cultural heritage sites. These efforts should encourage individuals and communities to reflect on their own perspectives of a site and facilitate the establishment of a meaningful bond with it. Ultimately, the goal is to spark interest, facilitate learning, enrich experiences, and encourage further exploration. Interpretation is crucial for unveiling the cultural significance of numerous sites that might not be readily discernible (Australia ICOMOS 2013). Heritage interpretation should facilitate deeper understanding and engagement while being culturally sensitive and appropriate.

The cultural significance of an historical artifact is often apparent and easily appreciated by the public. However, many historic buildings and sites have undergone alterations over time to some extent, and these changes are not easily understandable without assisted information-related systems. A careful interpretation strategy can help the community in understanding the significance of such artifacts. Therefore, heritage interpretation stands as a crucial aspect of conservation practice. Informative signage detailing the historical development of a place are the most common solution to convey information to visitors. Additional interpretive activities encompass a diverse range of media, such as on-site events, documentaries, guided and self-guided walks, audio guides, exhibitions, films, videos, brochures, books, catalogues, educational programs, and websites.

Heritage interpretation is taking on a new dimension through the integration of spatial computing. By leveraging those advanced technologies, heritage interpretation can be more immersive, interactive, and tailored to individual preferences and interests. This integration opens a myriad of possibilities, from personalized virtual tours and augmented reality (AR) experiences to gamified-narrated tours for real-time information and engaging storytelling. Ultimately, embracing spatial computing (SC) in heritage interpretation promises to enrich public engagement and foster a deeper understanding and appreciation of our cultural heritage.

Cultural heritage studies have undergone a significant shift with the adoption of technological advancements, particularly in augmented reality (AR), virtual reality (VR), and mixed reality (MR), which have emerged over the past decade. These technologies, which overcome the boundaries between physical and digital realms, have come to be known as SC (Greenwold 2003) as umbrella term, related to the safeguarding of cultural heritage, the reconstruction of cultural heritage within virtual environments, the establishment of digital museums, educational platforms, and the enrichment of cultural experiences (Ozer et al. 2016; Banfi et al. 2021; Li et al. 2021; Roumana et al. 2022; Chen et al. 2021).

In a study by Varinlioğlu and Halıcı (2019), the use of game mechanics using AR-compatible Android devices at archaeological sites was analyzed as a way to increase visitor interest and promote the dissemination of cultural heritage values. Krzywinska et al. (2020) utilized the same glasses to simulate telegraphing training during World War II at the Porthcurno Telegraph Museum in an escape room format. In the study by Chen et al. (2021), a combination of historical information related to the ancient Chinese city of Chaozhou was presented to visitors using HoloLens mixed reality glasses. The historical culture of the city was presented to visitors in an enjoyable and engaging manner using comic book-style characters and three-dimensional models. In the study by Banfi et al. (2021), the *Cerchia dei Navigli* in Milan (floodable defensive moat of the medieval walls of Milan) was recreated in a virtual environment through visual storytelling. The atmosphere of the daily life of the watersheds in ancient times was interpreted using AR technology. Another application, the Augmented Museum, proposes an application that allows visitors to explore digital artifacts using HoloLens mixed reality glasses (Giariskanis et al. 2022). During this interaction, visitors walk around the museum by following the scenario created with the gamification method and learn the history of the exhibited artifacts with the help of visuals displayed with the MR technology. MR is also used in intangible cultural heritage experiences.

## 8.4 Research Methodology

### *8.4.1 Game-Based Narratives and Spatial Computing Technologies*

To enhance the visitor experience and deepen appreciation of Yedikule Fortress, gamification techniques are integrated with advanced spatial computing technologies, including augmented reality (AR) and mixed reality (MR) using Android tablets for AR and Microsoft HoloLens 2 for MR, as shown in Fig. 8.1. As shown in Fig. 8.1, the study is designed as a between subject study, to compare the effect of gamification and SC technologies on user's experience. It involved four study groups. The first was the control group called one reality (OR) where visitors experience the site by using the paper guide without any intervention. The second is the physical gamified experience group, referred to as one reality with gamification (GOR), where users experience the site given a physical guide including game components. The third is the mixed reality (MR) group, composed of two subgroups based on the type of SC technology used, as augmented reality with Android tablet (MR-A) and mixed reality with HoloLens (MR-H). The fourth group, referred to as mixed reality with gamification (GMR) experiences the site with a narrative including gamification components and by using SC devices. It involves two subgroups as GMR-A and GMR-H referring to use of Android tablet and HoloLens.

A specific route was designed based on field research, historical analysis, social media content analysis, and workshops to (i) provide an engaging and educational experience; (ii) convey accurate historical and cultural information; (iii) create an immersive environment; and (iv) design gamification elements (Gül et al. 2023). The

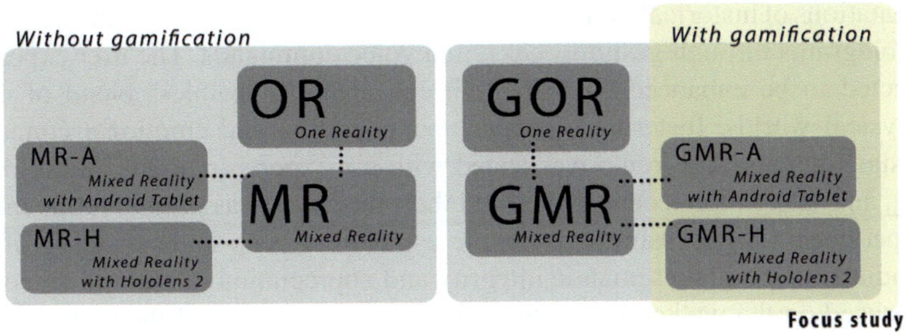


**Fig. 8.1** Four study groups within the project (own elaboration)

goal is to create a path that not only informs but also engages visitors through interactive game elements and narrative storytelling. This research methodology encompasses the processes of analysis, design, implementation, testing, and refinement, as shown in Fig. 8.2.

This study includes several interactive features to enhance visitor engagement and learning. Quiz-style tasks require visitors to answer questions related to the historical facts at each node, with correct answers unlocking further content and rewards. Treasure hunts provide digital clues that lead visitors to specific locations within the fortress, revealing additional historical narratives and visual content upon successful completion. Object completion tasks involve assembling digital artifacts or solving puzzles, offering a sense of accomplishment and deeper historical context. Android tablets provided a handheld AR experience. Visitors used these devices to view digital overlays on the physical environment, adding layers of historical information and visual enhancements. This is implemented by displaying historical facts, quizzes, and games (such as treasure hunts and object completion tasks on the tablets) to combine entertainment with practical objectives. Visitors engage with the content through touch-based interactions. The user experience is enhanced by AR making the site's history more tangible and engaging for the visitors. The Microsoft HoloLens 2 provides a more immersive MR experience. This head-mounted display allows visitors to see and interact with 3D holograms superimposed on the physical environment. This is implemented using MR headsets, which provide holographic

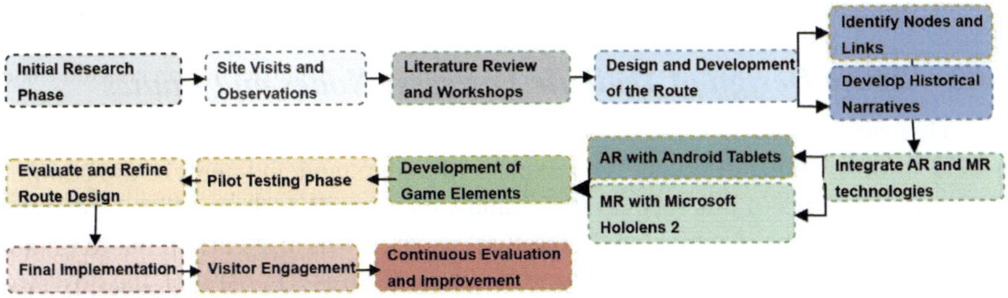


**Fig. 8.2** Process of analysis, design and implementation, testing, and refinement (own elaboration)

representations of historical events, characters, and artifacts. Visitors can interact with these holograms through gestures, gaze, and voice commands. The user experience is expected to be enhanced by MR, as it can create a seamless blend of digital and physical worlds, fostering a deeper understanding and emotional connection to the site's history. The route was tested with six experts in architectural history, gaming, and interaction technologies, and their feedback was used to refine the AV/VR experience and to ensure that people establish a deep understanding of their surroundings to maintain semantic integrity and appreciation of cultural assets. The tests focused on the walkability of the path, the effectiveness of the narratives, and the usability of the AR and MR devices.

Game elements and frameworks convey accurate, coherent, and relevant information to help individuals deeply understand their surroundings by ensuring that the information, narratives, and experiences presented align meaningfully with the cultural and historical context of the heritage site. The integration of game elements in cultural heritage is structured within certain frameworks. It is possible to consider how to tell a story to the user in the city, how the user will discover the important places of the city, understand its history, experiencing unique interactions, and offer social connections. Utilizing game elements will diversify the interaction as it will turn the city itself into an interactive game board. In this approach where gaming and cultural heritage intersect, AR and VR environments, gaming experience, storytelling, and cultural heritage awareness play a central role, as defined in literature (Dow et al. 2005; Kim et al. 2015; Volkmar et al. 2018). The starting point of using gamification is to offer visitors an interactive experience supported by different themes and game mechanics. The elements in heritage routes are quiz-based tasks, treasure hunts, object completion, points, rewards, and leveling system. While focusing on the impact of gamification in raising awareness in cultural heritage, this study also compares the development processes of two different technologies (an Android AR tablet for handheld devices and an MR head-mounted device for wearable devices) to enhance the route experience enriched through game-driven engagement.

At this stage, the narrative presented to the visitors, the information cards, and the 3D visuals and animations will increase the understanding of the cultural heritage in the historical context. Assessing the effectiveness of tools as information and visual layers, along with their strategic integration into the route design, has the potential to foster visitor engagement and encourage deep exploration of the historical site.

### *8.4.2 Route Design of Yedikule Fortress: Nodes and Routes*

In-field studies were carried out with experts to understand and analyze the components and potentials of this fortress under analysis, as well as the challenges and the existing tour patterns. Archival and literature research was also carried out to obtain accurate information about the history of Yedikule Fortress. In parallel, the observation of the behavior of visitors in the fortress, the paths they follow, and the points of focus was also important for designing the virtual route. Additionally, a content

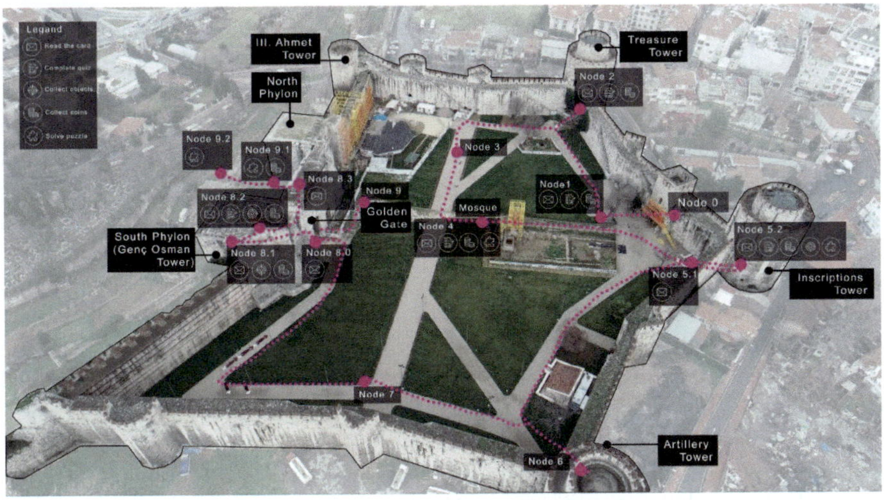


**Fig. 8.3** Route design for the on-site experience (own elaboration)

analysis of social media platforms revealed the most frequently shared content and the primary areas of interest for visitors during their visits (Gül et al. 2023).

The experience of the game elements on the route through two main components categorized as *nodes* and *links*. While the nodes represent the focal points of the visitors in the area, the links represent the paths that the visitors will follow between the nodes (Fig. 8.3). Once the nodes and links had been established, a series of narratives were devised to evoke the multi-layered structure of the fortress. These narratives were constructed to enhance visitor engagement and raise awareness of the site, both at nodes and along the connecting routes. Mini-games were designed by determining the timing, location, and components connected to the content of the relevant narratives. Throughout this process, experts collaborated to ensure historical accuracy and cultural sensitivity. As a result, the experience along the route that we designed was structured around geographical location rather than a chronological sequence of content.

### 8.4.3 *Mechanics, Narrative, Aesthetics, and Technology*

In examining the processes underlying the design of games, the following fundamental concepts emerge: *mechanics*, *narratives*, *aesthetics*, and *technology*. *Mechanics* is used to describe the various elements related to the gamified environment, including the specific goals, rules, and boundaries that are in place. The mechanics of a game remain consistent across all participants and applications, forming a repetitive cycle. At Yedikule Fortress, the game cycle is based on reading information cards, solving puzzles, answering questions, and collecting objects encountered, ensuring the continuity of the story. To ensure consistency across different technologies, the game mechanics were standardized to remain identical in both environments.

Based on the observations obtained from the field studies and pilot studies, the mosque and the old settlement in the center of the courtyard (the latter does not exist today) have been identified as nodes of great interest. The still existing Golden Gate and the two towers are also relevant. The fact that the foci of interest are nodal points creates mini-game areas where users can interact in the general game narrative. Users will collect '*sikkes*' (the old Ottoman gold coin) at the nodes by completing the tasks designed specifically for the nodes. The audio narrative will accompany and guide users to the nodes where they will complete tasks such as solving a puzzle or finding specific items. Table 8.1 shows the selected sixteen nodes and related gamified mechanics.

A series of short quizzes were defined to evaluate the knowledge acquired by the visitors (20 people each group, total of 120) through audio narration and information cards during the route experience. These questions are part of a question-and-answer procedure to assess visitors' understanding of the mechanics that make up the game loop. The purpose of these tests is to support education rather than assess performance. Therefore, the determination of correct *versus* incorrect answers has no impact on the outcome. The learning goal should be also achieved regardless of the visitors' performance in the tests, without the feeling that they are engaged in competitive endeavor. Certain diegetic elements and historical ornaments were also utilized to support the intrinsic learning objective and to increase the immersion of the route experience. The diegetic elements and historical ornaments help visitors not only to provide visual appeal but also to recall the historical narrative and context

**Table 8.1** Gamified mechanics of the nodes in the Android tablet and HoloLens environments

| No. of Node | Tablet (Augmented Reality) | | | | | Hololens (Mixed Reality) | | | | |
|---|---|---|---|---|---|---|---|---|---|---|
| | Read the card | Complete the quiz | Collect coin | Collect object | Solve puzzle | Read the card | Complete the quiz | Collect coin | Collect object | Solve puzzle |
| Node 1 | • | • | • | | | • | • | • | | |
| Node 2 | • | • | • | | | • | • | • | | |
| Node 3 | | | | | | | | | | |
| Node 4 | • | • | • | | • | • | • | • | | • |
| Node 5.1 | • | | | | | • | | | | |
| Node 5.2 | • | • | • | • | • | • | • | • | • | • |
| Node 6 | No interaction in this node, only animation | | | | | | | | | |
| Node 7 | No interaction in this node, only animation | | | | | | | | | |
| Node 8.0 | • | | | | | • | | | | |
| Node 8.1 | • | | • | • | | • | | • | • | |
| Node 8.2 | • | • | • | • | | • | • | • | • | |
| Node 8.3 | • | | | | | • | | | | |
| Node 9 | No interaction in this node, only animation | | | | | | | | | |
| Node 9.1 | | | • | | • | | | • | | • |
| Node 9.2 | | | | | • | | | | | • |

of the nodes and junctions they experience. Visitors are unwittingly engaged in a learning experience.

The puzzles play a crucial role in the game loop and are based on the mechanics of assembling puzzle pieces. The illustrations related to the Yedikule Fortress were organized as puzzle pieces, and visitors had to complete the images to progress to the next node. This approach integrates visitors' problem-solving skills and spatial awareness, allowing for a high level of interaction and motivation.

In addition to the physical conservation of cultural heritage, designing and implementing approaches that will enable interaction with users plays a critical role. In this context, mini-games, animations, and information cards have been designed to attract the attention of users, increase their awareness of cultural heritage, and motivate them to explore the heritage site. Based on the observations obtained from the field studies and pilot studies, the mosque and the old settlement in the center of the courtyard, which does not exist today, have been identified as nodes of great interest. The still existing Golden Gate and the two towers are also relevant. The fact that the foci of interest are nodal points creates mini-game areas where users will interact in the general game narrative. Users will collect '*sikkes*' (the old Ottoman gold coin), at the nodes by completing the tasks designed specifically for the nodes. The audio narrative will accompany and guide users to the nodes where they will complete tasks such as solving a puzzle or finding specific items.

The route that users experience forms the core of the gamified heritage experience. To maximize learning and visitors' historical interaction with the site, visitors will stop at node points along the route and perform actions and tasks guided by the audio narrative. The visitors on the route must collect the coins throughout the fortress, which will help to solve the mystery of the fortress. The coins contain clues for the visitors to solve the puzzle they will encounter at the end of the route. Once all the coins have been successfully collected, visitors will decipher the Latin text: 'Venice Navy Commander Stephan Alberti stayed here' on the Golden Gate and uncover its meaning (Fig. 8.4), and through a portal that will open, a 3D recreation of a past settlement that does not exist today.

In game mechanics, object collection is an important component of storytelling. Audio narration maximizes interaction by revealing the unique situations of the location at the nodes and connection points where visitors interact. Environmental elements and object collection mechanics are utilized to immerse visitors in the suggestive framework of the historical context as they navigate between locations. Environmental storytelling allows players to discover the story by exploring the game world. Environmental narrative elements are an approach that allows players to explore the game environment to find clues and background information. This approach shifts the focus from direct dialogue or cutscenes to visual cues embedded in the environment, fostering a sense of discovery. By integrating these visual elements, the historical narrative becomes more engaging, allowing visitors to actively participate in the experience and gain a deeper understanding of historical events. The main goal is for the environment to provide storytelling with visual clues and details instead of direct dialogue or cutscenes. Thus, the player is provided with an experience of discovery. Visual elements enable the story to be conveyed to the player

**Fig. 8.4** Inscription and design of the puzzle (black line) (own elaboration)

through the environment, allowing visitors to better understand historical events and take an active part in the game.

The concept of *aesthetics* in a gamified experience is closely related to the emotions and reactions intended to be elicited in participants. The objects that visitors collect during their route experience and the placement of environmental elements that support the narrative help create the necessary atmosphere. It is critical that the in-game objects (*diegetic elements*) are created and placed in harmony with the narrative for the game flow and participants' experiences. The consideration of *aesthetic* elements should extend beyond the notion of mere collection. Sound and animated elements augment the visitors' route experience, facilitating their sense of integration within historical site. The incorporation of aesthetic elements into the process was undertaken for evoking a range of emotions and reactions in visitors, such as curiosity, the desire to explore, and surprise.

#### 8.4.3.1 Cultural Route in Selected Nodes

The SC technologies can be classified as wearable technologies, exemplified by HoloLens glasses, and handheld technologies, exemplified by tablets. These technologies provide two distinct experiences and modes of interaction: one spatial and the other planar. In the Yedikule Fortress project, both AR via Android tablets and MR through Microsoft HoloLens 2 were employed to engage educational visitor experience. The integration of these technologies varied at each node along the cultural route (Fig. 8.3 and Table 8.1). These nodes are presented to present the insight of the discussion. Each technology which are leveraging its distinctive capabilities to facilitate enhanced visitor interaction and immersion, as indicated below:

- *Node 0*: AR and MR technologies gave visitors a unique introduction to Yedikule Fortress. The AR experience used Android tablets with a video overlay on the screen. Tablet's screen shows digital information right in front of the visitors, with interactive buttons to guide them through the tour. The MR experience with Microsoft HoloLens 2 had a holographic guide that welcomed visitors and gave instructions. This guide seemed to be seamlessly integrated in the physical space through spatial mapping, providing hands-free, immersive introduction that engaged visitors right from the start.
- *Node 2*: In the Treasury Tower, AR and MR provided different experiences. Those using Android tablets had the opportunity to view a 3D model of the tower, with interactive hotspots for learning more about the history. AR application overlaid the 3D model onto the real-world view through the tablet's camera, allowing visitors to engage with it via touch-based interactions. On the other hand, the MR experience offered a full-scale holographic reconstruction of the tower. Visitors can ideally walk around and explore the historical structure in a fully immersive 3D environment, thanks to the advanced spatial mapping and environmental understanding provided by the MR headset.
- *Node 5.1*: The AR and MR experiences at the Inscriptions Tower, located at the front door, offer distinct approaches to delivering historical information. The AR experience provided a comprehensive timeline of the tower's history, combining static images, text overlays, and simple animations to create an engaging, interactive narrative. On the other hand, the MR experience showcases holographic inscriptions to be carved into the tower's walls. Visitors could activate these inscriptions to listen to compelling stories about the prisoners held there. This MR approach utilized spatial anchors to accurately position the inscriptions and spatial audio technology to enrich the narrative with realism and depth.

A comparative analysis of AR and MR technologies at each node of Yedikule Fortress reveals the distinctive capabilities of each technology (Fig. 8.6). The use of AR with Android tablets facilitates accessible and interactive overlays that enhance the physical environment, whereas MR provides immersive experiences through accurate spatial mapping and holographic projections. The integration of these technologies results in a comprehensive and engaging visitor experience, effectively bringing the history of Yedikule Fortress to life.

#### 8.4.3.2 Refinement of Spatial Computing Devices Based on Expert-Driven Evaluation

Expert involvement aims to gather information on usability and user experience, impact of the game experience, technical and route-related issues, and participant feedback. To ensure the effectiveness and usability of this devices, expert studies

**Fig. 8.5** GMR-H and GMR-A interface scenes at each node (own elaboration)

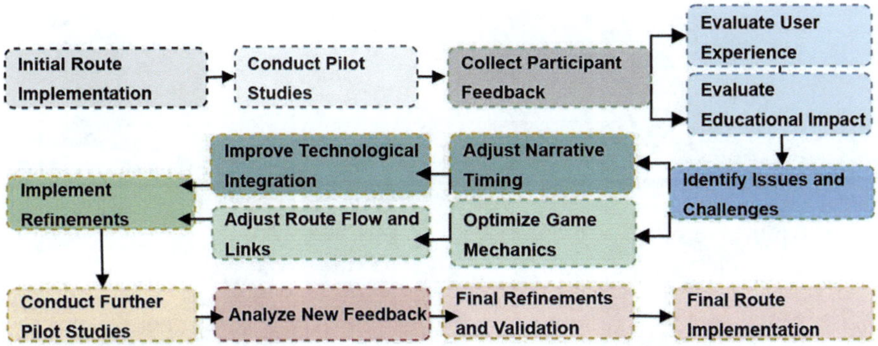


**Fig. 8.6** Refined route design following the expert evaluation (own elaboration)

were organized involving six experts in different research fields: two architectural historians and four professionals with an extensive knowledge on SC devices and gaming.

Usability issues included difficulties with the HoloLens 2 interface in bright outdoor environments and the discomfort of using an Android tablet for long periods of time. The technical challenges encountered by the experts regard the accuracy of Global Positioning System (GPS) data and the alignment of AR content, and delays in the rendering of MR holograms. Figure 8.6 shows the main requested improvements focused on adjusting narrative timing, optimizing game mechanics, and improving technological integration.

Most of the expert participants expressed positive and engaging experiences with AR and MR interactions. There was a consensus that the MR experience offered a more immersive experience.

The route experience was thus improved and made ready for the user experience, involving 120 visitors to test the gamified and non-gamified interfaces. Their experience is then analyzed, depending on the final outcomes, such as cognitive maps, surveys, and verbal feedback (Fig. 8.7).

Potential interactions with the tools and elements impacting user experience are analyzed, providing key insights for improving the application. At the end of the tour, a questionnaire is given to the experts to evaluate the overall experience. Table 8.2 shows the set of open-ended and 1–5 Likert scale questions addressing three topics: (i) heritage content (level of knowledge acquired by the visitor); (ii) travel route experience (ease of use and enjoyment); and (iii) application tool (comfort and performance).

**Fig. 8.7** Android tablet experiences (top), HoloLens MR device experiences at Yedikule Fortress (own elaboration)

## 8.5 Reflections on Heritage Interpretation Related to Yedikule Fortress

The conservation of architectural heritage is, at its core, an act of communication. The interpretation and presentation of cultural heritage sites are pivotal for promoting these sites and engaging with the public (Liu and Lin 2021). However, these activities can only achieve their purpose if the meaning of heritage is understood and recognized by local people and visitors (ICOMOS 2008). In this context, advanced digital technologies are increasingly being employed to enhance the promotion of heritage values to both local communities and visitors (King et al. 2016). The incorporation of these technologies is not merely a trend but a necessary evolution in heritage studies, driven by the need to make heritage more accessible, engaging, and relevant in the digital age.

Pilot studies gathered data on narrative timing, participants' movement times between nodes, their accuracy in identifying nodes from descriptions, and the fluency

**Table 8.2** Questionnaire regarding the experience

| |
|---|
| **Heritage content** |
| • *How do you evaluate the sate of preservation of the Yedikule Fortress?** |
| • Write the names of two historical figures you remember from the experience (open-ended) |
| • Write the names of two towers close to each other that you remember from your experience (open-ended) |
| • How would you describe the structure you are in?<br>(a) It is a masonry (stone) building built in the nineteenth century<br>(b) It is a wooden Ottoman structure built in the seventeenth century<br>(c) It is a masonry (stone) structure that was built in the fifth century during the Eastern Roman period, which has endured to the present day with various additions throughout history |
| • This experience changed my perspective on space* |
| • This experience made me feel the need to research and gain information about the historical structure* |
| **Travel Route Experience** |
| • How would you evaluate the experience route?* |
| – The tour route information was sufficient* |
| – I have read all the travel route information* |
| – I listened to all the narratives* |
| – I found the directions in the narrative inadequate* |
| – I did not find the content of the tour route sufficient* |
| – The travel narrative evoked a sense of discovery while touring the fortress* |
| – The travel narrative helped me visualize the place* |
| – The travel experience was made even more enjoyable with the device and application used* |
| **Application/tool** |
| • The device and the application supported the feeling of discovery* |
| • The travel route became more fun with the device and application given to me* |
| • While using the device and application given to me, I felt that my hands and arms were getting tired after a certain period of time* |
| • The device and application are easy to use* |
| • It is physically easy to control* |
| • The readability of the information on the application screen is low* |
| • Most people can easily learn to use the device and the app* |
| • I use the application confidently* |
| • I need to gain more experience to use the app effectively* |
| • *How successfully do you think you achieved the goals set by yourself or the researchers in completing the task? How satisfied are you with your own performance in achieving the goals mentioned?* |

*1-5 likert scale

of their navigation. Observations included expert feedback on the historical understanding of the fortification and overall impressions collected through post-tour interviews.

This research emphasizes heritage interpretation and communication through a game-based system comparing interaction devices. By integrating game elements into heritage experiences, the growing demand for interactive and immersive educational tools are addressed that resonate with contemporary audiences. This approach aligns with the increasing momentum in offering experiential opportunities that blend entertainment with education in cultural heritage (Mortara et al. 2014).

Communication-related historic sites have typically relied on static visual information or visitor brochures and audio guide, which offers concise historical accounts or images of reconstruction of the site. These methods, while informative, often fail to engage a broader audience and limited in their ability to convey the dynamic nature of heritage (Bartolini et al. 2016). This case study demonstrates the transformative potential of digital technologies in heritage communication. It can be challenging for a typical visitor to fully comprehend buildings of profound historical and architectural significance, especially when their functions have undergone significant changes over time (Andreoli et al. 2017).

This fortress, with its layers of changes, additions, and adaptations, presents a complex narrative that is ideally suited to exploration through digital means. By employing immersive technologies, visitors are provided a more engaging and nuanced understanding of the site's history, one that transcends the limitations of traditional interpretive methods. The quality of the narratives is crucial in elucidating the historical layers of the buildings and architectural elements, thereby enhancing the understanding of their uses over time. The design of audio narrative elements, including the amount of information and the length of the narrative, its relationship with the environment, and its integration with game elements, should be informed by a comprehensive understanding of the space itself.

### *8.5.1 A Brief Discussion of the Results*

These specific aspects were thoroughly discussed and optimized during the expert evaluations in this study. In addition to audio narration, a game-based application with a wealth of visual elements can guide visitors through the site, enhance their experience, stimulate interest and, most importantly, facilitate communication and interpretation of the heritage site. Like studies focused on enhancing the enjoyment of cultural heritage visits through gaming (Dow et al. 2005; Kim et al. 2015; Volkmar et al. 2018; Ćosović and Brkić 2020), this tour employed a variety of gaming elements as a supplementary visual layer to aid in understanding of the site's extensive history. This study was approached through a multidisciplinary lens, requiring a thorough examination of the historical layers of the castle in relation to its surrounding context and informed by scholars with expertise in its history. The spatial elements within the castle help guide the visitor; for instance, the visibility of tower doors encourages entry, while the distinct paving in the courtyard indicates the path.

The audio narrative related to Yedikule Fortress aims to create a sense of discovery for the visitor, linking different uses of the space while recounting historical events through guided exploration. For example, the audio narrative might say: 'Let us proceed to the Golden Gate via the Messe road, where you will observe an arched door on your right.' Such directions are meant to enrich the visitor experience by guiding them along the designed route, enhanced with visual decorations and animations where needed. The rich digital layer was experienced in relation to the accessibility and capabilities of the device in the visitor's hand. For instance, when depicting the occurrence of a fire in one of the towers and the destruction of the wooden floors and roof covering on the upper floor, tablet users viewed the animation by raising the tablet upwards, while the HoloLens 2 users simply raised their head upwards (Fig. 8.8). These devices are distinguished by their intrinsic characteristics, which give rise to distinct perceptions. One is regarded as an additional layer between the user and the surrounding space, whereas the other provides an embodied experience, as it is perceived as an extension of the body. The potential cognitive benefits of these sensory provisions will be the subject of future in-depth analytical studies.

Notably, one of the significant limitations identified by the participants was the glare issue with the HoloLens device in brightly lit environments. In such cases, the design of interface-related elements, such as the choice of visual color and the text size. Prolonged use of portable devices, such as tablets, can lead to arms and hands fatigue. To address it, the height of virtual objects should be adjusted to reduce excessive arm movement. While there are other aspects that could be discussed, it is essential to ensure the selected device aligned with the desired experience. The

**Fig. 8.8** Fire and destruction of the wooden floor animation in the Inscriptions Tower (own elaboration)

affordances of the devices should be thoroughly considered beforehand. The results of this research indicate that both devices elicit a high level of user interest and significantly enhance the overall experience as well as it stimulate users' interest in pursuing further exploration and learning about the history of the site in greater depth.

A significant number of participants expressed interest in further research development. These findings support the assertion that growing interest in fostering awareness and appreciation can serve as a crucial support in addressing fundamental challenges in heritage conservation. These challenges include ensuring public engagement, understanding the historical significance of the site, and considering its importance for long-term preservation and effective management.

## 8.6 Conclusion

This study explores the integration of wearable and portable devices in enhancing the interpretation and communication of architectural heritage. By focusing on the use of game-based systems, this research presents a novel approach to heritage interpretation beyond traditional methods, such as printed information boards or static displays. The findings resulting from this study emphasize the transformative role these technological applications can play, not only in engaging visitors but also in redefining the strategies and priorities of heritage conservation activities.

This case study demonstrates the potential of mixed reality (MR) technologies in conveying the layered history of heritage sites. By seamlessly integrating audio narratives with diegetic elements (visuals and animations) and thoughtfully considering the capabilities of the devices used, this study demonstrates how immersive experiences can be created to design complex yet accessible and comprehensive historical narratives. This approach not only enhances visitor engagement but also contributes to the broader objective of conserving heritage by advancing a deeper understanding and appreciation of the historical significance of each site.

More specifically, this study emphasizes the significance of diegetic elements, such as meticulously positioned visual cues and concise animations within the interface, in fostering an immersive and interactive engagement with the heritage site as memorable locations. While the audio narrative provided a linear and informative account of Yedikule Fortress's history, the diegetic visuals enabled participants to engage in active exploration of specific aspects of the site through direct interaction. Participants were able to engage with visual reconstructions (or animations) by navigating the interface. This creates a connection between often abstract historical narratives and tangible, location-specific representations. This combination of *passive auditory input* and *interactive visual elements* proved particularly effective in enabling participants to gain new insights into the site's history. By providing a means of exploration beyond static observation, the diegetic elements played a pivotal role in deepening participants' intellectual and emotional connections to the historical environment.

The application of these technologies to bring history to life and to bridge the gap between past and present is pivotal in sustaining public interest and supporting heritage conservation efforts. The positive feedbacks from participants encourage ongoing exploration and learning.

In the meantime, the authors discussed new challenges related to the effectiveness of these technologies. Considerations such as user interface design, device compatibility, and physical constraints must be carefully addressed to ensure that the technology enhances, rather than detracts from, the interpretation of heritage. Addressing these challenges is essential toward the optimization of the visitor experiences and ensuring that digital interventions align with the evolving priorities of heritage conservation.

Future research should continue to refine these approaches, with an emphasis on improving usability, accessibility, the interaction between visitors, and the enhanced representations of cultural heritage. By embracing new design solutions and approaches, heritage professionals can ensure that cultural heritage is not only preserved but also dynamically reimagined, engaging new generations and securing its resonance in the collective memory for the future.

**Acknowledgements** This study is a result of a research project supported by TÜBİTAK (The Scientific and Technological Research Council of Turkey, 1001, Project Number: 122K268). The authors would like to thank Fatih Municipality, expert participants for their support, the scholars Begum Moralıoglu Kaya, Varlık Yücel, Ayca Metin, and Ugur Onal for helping the development phase of the gamified interface. This project has 'ITU Social and Human Sciences Human Research Ethics Committee Approval' document number: 280 (19.09.2022).

## References

Andreoli R, Corolla A, Faggiano A, Malandrino D, Pirozzi D, Ranaldi M, Santangelo G, Scarano V (2017) A framework to design, develop, and evaluate immersive and collaborative serious games in cultural heritage. ACM J Comput Cultural Heritage 11(1):Article 4. https://doi.org/10.1145/306464

Ariza-Colpas PP, Piñeres-Melo MA, Morales-Ortega R-C, Rodríguez-Bonilla AF, Butt-Aziz S, Naz S, Contreras-Chinchilla LdC, Romero-Mestre M, Vacca Ascanio RA (2024) Sustainability in hybrid technologies for heritage preservation: a scientometric study. Sustainability, 16(5):1991. https://doi.org/10.3390/su16051991

Australia ICOMOS (2013) The Burra charter: the Australia ICOMOS charter for places of cultural significance (Original work published 1981)

Banfi F, Bolognesi CM, Bonini JA, Mandelli A (2021) The virtual historical reconstruction of the Cerchia Dei Navigli of Milan: From historical archives, 3D survey and HBIM to the virtual visual storytelling. In: The international archives of the photogrammetry, remote sensing and spatial information sciences, XLVI-M-1–2021, pp 39–46. https://doi.org/10.5194/isprs-archives-XLVI-M-1-2021-39-2021

Bartolini I, Moscato V, Pensa R, Penta A, Picariello A, Sansone C, Sapino M (2016) Recommending multimedia visiting paths in cultural heritage applications. Multimedia Tools Appl 75:3813–3842. https://doi.org/10.1007/s11042-014-2062-7

Chen F, Guo X, Lo T (2021) MR game for historical experience. Digital Heritage, pp 223–232

Ćosović M, Brkić BR (2020) Game-based learning in museums—cultural heritage applications. Information 11(1):22. https://doi.org/10.3390/info11010022
Çelebi HMZE (2008) Günümüz Türkçesiyle Evliyâ Çelebi Seyahatnâmesi: İstanbul: 1. Cilt-1. Kitap. Yapı Kredi Kültür Sanat Yayıncılık
Deterding S, Dixon D, Khaled R, Nacke L (2011) From game design elements to gamefulness: defining "gamification." In: Proceedings of the 15th international academic MindTrek conference: envisioning future media environments (MindTrek '11). Association for Computing Machinery, pp 9–15. https://doi.org/10.1145/2181037.2181040
Dow S, Lee J, Oezbek C, Maclntyre B, Bolter JD, Gandy M (2005) Exploring spatial narratives and mixed reality experiences in Oakland cemetery. In: Proceedings of the 2005 ACM SIGCHI international conference on advances in computer entertainment technology, pp 51–60
Eyice S (1993) Altın Kapı. In Dünden Bugüne İstanbul Ansiklopedisi, 1, 216–218. Türkiye Ekonomik ve Toplumsal Tarih Vakfı
Giariskanis F, Kritikos Y, Protopapadaki E, Papanastasiou A, Papadopoulou E, Mania K (2022) The augmented museum: a multimodal, game-based, augmented reality narrative for cultural heritage. In: ACM International Conference on Interactive Media Experiences, pp 281–286. https://doi.org/10.1145/3505284.3532967
Greenwold S (2003) Spatial computing. (Master's thesis). Massachusetts Institute of Technology
Gül LF, Kilimci ESY, Özer DG, Moralioğlu B, Coşkun E (2023) Fostering cultural heritage awareness through game elements. In: Proceedings of ASCAAD 2023 11th international conference of the arab society for computation in architecture, Art and Design, pp 653–666
Gül M (2025) Architecture and the Turkish City: an urban history of Istanbul since the ottomans, I.B. Tauris
Ham SH (2013) Interpretation: making a difference on purpose. Fulcrum Publishing
Ibrahim N, Mohamad Ali N (2018) A conceptual framework for designing virtual heritage environment for cultural learning. ACM J Comput Cult Heritage, 11(2), Article 11
ICOMOS (2008) Charter on the interpretation and presentation of cultural heritage sites
Kaya Dİ (2020) Architectural regeneration in Istanbul, Turkey. In: Orbaşlı A, Velinga M (eds) Architectural regeneration. John Wiley & Sons
Khan I, Melro A, Amaro AC, Oliveira L (2021) Role of gamification in cultural heritage dissemination: a systematic review. In: Advances in science, technology and innovation, pp 369–382. https://doi.org/10.1007/978-981-16-2377-6_37
Kim H, An S, Keum S, Woo W (2015) H-treasure hunt: a location and object-based serious game for cultural heritage learning at a historic site. Lect Notes Comput Sci (Including Subseries Lecture Notes in Artificial Intelligence and Lecture Notes in Bioinformatics) 9192:561–572
King L, Stark JF, Cooke P (2016) Experiencing the digital world: the cultural value of digital engagement with heritage. Heritage Soc 9(1):76–101. https://doi.org/10.1080/2159032X.2016.1246156
Krzywinska T, Phillips T, Parker A, Scott MJ (2020) From immersion's bleeding edge to the augmented telegrapher: a method for creating mixed reality games for museum and heritage contexts. J Comput Cult Heritage 13(4):1–20. https://doi.org/10.1145/3414832
Li Y, Yu L, Liang H-N (2021) CubeMuseum: an augmented reality prototype of embodied virtual museum. In: 2021 IEEE international symposium on mixed and augmented reality adjunct (ISMAR-Adjunct), pp 13–17. https://doi.org/10.1109/ISMAR-Adjunct54149.2021.00014
Liu Y, Lin H-W (2021) Construction of interpretation and presentation system of cultural heritage site: an analysis of the old city Zuoying. Heritage 4(1):316–332. https://doi.org/10.3390/heritage4010020
Mango C (2000) The triumphal way of Constantinople and the golden gate. Dumbarton Oaks Papers 54:173–188. https://doi.org/10.2307/1291838
Marques C, Pedro J, Araújo I (2023) A systematic literature review of gamification in/for cultural heritage: leveling up, going beyond. Heritage 6(8):5935–5951. https://doi.org/10.3390/heritage6080312

Marques CG, Pedro JP, Dionísio M, Almeida P, Pires da Silva C (2022) A systematic literature review of gamification in cultural heritage: Where are we? Where do we go? J Tourism Heritage Res 5(4):64–83. Retrieved from https://www.jthr.es/index.php/journal/article/view/417

Mortara M, Catalano CE, Bellotti F, Fiucci G, Houry-Panchetti M, Petridis P (2014) Learning cultural heritage by serious games. J Cult Herit 15(3):318–325. https://doi.org/10.1016/j.culher.2013.04.004

Nicholson S (2015) A recipe for meaningful gamification. In: Reiners T, Wood LC (eds) Gamification in education and business. Springer, pp. 1–20. https://doi.org/10.1007/978-3-319-10208-5_1

Ozer D, Nagakura T, Vlavianos N (2016) Augmented reality (AR) of historic environments: representation of Parion Theater, Biga, Turkey. A|Z ITU J Facul Arch 13(2):185–193. https://doi.org/10.5505/itujfa.2016.66376

Panzera E, De Graaff T, De Groot HLF (2021) European cultural heritage and tourism flows: the magnetic role of superstar World Heritage Sites. Pap Reg Sci 100(1):101–123. https://doi.org/10.1111/pirs.12562

Roumana A, Georgopoulos A, Koutsoudis A (2022) Developing an educational cultural heritage 3D puzzle in a virtual reality environment. Int Arch Photogrammetry, Remote Sens Spatial Inf Sci XLIII-B2–2022:885–891. https://doi.org/10.5194/isprs-archives-XLIII-B2-2022-885-2022

Sancak N, Uzun F, Turhan K, Saraoglu Yumni HK, Ozer DG (2023) Photogrammetric model optimization in digitalization of architectural heritage: Yedikule Fortress. Int Arch Photogrammetry, Remote Sens Spatial Inf Sci XLVIII-M-2:1403–1410

Tilden F, Craig RB, Dickenson RE (2008) Interpreting our heritage (4th ed.). The University of North Carolina Press

Varinlioglu G, Halici SM (2019) Gamification of heritage through augmented reality. Cultural Heritage 1:513–518

Volkmar G, Wenig N, Malaka R (2018) Memorial quest: a location-based serious game for cultural heritage preservation. In Proceedings of the 2018 annual symposium on computer-human interaction in play companion extended abstracts (CHI PLAY '18 Extended Abstracts). Association for Computing Machinery, pp 661–668

Xu J, Papangelis K, Tigwell GW, Lalone N, Zhou P, Saker M, Chamberlain A, Dunham J, Luna SM, Schwartz D (2024) Spatial computing: defining the vision for the future. In Extended abstracts of the 2024 CHI conference on human factors in computing systems. ACM

Yılmaz HF (1994) Yedikule Hisarı ve Zindanı. In: Dünden Bugüne İstanbul Ansiklopedisi, 7:460–462. Türkiye Ekonomik ve Toplumsal Tarih Vakfı.

# Chapter 9
# Documenting and Visualizing Heritage in Conflict Zones: The Underground Water Channel in Tel Gezer

**Rebeka Vital and Stella Sylaiou**

**Abstract** In regions of conflict, heritage sites often face threats of destruction, making documentation and visualization crucial for their conservation and dissemination. Traditional documentation methods encounter difficulties in accurately capturing and portraying significant archeological features, such as the amorphous shape of the water channel. This study examines the utilization of digital documentation techniques in showcasing and preserving cultural heritage sites in conflict zones, focusing on an Iron Age underground water channel at Tel Gezer in Israel. By utilizing laser scanning technology, this study demonstrates the effectiveness of digital documentation in creating architectural drawings and visualization models. A detailed point cloud generated from laser scanning offers a comprehensive digital record of the water channel's intricate features. From this dataset, architectural drawings were derived, enabling precise analysis and interpretation by experts in the field. Additionally, advanced visualization techniques were employed to create a three-dimensional model, making the site's complexity and history accessible and immersive for a global audience. This research addresses the challenges posed by the unique morphology of the underground water channel and underscores the importance of technology in bridging the gap between archeological research, heritage preservation, and public engagement, particularly in areas that are difficult to access and affected by conflict.

**Keywords** Digital documentation · Laser scanning · Cultural heritage · Water channel · Conflict zones · Tel Gezer

R. Vital (✉)
Department of Interior Building and Environment Design, SHENKAR—Design Engineering Arts, Ramat Gan, Israel
e-mail: rebekavital@gmail.com

S. Sylaiou
Department of Surveying and Geoinformatics Engineering, International Hellenic University, Thermi, Greece
e-mail: sylaiou@gmail.com

 
S. Stellacci and S. Aydin (eds.), *Endangered Heritage Sites*, Springer Series on Cultural Computing, https://doi.org/10.1007/978-3-031-91949-7_9

## 9.1 Cultural Heritage Preservation in Conflict Zones

In conflict zones around the world, the preservation of cultural heritage emerges as a critical concern among the chaos of war and violence. Archeological sites, museums, and other repositories of human culture and history face the dual threats of deliberate destruction and collateral damage. This endangers irreplaceable artifacts and monuments that bear witness to our collective past and individual experiences. The tragic loss of cultural treasures during conflicts, such as World War II and ongoing turmoil in regions like the Middle East, underscores the urgency of effective documentation and preservation strategies.

Among these challenges, the emergence of digital documentation and visualization technologies offers an efficient solution, providing innovative tools to capture, record, and disseminate cultural heritage in high fidelity. By digitally documenting artifacts, structures, and landscapes, archeologists, and conservationists and other heritage professionals can create comprehensive records that transcend the limitations of traditional methods, even amidst the chaos of conflict.

In "Cultural Heritage and Preservation: Lessons from World War II and the Contemporary Conflict in the Middle East," Moustafa (2016) explored the parallels between efforts to preserve cultural heritage during the Nazi occupation of Europe, as well as similar initiatives during modern conflicts in the Middle East. This study underscores the necessity of proactive measures, like the disaster management plans, to mitigate the risks posed by armed conflicts to libraries, museums, and archives and discusses strategies, such as international cooperation and policy support that can significantly contribute to the preservation of cultural heritage in conflict zones. Levin et al. (2019) utilized big data and remote sensing technologies to explore their potential for identifying threats to World Heritage sites in near real-time. Hammer et al. (2018) analyzed spatial and temporal patterns to investigate looting, agricultural activity, military occupation, urban growth, and mining, examining their impact on the destruction of archeological sites in the Islamic Republic of Afghanistan. Pütt (2018) presented a digital archive with more than 200,000 photographs, plans, and documents concerning Syrian heritage and built environment that is hosted by the Museum of Islamic Art in Berlin and the German Archeological Institute.

Digital technologies can provide valuable help to cultural heritage preservation in times of conflict. Stobiecka ( 2020 ) carried out a study that sought to establish how digital colonialism[1] has affected the archeological heritage with reference to the Syrian Arch of Triumph replica.[2]

---

[1] Digital colonialism refers to the extraction, ownership, and control of data from individuals—often without their explicit consent—through digital infrastructure and communication networks that are developed, operated, and dominated by Western technology companies. This phenomenon extends beyond mere data collection, encompassing the influence these corporations exert over digital ecosystems, knowledge production, and even economic and political structures in regions where they operate.

[2] In 2015, the original arch was destroyed, and it underwent digital documentation and restored in Egyptian marble, travelling in different western countries but never going back to Syria. The study

Technological advancements in spatial documentation add to the toolbox of strategies to safeguard heritage in areas of conflict. A digital documentation database gives a robust base for creating the virtual reconstruction of heritage sites and represents such sites through innovative and user-friendly tools as Virtual Reality (VR) and other online platforms. This approach, exemplified by the virtualization project of the Motilla del Azuer archeological site in Spain[3] (Torres Mas et al. 2022), integrates advanced technological tools like photogrammetry, laser scanning, and 3D spherical photography to capture intricate details of the architecture of the site. By leveraging VR installations equipped with motion controllers and immersive software, accessibility to the Motilla del Azuer site is enhanced, offering a realistic virtual tour experience to visitors, including those with reduced mobility. This initiative not only promotes tourism and cultural appreciation, but also revolutionizes heritage management and public engagement practices.

This study examines the case study of one such site of significance in an area that is often in conflict.[4] The settlement of Tel Gezer is an archeological site with a rich history dating back to the Iron Age, located in Israel, in the foothills of the Judaean Mountains, roughly halfway between Jerusalem and Tel Aviv. Tel Gezer's strategic location and historical importance make it a focal point for archeological research, ongoing excavations, and heritage preservation efforts. Exploring the intersection of conflict, cultural heritage, and technology, the case study of Tel Gezer provides a compelling lens to examine the challenges and opportunities in safeguarding our shared heritage for future generations.

## 9.2 The Site of Tel Gezer and Its Excavation

The archeological site of Tel Gezer boasts a rich and diverse history, dating back to the second millennium BCE. Initially established around 3500 BCE, Gezer flourished as a walled city during the Middle Bronze Age (ca. 2000–1500 BCE), evidenced by the construction of significant fortifications and the establishment of a 'high place' or 'tel'. Throughout the Late Bronze Age, Gezer came under Egyptian hegemony, as indicated by the presence of palaces and residences, and it garnered mention in

investigates cultural political as well as moral issues surrounding these digitalized practices used by post-colonial theory and technology studies which brings out their merits and demerits.

[3] La Motilla del Azuer is one of the most unique archaeological sites in Spain. Dating from the Bronze Age, it is a fortification with a central plan, formed by three lines of concentric walls distributed around a central tower. Inside, the labyrinthine shape of the access systems is remarkable, made up of narrow corridors, stairs, and ramps. This defensive enclosure allowed the protection and control of essential products for the people of the Bronze Age. Its true uniqueness lies in the fact it houses a monumental water well more than 15 m deep (Torres Mas et al., 2022).

[4] The area has been affected by the Arab-Israeli conflict, which is a prolonged and complex struggle between Israelis and Arabs, mainly over territory and national identity. Originating in the early twentieth century, the conflict has included several wars, uprisings, and ongoing disputes that continue to the present day.

historical texts such as the annals of Thutmose III and the Amarna letters. The city continued to evolve through the Iron Age, witnessing various phases of occupation and destruction. Notably, it played a role in biblical narratives, featuring in accounts of conflicts between Canaanites, Israelites, and Philistines. Under Solomon's reign, Gezer became fortified alongside other key cities, marking its significance within Israelite territory. Excavations, particularly those by the Hebrew Union College, have provided valuable insights into the Iron Age strata of Gezer, revealing layers of occupation and destruction, shedding light on its importance as a cultural and administrative center in antiquity (Ortiz and Wolff 2012).

Excavations at Tel Gezer commenced in 1902 under the direction of Macalister, spanning until 1909. Despite employing traditional methods, Macalister managed to excavate nearly forty percent of the site, identifying eight distinct levels of occupation (Macalister 1912). Following Macalister's efforts, Raymond-Charles Weill conducted excavations in 1913–1914 and 1923–1924, with renewed interest in 1934 under Alan Rowe's direction. A significant breakthrough occurred with the inception of the American Gezer Project in 1964, led by William G. Dever and J. D. Seger. Their meticulous work during the first phase I (1964–1971) and the second phase (1972–1974) revealed twenty-one stratigraphic levels, spanning from the Late Chalcolithic to the Roman period. Notable findings included the redating of city defenses, investigation of the 'high place', and clarification of Bronze Age domestic levels. The project's impact extended beyond excavation, contributing to scholarly understanding through the publication of several volumes detailing their discoveries. Additional seasons in 1984 and 1990 further enriched the data pool (Ortiz and Wolff 2012).

The Tel Gezer site includes a water system that has been continually excavated since the early 1900s. The ongoing Water System Project at Gezer challenges previous dating hypotheses proposed by William G. Dever, suggesting that the water system actually dates to the Middle Bronze Age (MBA) based on pottery findings from the 2015 season. Co-director Dan Warner, from Michael and Sara Moskau Institute of Archaeology—Center for Archaeological Research, at New Orleans Baptist Theological Seminary, indicates a clear transition from Late Bronze Age to Middle Bronze Age pottery, supporting the MBA dating. The system's construction, possibly as early as 2000 B.C., was revealed to have been cut through rock using bronze and flint tools, with its preservation attributed to a causeway built by Macalister during early twentieth century excavations, inadvertently protecting the basin from debris when a retaining wall collapsed. In 2014, the New Orleans Baptist Theological Seminary, the Israel Parks Authority, and the Israel Antiquities Authority,[5] in collaboration with Shenkar College of Design & Engineering,[6] executed a digital documentation of the Tel Gezer water system.

The interiors of the water channel were documented through laser scanning. The laser scanning methodology employed Leica C-10 ScanStation with resolution settings optimized for detailed point cloud generation in a distance of up to 100 m.

[5] https://www.biblicalarchaeology.org/dig/tel-gezer-water-system/#detailsSec

[6] https://www.shenkar.ac.il/en/

The workflow started on-site with an initial understanding of the geometry of the water channel and sketching the locations of the scan-stations and the targets that would allow for compiling the individual point clouds into one comprehensive point cloud of the whole geometry. The scan stations were defined to produce multiple scan points, in a way that there is an overlap of geometry and overlap of minimum three common targets from scan to scan, to ensure the accurate connection of the point clouds. After the scans were executed, the workflow continued in the office, where the individual scans were compiled into one comprehensive point cloud. The resulting point cloud served as a base for accurate two-dimensional drawings, as well as for a three-dimensional visualization model.

### *9.2.1 How Conflict Affects the Archeological Site of Tel Gezer*

The Israel–Gaza War has significantly impacted the excavation project, preservation efforts, and accessibility of the heritage site in Tel Gezer.[7] The 2023 conflict has posed immediate threats to the safety of archeologists and staff involved in the excavation, leading to disruptions and delays in ongoing research and documentation. Moreover, the heightened security risks and restricted access to the region have hindered conservation initiatives, leaving the site vulnerable to decay and damage. The war has also impeded public accessibility to Tel Gezer, limiting educational and cultural exchange opportunities for visitors and scholars alike. As the conflict persists, urgent measures are needed to safeguard the site's rich archeological heritage and ensure its preservation for future generations among the ongoing challenges posed by armed conflict.

## 9.3 Challenges in Documenting Heritage in Conflict Zones

### *9.3.1 Threats to Heritage Sites in Conflict Zones*

In regions affected by conflict, cultural heritage sites often are caught in the crossfire, facing imminent threats of destruction, looting, and irreversible damage. The preservation of these sites becomes not only a matter of historical importance but also a symbol of resilience and identity for affected communities and cultures. However, documenting heritage in such volatile environments presents many challenges, ranging from security risks to logistical hurdles. This section examines the

[7] The Israel–Gaza war is an ongoing conflict characterized by periodic escalations of violence between the Israeli military and Palestinian militant groups in Gaza, that are rooted in deep-seated historical, political, and territorial disputes. The latest escalation followed the October 7th, 2023, attack by Hamas militants on Israeli territory and massacre of civilians, resulting in severe retaliatory strikes, increased tensions, significant casualties, and a humanitarian crisis.

multifaceted threats posed to heritage sites in areas of conflict and explores the daunting obstacles encountered in the documentation and preservation efforts within the chaos and upheaval of war.

In areas of conflict, heritage sites face a multitude of threats that endanger their survival and integrity. These threats encompass both deliberate acts of destruction and unintentional damage resulting from the chaos of war. Deliberate targeting by armed groups seeking to erase cultural identities and symbols exacerbates the vulnerability of heritage sites, leading to irreversible loss of historical treasures. Moreover, the presence of military operations and armed conflict increases the risk of collateral damage, as heritage sites become casualties of warfare.

An unfortunate example of such destruction is the archeological site of Palmyra in Syria between 2015 and 2017. Palmyra holds immense historical and cultural significance, serving as a testament to the rich heritage of humanity. This ancient city, inscribed as a UNESCO World Heritage Site in 1980, and placed on the List of World Heritage in Danger in 2013, once thrived as a vital hub of trade and civilization, bridging the gap between the East and West during the Roman era. Its temples, theaters, and diverse architectural marvels bore witness to centuries of cultural exchange and innovation. However, the tranquility of Palmyra was shattered by the devastating conflict that engulfed Syria, particularly with the occupation of the city by ISIS in May 2015. The ruthless actions of the terrorist group resulted in the deliberate destruction and looting of cultural heritage on a massive scale, including the iconic temples of Bel and Baalshamin, the Monumental Arch, and numerous tower tombs. The local museum that was housing invaluable artifacts was vandalized, with precious statues and relics smashed and scattered to debris. Tragically, Palmyra's irreplaceable treasures, symbols of humanity's shared history, fell victim to the ravages of war, underscoring the urgent need for global efforts to protect and preserve our cultural heritage (Abdulkarim 2020). As Bevan (2006) mentioned in *The Destruction of Memory: Architecture at War*, heritage often is destroyed during conflict with the purpose to erase the heritage from the collective memory: "In these circumstances structures and places with certain meanings are selected for oblivion with deliberate intent. This is not 'collateral damage'. This is the active and often systematic destruction of building types or architectural traditions that happens in conflicts where the erasure of the memories, history and identity attached to architecture and place- enforced forgetting is the goal itself."

A key initiative in the effort for documenting and preserving the site's legacy, is the Palmyra Portrait Project at Aarhus University. Since 2012, the project has been compiling a comprehensive corpus of Roman period funerary portraits from Palmyra, now the largest outside of Rome. This project has utilized fieldwork diaries and archival materials from Danish archeologist Kai Harald Ingholt, who worked in Palmyra between 1924 and 1935. These materials have been digitized to reconstruct in-situ contexts that no longer exist, such as the monumental underground tomb of Ḥairan. Such digital reconstructions have become a primary method for preserving and studying Palmyra's heritage. These reconstructions offer a way to visualize and understand the site's historical and cultural significance despite the inability to conduct physical restoration on-site due to the conflict (Bobou et al. 2020).

The Convention for the Protection of Cultural Property in the Event of Armed Conflict, established in 1954,[8] was an initiative that aimed to safeguard cultural heritage during wartime. Still, it is ignored during war and even in the aftermath of war. It overlooked certain threats like the ones from landmines and explosive remnants of war that continue to damage archeological sites, for example in regions like Croatia. Despite international efforts to ban landmines through treaties like the Ottawa Convention, their negative impacts persist, underscoring the need for better post-conflict heritage management strategies to address these overlooked threats (Kulenovic et al. 2020).

In addition to direct physical harm, heritage sites in conflict zones are also susceptible to raiding and illicit trafficking of cultural artifacts. The breakdown of law and order provides fertile ground for opportunistic looters to exploit these sites for financial gain, further depleting the cultural heritage of affected regions. The loss of these artifacts not only erases valuable historical narratives but also deprives communities of their cultural identity and connection to the past.

In the chaos and upheaval of conflict, efforts to document and preserve heritage sites encounter daunting obstacles. Security concerns pose significant challenges for archeologists, conservationists, and researchers, limiting access to sites and hindering documentation efforts. The lack of infrastructure and resources in conflict-affected areas complicates conservation initiatives, impeding the implementation of preventive measures and emergency response protocols.

### *9.3.2 Limitations of Traditional Documentation Methods and Advantages of Digital Documentation*

Traditional documentation methods are time-consuming and require accessibility to the site for extended continuous time periods. In areas of conflict, this is a significant limitation due to the volatile and hazardous nature of these environments. The reliance on manual surveying techniques and physical documentation poses challenges in terms of safety and accessibility for archeologists and researchers operating in conflict zones. Additionally, the rapid pace of destruction, decay, and raiding during armed conflicts outpaces the ability of traditional methods to capture and preserve vital information about cultural heritage sites. These limitations underscore the urgent need for innovative, rapid, and remote documentation approaches that can overcome the obstacles presented by conflict environments, while ensuring the preservation and accessibility of heritage for future generations.

In conflict zones, documenting cultural heritage is fraught with challenges such as restricted access, safety risks, and logistical hurdles. Digital methods like laser scanning offer practical solutions to these issues, enabling researchers to safely and efficiently capture detailed data without prolonged exposure to danger. The portability of modern laser scanning equipment allows teams to work in confined or

[8] https://www.unesco.org/en/heritage-armed-conflicts/convention-and-protocols/1954-convention

otherwise inaccessible spaces, navigating logistical and environmental challenges with greater ease. By creating precise digital records, these methods not only protect the information for future study but also ensure that even if physical access to the site becomes impossible, the cultural heritage can still be preserved and appreciated. Digital documentation through laser scanning, photogrammetry, and remote sensing offers a transformative approach to heritage site preservation and archiving. By capturing highly detailed and accurate 3D models of heritage sites, these technologies ensure the comprehensive documentation and preservation of cultural and historical assets. Laser scanning and photogrammetry enable precise measurements and detailed renderings of structures, artifacts, and landscapes, providing scholars with invaluable data for research and analysis. Additionally, remote sensing allows for the monitoring of site conditions and environmental changes over time, enhancing conservation efforts. By compiling these digital datasets into a structured database, accessible to scholars and the broader public, these technologies facilitate immersive visualization experiences that bring heritage sites to life. This accessibility not only enriches scholarly research but also fosters public engagement and appreciation for cultural heritage, ensuring its continued significance and preservation for future generations (Levin et al. 2019).

Since the 1990s, laser scanning and digital aerial and terrestrial photogrammetry have been essential tools for metric data acquisition in cultural heritage documentation. These advanced technologies have significantly enhanced the accuracy and efficiency of preserving historical sites and artifacts, ensuring that detailed records are maintained for future generations. The evolution of these methods has been driven by rapid technological advancements and the increasing accessibility of digital equipment, which have collectively revolutionized the field of cultural heritage documentation (Moullou et al. 2023). Currently, documentation methods are categorized into image-based, non-image-based, and combinatory techniques. Image-based methods, such as photogrammetry, rely on photographic images to create detailed 3D models and maps of heritage sites (Stylianidis et al. 2016). These methods are further divided into panoramic, close-range, and UAV-based types (Remondino and Stylianidis 2016). Non-image-based methods, including laser scanning, provide highly accurate geometric data but often require specialized equipment and expertise. Techniques that integrate both image-based and non-image-based methods leverage the strengths of each to produce accurate documentation.

Photogrammetry, an image-based method, is divided into three main types: panoramic, close-range, and UAV-based. Panoramic photogrammetry involves capturing wide-angle images that encompass large areas, making it ideal for documenting expansive archeological sites or landscapes. Close-range photogrammetry focuses on capturing detailed images of smaller objects or specific features of a site, providing high-resolution data that is crucial for intricate analysis. UAV-based photogrammetry utilizes drones equipped with cameras to capture aerial images, offering a unique perspective and the ability to document hard-to-reach areas quickly and efficiently (Castillo et al. 2019; Karachaliou et al. 2019).

One of the most transformative developments in digital documentation is the structure from motion (SfM). SfM is a photogrammetric technique that reconstructs

3D structures from 2D image sequences, making it particularly valuable for cultural heritage modeling (Brandolini and Patrucco 2019). Its ease of use and low cost have made it a popular choice among researchers and conservators, allowing for the creation of accurate 3D models without the need for expensive equipment or extensive training. Unmanned aerial vehicles (UAVs) provide fast, cost-effective, high-resolution data capture, allowing for the efficient documentation of large sites or difficult-to-access areas. UAV-based photogrammetry has proven to be especially useful in archeological surveys, historical site mapping, and monitoring changes over time (Fallavollita et al. 2013; Themistocleous 2019; Pecci 2020).

## 9.4 Methodology

Terrestrial laser scanning as opposed to UAV or vehicle-based platforms has some self-evident advantages in closed or restricted spaces, and therefore, its use for CH documentation in the last two decades, has increased (Remondino and Campana 2014; Karagianni 2021; Ruiz et al. 2021; Sylaiou et al. 2021; Ulvi 2021; Stylianidis et al. 2022; Fellas and Demosthenous 2023; Kompoti et al. 2023; Liu et al. 2023; Gutierrez et al. 2024) given that in combination with photographic imagery realistic and accurate representations/3D models can be created. As such, laser scanners generate point clouds, in turn used to create 3D models and are considered non-image-based methods. A key strength of terrestrial laser scanning is that it offers rapid data acquisition with hundreds of points per second (Drap et al. 2003; Lercari 2019; Vital and Sylaiou 2022). When combined with imagery acquired by cameras, accurate and appropriately textured digital twins of cultural sites may accrue. Laser scanners are computer-controlled and can integrate Global Navigation Satellite System (GNSS), producing detailed 3D models. Terrestrial laser scanners, being robotic, are effective in confined spaces, providing accurate documentation in short periods. This is precisely the reason behind opting for this combination of methods in documenting and rendering the Tel Gezer site. However, they struggle with rendering detailed edges, colors, and minor surface features like cracks. LIDAR is suitable for area scanning via UAVs but still faces challenges in visual representation.

Structured-light techniques, which combine cameras and scanners, have emerged to address these limitations by integrating software and technological solutions, such as those used in virtual museums and serious games. Despite requiring highly trained personnel and being time-consuming, these methods, especially combinatory ones, offer rich and accurate visualizations. The need for seamless, cost-effective digital processing of the entire workflow is critical but remains challenging.

As noted by Patias et al. (2008), each case is unique, necessitating tailored approaches to documentation. The products of CH documentation are equally varied. They range from architectural analyses of monuments at different scales to conservation and restoration plans, studies of artifacts, and specialized assessments, such as structural stability and humidity studies. Additionally, urban planning and archeological documentation often require detailed and accurate records. Researchers like

Patias (2006) and Eppich and García Grinda (2015) highlighted the breadth of applications, emphasizing the importance of flexibility in choosing the appropriate documentation method. Hybrid methods that integrate laser scanning and photogrammetry offer a robust solution, combining the best features of both technologies. While these methods present challenges, such as data synchronization and the need for traditional survey measurements, they are increasingly effective thanks to advances in software and techniques.

The documentation of the Tel Gezer archeological site through laser scanning involved multiple stages to ensure comprehensive data acquisition and detailed analysis. Each stage was essential in capturing the site's geometry and creating accurate digital models for preservation, research, and educational purposes. The initial phase, planning and preparation, requires researchers to define the specific objectives of the documentation, whether for preservation, research, or educational purposes. A preliminary survey was conducted to understand the site's layout, size, and distinctive features, which informs the selection of the most suitable equipment based on the site's requirements and the desired level of detail. Furthermore, researchers obtained the necessary permissions from local authorities and stakeholders to proceed with the scanning process. The most critical phase, data acquisition, involved several key steps: (a) setting up the scanners at various locations to ensure comprehensive site coverage, and (b) performing the scanning process from multiple angles. During scanning, laser beams reflect off surfaces, allowing for the creation of detailed point clouds that represent the site's three-dimensional coordinates.

At Tel Gezer, the Leica C-10 ScanStation was utilized for the laser scanning methodology. This equipment is a versatile tool capable for doing high-accuracy, long range scanning plus fast, full-dome interior scanning. The scanning process began with an on-site survey to analyze the unique geometry of the water channel, identifying critical areas requiring detailed documentation. The initial phase involved sketching a comprehensive layout of scan-station locations and strategically positioning targets to ensure proper alignment of individual scans. These targets, typically reflective spheres or flat markers, were carefully placed to maintain at least three common reference points between consecutive scans, enabling precise registration of overlapping geometry. Overlap between scan areas was carefully calibrated to exceed 30%, ensuring seamless integration of data and eliminating blind spots.

Upon completion of the fieldwork and following data acquisition, the workflow continues with the data processing and registration phase, which takes place in the office using Leica software. Here, the collected data are processed to remove noise and correct any errors within the point cloud. During registration, multiple point clouds were aligned and compiled into a unified dataset with a single coordinate system using reference points. Subsequently, the collected data are combined, and the point clouds are merged to create a complete 3D model that accurately reflects the spatial relationships and dimensions of the site. At last, the final product served as a detailed and accurate digital representation of the site that served as a basis for producing two-dimensional drawings and rendered into detailed 3D models with textures. The process of converting point clouds into two-dimensional architectural drawings involved manual segmentation in CAD software, ensuring minimal data loss by tracing accurately over the point cloud in plan and section (scale 1:20).

Laser scanning offers some unique features that render it an ideal method in confined spaces that lack sunlight. Laser scanning generates a point cloud by means of emitting laser beams, which accurately recreate the surfaces scanned and may also recreate complex structures with the addition of textures that are not recorded but artificially produced to match the visual appearance of the original. In ancient tunnels, for example, laser scanning is proved to be an optimal method of documentation often in conjunction with other approaches. A structure similar to Tel Gezer, though on a much larger scale and sophistication due to its more recent construction, is the Eupalinos tunnel or Eupalinian Aqueduct, a marvel of ancient engineering (Zambas 2019), which has been the subject of several research and documentation projects, the most recent of which involved laser scanning (Tokmakidis 2009). Laser scanning may have advantages over photogrammetry especially in underground archeological sites (see also Roman tunnels in Clini et al. 2013) but as is the case with Eupalinos tunnel, in very confined spaces the size and placing of the necessary equipment can pose challenges: Tokmakidis, e.g., mentions that the team had to cover 800 out of 1036 m of the tunnel as they could not use their equipment in narrower segments of the tunnel (which for the most part is fairly wide). Likewise, laser scanning has been used in closed spaces such as the section under the roof, e.g., of old cathedrals, proving an accurate model of the timber structures supporting the roofing (Bassier et al. 2016). In other instances, nevertheless, laser scanning has been used to safeguard places of worship that are either structurally vulnerable, systematically neglected or both, as is typically the case with churches in Turkey (Sidiropoulos et al. 2014). In the latter case, researchers used a combination of topographical measurements and laser scanning to capture highly complex features or objects, combining the best of both methods. Topographic method can be very accurate, but laser scanning is way faster, straightforward, needs less technical knowledge and staff, while it can obtain detail under a 0.25 mm with special equipment, therefore can be more appropriate for intricate (e.g., ornamental) heritage artifacts. One characteristic example of the methodology typically employed in relation to the use of laser scanning in cultural heritage buildings is published by Tokmakidis (2009).

The 3D models are used for precise measurements and to create maps or plans. Furthermore, they can be used for the identification of features and details not easily visible during scanning. The new 3D models are used for comparison with previous 3D models to understand historical context and changes over time. The documentation and the archiving of the 3D models ensure long-term preservation and accessibility for future research and re-analysis (Tavantzis et al. 2023). They can be shared with the community for public engagement and education purposes as well as for conservation and restoration purposes, damage assessment, restoration planning, and for monitoring changes. 3D interactive visualizations of archeological monuments and sites can be used for virtual tours and remote exploration, and the enhancement of the cultural experience through the creation of educational materials for schools, universities, and museums.

**Fig. 9.1** Point Cloud of the Tel Gezer water channel (photo by research team at Shenkar - Design. Engineering. Arts in 2014)

### *9.4.1 Comprehensive Digital Record of the Water Channel's Features*

Digital documentation through laser scanning enabled the creation of a high-resolution point cloud, resulting in a comprehensive digital record of the water channel's features. By employing laser scanning technology, the surveying team captured precise three-dimensional data points at a rapid pace, documenting the underground water channel's morphology and dimensions. This approach provided a detailed documentation of the channel's layout and structure that included features in wall surfaces that were used for ritual practice, according to the archeological team (Fig. 9.1).

However, documenting an underground amorphic water channel presented several challenges, particularly the need to operate in a confined and often inaccessible environment. The uneven and sloping wet ground further complicated the documentation process, requiring meticulous planning and execution to ensure the accurate capture of data points while navigating challenging terrain. Despite these obstacles, the use of laser scanning technology overcomes the limitations of traditional documentation methods, ultimately resulting in a comprehensive digital record of the water channel's features and geometry.

From the point cloud database generated by laser scanning, precise and accurate architectural drawings were produced through a meticulous process of drafting within the point cloud. Using CAD software, the three-dimensional point cloud was used to extract specific features and measurements related to the architecture and morphology of the site. By segmenting the point cloud and identifying key elements such as niches in the walls of the water channel and by cutting through the slopped ground and walls, detailed two-dimensional plans and elevations were generated (Fig. 9.2).

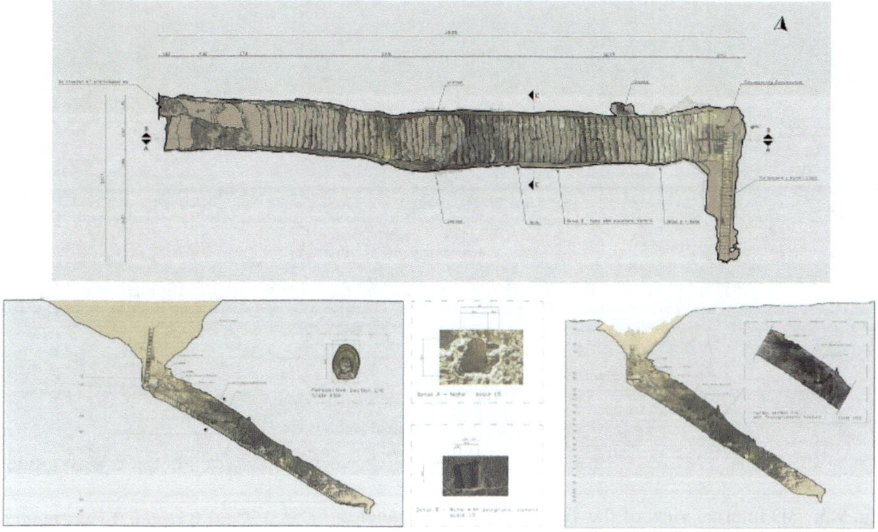

**Fig. 9.2** Plan and sections of the Tel Gezer water channel (drawing by research assistants at Shenkar - Design. Engineering. Arts in 2014)

These architectural drawings provided a clear and comprehensive representation of the site's layout, levels, and dimensions, offering invaluable insights for further analysis and interpretation by researchers and archeologists. The importance of this two-dimensional record cannot be overstated, as it serves as a fundamental tool for understanding and documenting the architectural heritage of the site. By translating complex three-dimensional data into two-dimensional drawings, the architectural drawings facilitate communication and collaboration among stakeholders involved in the preservation and management of the site. Moreover, these drawings serve as a crucial reference for future research, restoration, and conservation efforts, providing a baseline for monitoring changes to the site over time. Ultimately, the precise and accurate architectural drawings retrieved from the point cloud contribute to the comprehensive documentation and long-term preservation and accessibility of the site's architectural heritage, ensuring its cultural significance is safeguarded for future generations.

In addition to the architectural documentation, a three-dimensional visualization model was created to provide an immersive and accessible showcase of the historical significance of Tel Gezer to the broad public. This visualization model offers a dynamic and interactive experience, allowing users to explore the site virtually and gain a deeper understanding of its historical context and architectural features (Fig. 9.3). While the architectural documentation primarily addresses professionals and researchers, the visualization model caters to the layman by presenting complex information in a visually engaging and easily understandable format. Using interactive elements such as virtual tours, animations, and annotations, the visualization model brings the history and culture of Tel Gezer to life, making it accessible to a

**Fig. 9.3.** 3D internal view of the Tel Gezer water channel

wider audience beyond academia, around the world. This offsets the disconnection to the site during times of conflict and not only enhances public engagement and awareness of cultural heritage but also fosters a sense of connection and appreciation for the site's historical significance, ultimately contributing to its preservation and long-term sustainability.

In the visualization model, the viewer steps into the virtual realm and finds themselves transported to the heart of this iron age settlement, to the water channel system that was both an important source of survival for the community and a place for rituals. Through innovative VR experiences, visitors can not only observe but fully immerse themselves in the cultural heritage site, interacting with its surroundings in ways previously unimaginable. From the comfort of their own homes, users can visit sites in dangerous locations, embark on guided tours led by expert archeologists, engage in activities to understand the history of the site, and experience the space in an immersive three-dimensional manner, in real-time. By harnessing the power of technology, VR transforms the way we experience cultural heritage, transcending physical boundaries and their disadvantages, while preserving the wonders of the past for generations to come.

## 9.5 Discussion

Tel Gezer, or for the same matter Eupalinos tunnel, may be fascinating but also daunting or in some segments, prohibitive for visitors to experience in person, on-site, for very different reasons in each case. While efforts are being made to make such ancient structures visitor-friendly, the measures taken to actually protect tourists

**Fig. 9.4** Cross-section of the tunnel with the water channel containing the actual water-pipe (1), layout of site (2), and a vertical shaft (3)

can be intrusive or outright destructive for the monument itself, as is the case with the extensive metal caging that line open shafts in Eupalinos tunnel, or until recently (2016) inhibited access beyond a point. As Papantonopoulos (2022, pg. 597) noted: 'The Eupalinos tunnel built in Samos Island, Greece, in the sixth century, is considered as one of the most important engineering achievements of antiquity (Fig. 9.4). The tunnel, which is the central part of an aqueduct, was excavated from two portals, set about 1 km apart: the two bores met with a high degree of accuracy at a depth of 175 m under the ancient fortifications of the Kastro Hill'. Papantonopoulos described the various aspects of the restoration interventions undertaken between 2013 and 2016, including structural restoration, geological consolidation, enhancement of the monument, and illumination. This project enabled the visitor to 'admire the design and the construction of the tunnel in its full length and understand the ingenious engineering of Eupalinos' (Papantonopoulos 2022, pg. 597).

Beyond the intervention and actual barriers that, more often than not, are present in ancient structures such as tunnels and underground aqueducts, even when access to the whole length is restored after careful interventions, as is the case with the Eupalinos tunnel after 2016, the nature of the monuments poses severe challenges. The tunnel is 1,036 m long, with the average dimensions of 1.80 m highlight and width, but in some sections the height drops to 1.50 m and the width narrows to 0.42 m. 'The rocky, uneven floor is wet and slippery in some areas and from the ceiling is dripping water in some parts. (...) Therefore, overweight people, visitors suffering from claustrophobia, panic attacks, lumbago, cardiac or respiratory problems, spinal diseases, musculoskeletal disorders causing moving difficulties are strongly advised not to enter' (Odysseus, Tunnel of Eupalinos). This issued set of restrictions and warnings apposite as they may be, still highlight the limitations of the physical visit even by people who are feeling comfortable in such environments in terms of access to information, lack of guides' descriptions inside the monument. This is an indication of the potential of proper Virtual/Extended Reality experiences to complement such visits or to offer digital tourism alternatives to those who may prefer for their own reasons to experience the site through digital means (as well).

Apart from the apparent benefits of recording heritage sites in minute detail, thereby creating digital twins in effect, that help monitoring and safeguarding these cultural treasures, 3D reconstructions can also foster virtual tourism or virtual tours to these sites offering unobtrusive accessibility even from the comfort and safety of one's home. While being on-site can provide a mesmerizing experience of the actual scale, exact nature of the excavated rock, and sensuous input such as smell and temperature, that may help absorb the atmosphere and ambient of the actual site, and help connect more deeply with (or reflect on) those who originally built or used it, virtual worlds that are accurate and scientifically sound can offer another layer of understanding and a different way of engaging with such places. A virtual reconstruction with adequate user interface and navigation provisions can offer the ability to users to gain access to multiple layers of information, bird eye-view maps, diagrams, and other visual or textual resources. These interactive elements can enhance engagement with the site's history information and highlight aspects of such heritage sites that often are also miracles of ancient engineering, in ways that would not be feasible or practical in the actual archeological site. Teleportation, nonlinear speed of virtual transfer from point to point of interest, can offer alternative ways of experiencing the site which may combine increased levels of knowledge acquisition with enjoying smart interfaces that can accommodate innovative ways of experiencing the virtual yet accurate reconstruction of the space.

## 9.6 Conclusion

Laser scanning documentation of archeological sites involves meticulous planning, data acquisition, processing, and analysis. Each stage is crucial for accurate digital modeling, preservation, and public engagement. Despite challenges, advancements in technology and methods continue to enhance the documentation and preservation of cultural heritage. The theory of multimodality (Kress and Leeuwen 2001; Kress 2005) suggests that there are always gains and losses when switching from one modality to another; this broadly speaking can be the case also when experiencing a site in its actuality as opposed to visiting a virtual world inhabited by its digital twin. While the importance of the full sense of being-there inside an underground structure cannot be overestimated, the potential of experiencing through extended reality, digital reconstructions which may offer a wealth of contextual information and visualizations, features such as virtual guides, and digital narratives, maps, soundscapes, real-time access to contextual resources, can complement the 'real thing' and enhance it either with the use of on-site devices, with apps designed for portable devices or AR googles or remotely through Virtual Reality.

Spaces like Tel Gezer may seem unique, but similar sites are more common than one might think. According to Valipour et al. (2020), Alexandria alone has over 100 ancient cisterns. Many of these cisterns feature remarkable structures. For example, the El-Nabih cistern includes three floors of columns with slightly arched beams. Another example is the sixth-century Royal Cistern in Constantinople, just 150 m from the Hagia Sophia. This cistern is an engineering and cultural marvel, with hundreds of 9-m-high columns showcasing a blend of diverse architectural styles.

A virtual world that would allow this otherwise challenging physical environment to be experienced while allowing well-designed modes of movement (e.g., flight mode) and interaction with resources, sounds, and virtual humans of that bygone era, can offer glimpses into the reality of the past with tools heralding future capabilities, sensibilities, and holistic understandings in a non-antithetical perception of the digital and the actual.

## References


Abdulkarim M (2020) Palmyra: from war and destruction to rehabilitation. In: Nagaoka M (ed) The future of the bamiyan buddha statues: heritage reconstruction in theory and practice. Springer, Cham, pp 113–122

Bassier, M., Hadjidemetriou, G., Vergauwen, M., Van Roy, N., & Verstrynge, E. (2016). Implementation of scan-to-BIM and FEM for the documentation and analysis of heritage timber roof structures. Digital Heritage. Progress in Cultural Heritage: Documentation, Preservation, and Protection, pp. 79–90. Springer International Publishing. https://doi.org/10.1007/978-3-319-48496-9_7

Bevan R (2006) The destruction of memory: architecture at war. Reaktion Books (distributed by the University of Chicago Press)

Bobou, O., Kristensen, N.B., McAvoy, S., Raja, R. (2020). Archive archaeology in Palmyra, Syria a new 3D reconstruction of the tomb of Ḥairan. Digital applications in archaeology and cultural heritage, Elsevier. https://doi.org/10.1016/j.daach.2020.e00164

Brandolini, F., & Patrucco, G. (2019). Structure-from-motion (SFM) photogrammetry as a non-invasive methodology to digitalize historical documents: A highly flexible and low-cost approach? Heritage, 2(3):2124–2136. MDPI AG. https://doi.org/10.3390/heritage2030128

Castillo LJ, Serván F, Patroni K (2019) Documenting archaeological sites on mountains and slopes with drones. Adv Archaeol Pract 7(4):337–352. Cambridge University Press (CUP). https://doi.org/10.1017/aap.2019.35

Clini, P., Nespeca, R., & Bernetti, A. (2013). *All-in-one laser scanning methods for surveying, representing and sharing information on archaeology Via Flaminia and the Furlo Tunnel Complex.* The International Archives of the Photogrammetry, Remote Sensing and Spatial Information Sciences: Vol. XL-5/W2 (pp. 201–206). Copernicus GmbH. https://doi.org/10.5194/isprsarchives-xl-5-w2-201-2013

Drap P, Seinturier J, Long L (2003) Archaeological 3D modeling using digital photogrammetry and expert system: the case study of Etruscan amphorae. In: Paper presented at the sixth international conference on computer graphics and artificial intelligence, Limoges, France

Eppich R, García Grinda JL (2015) Management documentation indicators & good practice at cultural heritage places. In: Proceedings of the 25th international CIPA symposium 2015, 31 August–04 September 2015, Taipei, Taiwan. Conference Volume. International Society of Photogrammetry and Remote Sensing (ISPRS), Sydney, 140p

Fallavollita, P., Balsi, M., Esposito, S., Melis, M. G., Milanese, M., & Zappino, L. (2013). UAS for archaeology-New perspectives on aerial documentation. In: The international archives of the photogrammetry, remote sensing and spatial information sciences, Vol. XL-1/W2 (pp. 131–135). Copernicus GmbH. https://doi.org/10.5194/isprsarchives-xl-1-w2-131-2013

Fellas, A., Demosthenous, M. (2023). Comparing the methods of terrestrial laser scanning and photogrammetry for the geometric documentation of stone bridges through the case study of Tzelefos bridge. In: Moropoulou A, Georgopoulos A, Ioannides M, Doulamis A, Lampropoulos K, Ronchi A (eds) Transdisciplinary multispectral modeling and cooperation for the preservation of cultural heritage. TMM_CH 2023. Communications in Computer and Information Science, vol 1889. Springer, Cham. https://doi.org/10.1007/978-3-031-42300-0_3

Gutierrez I, et al (2024) Building a Mycenaean chamber tomb catalogue from terrestrial laser scan data. Dig Appl Archaeol Cult Heritage 32:e00319
Hammer, E., Seifried, R., Franklin, K., Lauricella, A. (2018). Remote assessments of the archaeological heritage situation in Afghanistan. In J. Cult Herit 33, 125–144. https://doi.org/10.1016/j.culher.2017.12.008
Karachaliou E, Georgiou E, Psaltis D, Stylianidis E (2019) UAV for mapping historic buildings: from 3D modelling to BIM. Int Arch Photogrammetry, Remote Sens Spatial Inf Sci XLII-2/W9:397–402, https://doi.org/10.5194/isprs-archives-XLII-2-W9-397-2019
Karagianni A (2021) Terrestrial laser scanning and satellite data in cultural heritage building documentation. Int Arch Photogrammetry, Rem Sens Spat Inf Sci. XLVI-M-1:361–366. https://doi.org/10.5194/isprs-archives-XLVI-M-1-2021-361-2021
Kompoti A, Kazolias A, Panagiotidis VV, Zacharias N (2023) 3D Laser scanning and UAVs in cultural heritage: the case of old Navarino castle in Pylos, Greece. J Archaeol Sci: Rep 52, p. 104223. Elsevier BV. https://doi.org/10.1016/j.jasrep.2023.104223
Kress G (2005) Gains and losses: new forms of texts, knowledge, and learning. Comput Compos 22(1):5–22
Kress G, Van Leeuwen T (2001) Multimodal discourses. Arnold, London
Kulenović N, Kulenović I, Sirovica F (2020) The war damage on archaeological heritage after the war: archaeological heritage and landmines. Conserv Manage Archaeol Sites 22(1–2):74–92
Lercari N (2019) Monitoring earthen archaeological heritage using multi-temporal terrestrial laser scanning and surface change detection. J Cultural Herit 39:152–165. Elsevier BV. https://doi.org/10.1016/j.culher.2019.04.005
Levin N, Ali S, Crandall D, Kark S (2019) World Heritage in danger: big data and remote sensing can help protect sites in conflict zones. Global Environ Change, vol 55, pp 97–104. Elsevier BV. https://doi.org/10.1016/j.gloenvcha.2019.02.001
Liu J, Willkens D, Gentry R (2023) A conceptual framework for integrating terrestrial laser scanning (TLS) into the historic american buildings survey (HABS). Architecture 3(3):505–527. https://doi.org/10.3390/architecture3030028
Macalister SRA (1912) The excavation of Gezer: 1902–1905 and 1907–1909. The Committee of The Palestine Exploration Fund, London
Moullou D, Vital R, Sylaiou S, Ragia L (2023) Digital tools for data acquisition and heritage management in archaeology and their impact on archaeological practices. Heritage 7(1):107–121. MDPI AG. https://doi.org/10.3390/heritage7010005
Mustafa LH (2016) Cultural heritage and preservation: lessons from world war II and the contemporary conflict in the middle east. Am Arch 79(2):320–228
Odysseus, Tunnel of Eupalinos, http://odysseus.culture.gr/h/3/eh352.jsp?obj_id=818. Last accessed 1 June 2024
Ortiz S, Wolff S (2012) Guarding the border to Jerusalem: the iron age city of Gezer. Near Eastern Archaeol 75(1):4–19
Papantonopoulos C (2022) The restoration of the Eupalinos tunnel: The many faces of a composite project. In: Vayas I, Mazzolani FM (eds) Protection of historical constructions. PROHITECH 2021. Lecture Notes in Civil Engineering, vol 209. Springer, Cham. https://doi.org/10.1007/978-3-030-90788-4_47
Patias P, Grussenmeyer P, Hanke K (2008) Applications in cultural heritage documentation. In: Arabatzi L, Pagounis V, Tsakiri M (eds) Experiences from cultural heritage documentation using modern geodetic techniques (Paper TS06E, pp 1–11). FIG Working Week 2011, Marrakech, Morocco
Pecci A (2020) Digital survey from drone in archaeology: potentiality, limits, territorial archaeological context and variables. In: IOP conference series: materials science and engineering, vol 949, no 1, p 012075. IOP Publishing. https://doi.org/10.1088/1757-899x/949/1/012075
Pütt K (2018) Documentation and digital preservation of Syrian heritage. In: The Public Historian 40(4):107–128. University of California Press. https://doi.org/10.1525/tph.2018.40.4.107

Remondino F, Stylianidis E (2016) Cultural Heritage documentation with RPAS/UAV. In: Stylianidis E, Remondino F (Eds) 3D recording, documentation and management of cultural heritage, pp 369–381
Remondino F, Campana S (2014) 3D recording and modelling in archaeology and cultural heritage—Theory and best practices. BAR International Series, Oxford
Ruiz RM, Torres MTM, Allegue PS (2021) Comparative Analysis between the main 3D scanning techniques: photogrammetry, terrestrial laser scanner, and structured light scanner in religious imagery: The case of the holy christ of the blood. J Comput Cult Heritage 15(1):1–23. Association for Computing Machinery (ACM). https://doi.org/10.1145/3469126
Sidiropoulos A, Lakakis K, Tokmakidis K (2014) Laser scanners technology applications-the case of church of holy trinity and figure of Panagia Pafsolipi, Heybeliada Turkey. Civil Eng Archit 2(9):330–337. https://doi.org/10.13189/cea.2014.020904
Stobiecka M (2020) Archaeological heritage in the age of digital colonialism. Archaeol Dial **27**(2), 113–125. Cambridge University Press (CUP). https://doi.org/10.1017/s1380203820000239
Stylianidis E, Georgopoulos A, Remondino F (2016) Basics of image-based modelling techniques in cultural heritage 3D recording. In: Stylianidis E, Remondino F (eds) 3D recording, documentation and management of cultural heritage. Whittles Publishing, pp 253–304
Stylianidis E, Evangelidis K, Vital R, Dafiotis P, Sylaiou S (2022) 3D documentation and visualization of cultural heritage buildings through the application of geospatial technologies. Heritage 5(4):2818–2832. https://doi.org/10.3390/heritage5040146
Sylaiou S, Androudis P, Tsiapali M, Trivizadakis N, Ramnalis D, Polychronos V, Efopoulos V, Evangelidis K (2021) Cultural heritage documentation: the case study of the ottoman bath in Apollonia, Greece. In Emerging technologies and the digital transformation of museums and heritage sites. Springer International Publishing, pp 97–110. https://doi.org/10.1007/978-3-030-83647-4_7
Tavantzis I, Tsifodimou ZE, Skalidi I, Karachaliou, E, Giannaris I, Bakousi A, Skondras A, Katakalos K, Stylianidis E (2023) Restoration workflows by means of photogrammetry: the case study of pashas bridge. In: The international archives of the photogrammetry, remote sensing and spatial information sciences: Vol. XLVIII-M-2–2023. Copernicus GmbH, pp 1543–1548. https://doi.org/10.5194/isprs-archives-xlviii-m-2-2023-1543-2023
Themistocleous K (2019) The use of UAVs for cultural heritage and archaeology. Remote sensing for archaeology and cultural landscapes, pp 241–269. Springer International Publishing. https://doi.org/10.1007/978-3-030-10979-0_14
Tokmakidis K (2009) Surveying the Eupalinian aqueduct in Samos Island. In: Proceedings of 22nd international CIPA symposium digital documentation, interpretation and presentation of cultural heritage, Kyoto. https://www.cipaheritagedocumentation.org/wp-content/uploads/2018/12/Tokmakidis-Surveying-the-Eupalinian-Aqueduct-in-Samos-Island.pdf
Torres Mas M, López-Menchero Bendicho VM, López Tercero J, Torrejón Valdelomar J, Maschner H (2022) Digitization and virtual reality projects in archaeological heritage. The case of the archaeological site of Motilla del Azuer in Daimiel (Ciudad Real). Virt Archaeol Rev 13(26):135–146
Ulvi A (2021) Documentation, three-dimensional (3D) Modelling and visualization of cultural heritage by using Unmanned Aerial Vehicle (UAV) photogrammetry and terrestrial laser scanners. Int J Remote Sens **42**(6), 1994–2021. https://doi.org/10.1080/01431161.2020.1834164
Valipour M, Ahmed AT, Antoniou GP, Sala R, Parise M, Salgot M, Sanaan Bensi N, Angelakis AN (2020) Sustainability of underground hydro-technologies: from ancient to modern times and toward the future. Sustainability 12(21):8983. https://doi.org/10.3390/su12218983
Vital R, Sylaiou S (2022) Digital survey: how it can change the way we perceive and understand heritage sites. Digital Appl Archaeol Cultural Heritage, 24:e00212. https://doi.org/10.1016/j.daach.2022.e00212
Zambas C (2019) More light in the tunnel of Eupalinos. Mitteilungen des deutschen Archaologischen Instituts - Athenische Abteilung 131(132):99–145

# Chapter 10
# Digital Engagement with Remote Architecture 'Furthest from the Sea': A Virtual Heritage Approach

**Serdar Aydin and Marc Aurel Schnabel**

**Abstract** This research addresses a computational analysis of the architectural heritage in Kashgar, the westernmost city in China and the easternmost part of Central Asia. Relevant to its culture and historical features, Kashgar is home to distinctive forms of mudbrick architecture that are furthest from the sea. Most historical mudbrick houses in the old town were replaced with replicas during a large-scale renewal project, initiated in 2009 and lasting for a decade. While the high risk of earthquakes made demolishing the original buildings seem like a practical solution for preserving local heritage, it also created a rare opportunity to digitally document the disappearing structures before their destruction. Based on an insightful review of methods used in 3D digital documentation and representation, this study provides new perspectives on computational studies of heritage sites. This study presents a set of 3D photogrammetric reconstructions of the narrow alleys in the old town, focusing on the role of user participation in the evaluation and interpretation of heritage. By investigating user-generated content in this unique cultural context, this research shows how novel research approaches are required to evaluate and interpret the inherent values of endangered heritage sites through participatory practices.

**Keywords** Virtual reality · Digital heritage · User participation · Simulated authenticity · Kashgar · Mudbrick architecture

---

S. Aydin (✉)
Department of Architecture, Mardin Artuklu University, Mardin, Türkiye
e-mail: serdaraydin@artuklu.edu.tr

M. A. Schnabel
Design School, Xi'an Jiaotong-Liverpool University, Suzhou, China
e-mail: MarcAurel.Schnabel@xjtlu.edu.cn

S. Aydin
School of Architecture, Victoria University of Wellington, Wellington, New Zealand



S. Stellacci and S. Aydin (eds.), *Endangered Heritage Sites*, Springer Series on Cultural Computing, https://doi.org/10.1007/978-3-031-91949-7_10

## 10.1 Introduction

Architectural heritage preservation and conservation are regulated by the documents of international communities, which include guidelines on the use of digital heritage.[1] 'Authenticity' is among the fundamental parts of these guidelines that emphasise 'archaeology (*to be extended to architecture*) is complex and not an exact and irrefutable science' while digitally reconstructing heritage environments for alternative interpretations[2] (ICOMOS 2017). Preliminary joint efforts and EU-funded projects (e.g. Charatzopoulou et al. 2016; Euromed 2020; Rainey et al. 2022) have been made to challenge the methodological rigour and to contribute to the scientific reliability behind alternative user-based interpretations, alongside the exploration of the theoretical underpinnings of inclusivity, such as 'unmediated cultural heritage' and 'authorised heritage institutions' (Smith 2006).[3]

Within this context, this research focuses on content-making processes in participatory digital heritage platforms while performing advanced and hybrid virtual reality applications.[4] In a wider spectrum, the results of the exploratory participatory project, using the unique case of Kashgar (in China), are relevant to researchers, policymakers and any heritage-related entities that are interested in the decentralisation of content-making processes in digital heritage, while guaranteeing methodological integrity.

The region where Kashgar is marked by unique geographical features, such as the Eurasian pole of inaccessibility (i.e., furthest point from sea access,[5] the highest peaks on earth), the Karakoram Range's (K1 and K2 reaches 8611m), and one of the lowest places on earth (Ayding Lake in the Turpan Depression, with 154m below the sea level). On the world's political map, it is the westernmost city in China and the easternmost part of Central Asia. The geographical uniqueness of Kashgar has contributed significantly to its historical importance as a major hub in the middle of the ancient Silk Road. Therefore, its architecture and urban character make Kashgar a relevant case study for the research community interested in endangered heritage sites and related cultural values at risk.

---

[1] For instance, the relevance of addressing heritage analysis through computational means is emphasised in London Charter for the Computer-based Visualisation of Cultural Heritage, aimed to ensure methodological integrity among the research community (Bentkowska-Kafel 2013).

[2] The Principles of The Seville Charter (later, The Seville Principles: International Principles of Virtual Archaeology) features eight main principles for virtual archaeology: interdisciplinarity, purpose, complementarity, authenticity, historical rigour, efficiency scientific transparency, and training and evaluation (Lopez-Menchero and Grande 2017).

[3] Smith (2006) introduces the concept of 'authorised heritage institutions', while stressing the novel side of inclusiveness embedded in the use of new technologies in cultural heritage. Cultural Heritage in a Changing World collects unique insights on the relationship between heritage institutions and individual content making processes (Borowiecki et al. 2016).

[4] This research is a part of Serdar Aydin's PhD under the supervision of Marc Aurel Schnabel at the School of Architecture, Victoria University of Wellington located in Wellington, New Zealand between 2015 and 2018 (Aydin 2018).

[5] 46°17′N 86°40′E.

This research explores two main interrelated aspects: how architectural heritage can be decoded into creative digital forms and how immersive virtual reality applications can enhance public engagement through creative virtual experiences. It is structured around three main areas: documentation, representation and dissemination, which typically are viewed as the three main research pillars (Addison 2000; Rahaman 2012). It shows how to undertake these three phases while examining cutting-edge technologies and the development of respective tools for inclusive virtual heritage applications.

After, the 'Introduction', which contextualizes this research in an extensive body of literature related to virtual heritage, a brief historical analysis is provided to show the key features of the case study. Then, the 'Documentation, Representation and Dissemination' sections show the computational methods used in this study, namely: (i) non-invasive approach applied to analyze and virtually reconstruct the architectural heritage of the narrow streets[6]; (ii) interpretative reconstructions; and (iii) user-generated content assessment for the interpretation of heritage values. Finally, the 'Results and Discussion' section reviews the concept of user participation in the field of digital virtual heritage for further applications.

The praxis of digital heritage and humanities operates through customary, innovative, and cyclic procedures, processes and methods. Digital heritage studies include using different advanced technologies, such as photogrammetry, laser scanning, virtual and augmented reality, and high-fidelity sound recording. These methods interchangeably provide rich content for documentation, representation and dissemination. This study offers a novel interpretation of the digital heritage processes by searching relations within user-generated data as part of virtual reality engagement.

## 10.2 Context Furthest from the Sea: Historic Urban Landscape of Kashgar's Mudbrick Architecture

Once a major city along the Silk Road, Kashgar faced limited accessibility and was vulnerable to extreme environmental and political conditions. As the westernmost city in China, Kashgar is situated at the convergence of Central Asia to the West, the Indian subcontinent to the South and China to the East. Its history showcases ancient civilizations (e.g. the Chinese, the Tibetans, the Mongols, the Indians and the Turks), with their religions (e.g. shamanism, Buddhism and Islam), as well as modern nations (e.g., Russia, England, Japan, China and a discontinued Uyghur state of the 1940s). At present, it is a place of conflict between Uyghur separatists and the Chinese security forces. This condition limits access to the city, implying a significant obstacle to conducting on-site research.

[6] In heritage studies, on-site limitations and sensitivities may prioritise the use of methods as non-invasive as possible due to security and ethics concerns, as discussed, among others, by Colley (2015).

At the same time, Kashgar is a place of growing tourist attraction due to being one of the gates of China to the rest of the world. A worldwide campaign of the Silk Road Economic Belt (*Aka Belt and Road Initiative*) is being widely promoted to which Kashgar is historically related. However, high economic development causes high pressure on the preservation of this cultural heritage site. A large-scale renewal project subjected nearly 80% of the houses in the Kashgar Old Town to demolition and reconstruction. Local people were arguably disengaged from inclusive decision-making processes (Bellér-Hann 2014; Holdstock 2015; Pawan and Niyazi 2016). The demolition of the Kashgar old town represents a worldwide problem of state-led mechanisms to 'manipulate' minority heritage (Aygen 2012: 28). Cultural heritage of ethnic and political minorities suffers lack of participation. In this context, digital methods help consider designing new means of participatory heritage preservation in Kashgar. These constructions seem sufficiently timeworn and soiled due to the application of exterior stucco onto modern concrete structures.

The architectural heritage of Kashgar Old Town is based on compact residential building blocks organized around a courtyard attached to each other along narrow alleys. The architectural layout of Uyghurs' domestic spaces significantly impacts the definition of family. The concept of household in Kashgar's old town is a broader definition of family that extends beyond kinship, as studied by Steenberg (2014). Other works, for example, those undertaken by Pawan and Niyazi (2016), analyzed the existing narrower relations between the neighbourhood and the market. Different functions around the courtyard prove a strong connection to water and thermal comfort in shaping the configuration of those houses, as in-depth analyzed by Florenzano et al. (2010). The configuration of outdoor spaces depends on water resource channels for irrigation as well as for living.

The narrow roads of the old town of Kashgar foster a strong sense of community. It remains unclear what associations between material features (e.g. textural, orange peel effect, brick thickness) and functional connections (e.g. between narrow roads and courtyards) have contributed to fostering the sense of neighbourhood in the old town of Kashgar.

Several researchers from different domains within social sciences and humanities, such as modern and classical languages, anthropology, archaeology, history, comparative religion, culture studies, political science and architecture, have documented the cultural heritage in Kashgar (Bellér-Hann 2008; Steenberg 2014; Pawan and Niyazi 2016), yet digital documentation activities have been limited to only a few cases. For instance, *The Kite Runner* (2008) movie may be the first of its kind to use aerial photography, digital modeling and post-production to map Kashgar's old town. The movie scenes are refined using advanced photogrammetry and 360° matte painting. Prince (2012) focuses on the reconstruction of 'authentic' places that resemble the city of Kabul in Afghanistan, where the movie was based. Other studies on this context include a 3D model of an old town area embedded with survey information regarding each house, created by Wang et al. (2014), a study of cultural heritage sites in Kashgar with Geographic Information System (GIS) and spatial modeling techniques developed by Gilad (2009), a morphological and typological

**Fig. 10.1** Narrow alleys in Kashgar (photos by Aydin 2018)

analysis of houses in Kashgar old town using digital techniques, such as photogrammetry and web-museum by Florenzano, Courel and De Domenico (2010), and a study of dynamic monitoring of changes in the urban pattern between 2002 and 2009 by remote sensing, carried out by Tang and Zhou (2013).

In a maze-like built environment, mind-boggling vistas grow and unfold in a fractal sense. Mapping these unique aspects of these alleys in digital formats requires effort and a thorough analysis of their configuration. Such research would be hardly feasible with physical traditional preservation techniques since it would require a considerable investment of time and budget. The outdoor space comprises narrow alleyways measuring more than a kilometre long and two to three meters wide. They are defined by single to three-storey high house walls that are occasionally linked with house units overpassing the alley to create tunnel-like passages underneath, as shown in Fig. 10.1.

## 10.3 Virtual Heritage: Related Works

Scholars recognize the value of transferring architectural methods into digital heritage. The use of high-fidelity documentation methods advances the means of the technological interpretation of digital heritage. Research on the architectural interpretation of digital heritage has focused on different aspects, including 3D documentation and visualisation. Affleck and Kvan (2005) and, later, Kalay et al. (2007) contributed to the theorisation of digital heritage. Datta and Beynon (2014) discussed the role of 3D reconstructions in understanding the values embodied by tangible architectural heritage. Webb and Brown (2011a, b, 2016) devised the expression of 'digital forensics' as a tool for enriching traditional architectural analysis. The 'Digital Documentation and of Ksar Said' Project articulated new technologies to combine tangible and intangible heritage in Said Palace in Tunis (Di Giuseppantonio Di Franco et al. 2019). These researchers use a user-centred approach to examine the learning objectives of co-creation processes and engagement with virtual heritage reconstructions.

Directed by Jeffrey Shaw and Sarah Kenderdine, the *Applied Laboratory of Interactive Visualisation and Embodiment (ALiVE)* is described as 'an incubator and innovations showcase for new forms of creativity and at the cutting edge of digital media in society', stating that 'ALiVE promotes an integrated scientific and artistic research strategy' via embodied multimedia models to 'enable the interpretation of tangible and intangible cultural knowledge' for museums (ALiVE 2017). Set up in the Hong Kong Science Centre premises of the City University of Hong Kong, the visualisation systems of ALiVE include 360-degree stereoscopic interactive visualisation environments (AVIE and PLACE) and hemispherical projection systems (iDome and MediaDome). ALiVE's display systems have made a significant contribution to research and practice in digital heritage, aligning with the progress made in the New Museology movement (Schettino and Kenderdine 2011; Kenderdine 2015; Kenderdine and Shaw 2014).

The heritage artefact is valued most in this user-oriented approach, while user-generated data remains complementary to any technological improvements. 'Reality-Virtuality (RV) continuum' developed by Milgram et al. (1995) is a highly influential work to be referenced. The RV Continuum is grounded on a linear relationship between reality and virtuality. As described by Milgram et al. (1995), it is 'limited strictly to visual displays' (Ibid, 282). On the theoretical side of the discussion, the increased use of digital applications has mitigated the entrenched dualism between 'real' and 'virtual' in recent years (Kenderdine, 2013). Richens (2014) showed the incapability of RV Continuum to describe the complexity of the 'Matters of Medium.' His Virtuality Matrix (VM) is based not only on technology but in a trifold relation to visitor-site-content aspects, as shown in Table 10.1, using the approach adopted by Richens (2014).[7]

Engagement types in digital heritage may shift their focus from the emphasis on the object itself (i.e., 3D reconstructions) to more authoritative forms that prioritise the role of users in the interpretation of heritage (Adair et al. 2011). In *Playing with the Past*, Champion (2011) connected digital heritage to the integrated concepts of architectural place-making and serious games, whereas a previous work (Aydin et al. 2017) emphasized more creative approaches to content production.

Rushton and Schnabel (2022) investigated how new realities alter the experience of the tangible and intangible in virtual environments and how meaning can be constructed to compensate for this, while Rogers et al. (2018) evaluated the 'five-dimensional' qualities of virtual reality environments to create an authentic, immersive virtual reality experience that will define the future of virtual heritage.

[7] Richen's classification is presented at the keynote speech of CAADRIA 2014 held in Kyoto, Japan.

**Table 10.1** Virtuality matrix (VM) adapted from Richens (2014) by the authors

| Visitor | Site | Content | Definition by Richens (2014) |
|---|---|---|---|
| Real | Real | Real | Reality |
| Real | Real | Virtual | Augmented reality |
| Real | Virtual | Real | Mixed reality |
| Real | Virtual | Virtual | – |
| Virtual | Real | Real | Telepresence |
| Virtual | Real | Virtual | – |
| Virtual | Virtual | Real | Virtual museum |
| Virtual | Virtual | Virtual | Virtual reality |

Bentkowska-Kafel (2013, 38) stated that digitizing historical knowledge presents a paradox of two distinct views about digital heritage forensics, which are 'a mode of inquiry' and a 'form of communication'. This can be further related to the 'creativity versus preservation' paradigm (Delve and Anderson 2014, 1) and even to the nineteenth-century division of architectural heritage between Ruskin's romanticism and Viollet-le-Duc's restoration (Howard 2003). Bentkowska-Kafel (2013) reframed the issue on an ethical basis around the request for para data. This view on para data is similar to that of the London Charter (version 2.1) ([2006] 2009, article 4.6), that 'should be disseminated in such a way that the relationship between research sources, implicit knowledge, explicit reasoning and visualisation-based outcomes can be understood'.

A gap in knowledge arises from the requirement for new insight into unified and associative processes, which may help better understand the effectiveness of digital heritage studies. This contribution explores the evaluative, analytical, deductive, interpretative and creative decisions and their derivative para data information generated while processing heterogeneous sets of methods during documentation, representation and dissemination processes.

## 10.4 Documentation

Various methods can be undertaken to document an architectural heritage site. In most cases, the selection of the type of technology depends on the context, the level of accuracy and the required amount of detail. Based on a review of different methods used in 3D digital documentation, Pavlidis et al. (2007) defined the following criteria for choosing an appropriate documentation system: (i) cost; (ii) material; (iii) size; (iv) portability of equipment; (v) accuracy of the system; (vi) texture acquisition; (vii) productivity; (viii) required skills; and (ix) compliance of outcome with standards. The research methodology for documentation is customized to guarantee accuracy and the required level of detail. The challenges include, but are not limited to, dealing

**Table 10.2** Methods, data sources, expected use and location

| Method | Data source | Expected use | Location |
|---|---|---|---|
| Unstructured interviews and on-site observations | Local inhabitants in Kashgar | N/A | Throughout the entire old town of Kashgar |
| CAD drawings | Published and unpublished materials retrieved by local administrative repositories | 3D modeling | Entire old town, focus on the study area |
| Sound recording | Field recordings from shops, streets, houses and public areas | Interactive design, virtual environment modeling with sound | Throughout the entire old town of Kashgar |
| Photography | Houses, streets and public areas | 3D modeling, interaction design | Throughout the entire old town, focus on the study area |
| Aerial video recording | Neighbourhood from above with > 30 m distance in accordance with the ethics and legislative regulation | 3D modeling, interactive design | Only the study area |

with the security measures in the region and optimization of time and available budget required to finalize data collection and data processing.

### 10.4.1 Fieldworks in Kashgar

The fieldworks for data collection in Kashgar focused on the *Köziciyerbişi*[8] neighbourhood separated from the rest of the old town by a crossing motorway. Social and cultural patterns within the context were examined in this study. Data collection included Computer-Aided Design (CAD) plan drawings (*.dwg*), on-ground and aerial photographic data, video and sound recordings, and textual resources related to local culture and architecture. A flexible methodology design integrating different approaches and tools was adopted to overcome each representation method's specific limitations and address context-related challenges. Table 10.2 identifies each method for documenting the *Köziciyerbişi* neighbourhood. The information was collected during three fieldworks carried out between April 18 and May 18, 2015; September 17 and 27, 2015; and October 16 and 26, 2015.

[8] Ch. 高台; pinyin. Gaotai; U. رايچىزوك ىشېب

**Fig. 10.2** Impact of large-scale urban renovation project (*first row*) and impact of sandstorm in Kashgar (*second row*) (photos by Aydin 2018)

### *10.4.2 On-Ground and Aerial Photographic Data Collection*

Conducting fieldwork in Kashgar is challenging due to its remote location and the political circumstances. On the one hand, high-level security measures in this geo-cultural context would not help a foreign researcher move around as freely as planned. On the other hand, natural phenomena, such as the frequent sandstorms[9] (which occurred, for example, during three days of fieldwork), brought difficulties, as shown in Fig. 10.2. Documentation was limited to fast and hybrid recording techniques with a digital mirrorless camera and two UAV devices.[10]

As personal UAV devices become increasingly common for laypeople, authorities set up rules to ensure a safer experience for everybody. Local regulations were enacted to control GPS signals, which is even more limited in Kashgar due to the political conflict in the region. New regulations that were enacted before Fieldtrip II resulted in the new DJI Phantom 3 no longer being able to fly over the study area. Due to time restrictions, it was not possible to obtain official permission for the device ID to be recognized in the system for GPS tracking. Another UAV with a registered ID for safely flying within China was rented on-site. Computational heritage studies in similar areas of conflict, which need to use UAVs, must ensure the latest national

---

[9] Sandstorms in Kashgar happen annually, moving westward from Taklimakan, one of the largest deserts on earth and located on the east side of Kashgar.

[10] To swiftly gathering image-based data of thousands of photographs for 3D photogrammetric modeling, Sony α6000 is used considering cost, size, and quality for fast focus and shutter speed. Additionally, data collection in this sensitive region must respect privacy matters and avoid intrusive methods. Fast focus and advanced shutter speed of the camera prevented suspicious gazes from the surrounding. UAV devices were DJI Phantom.

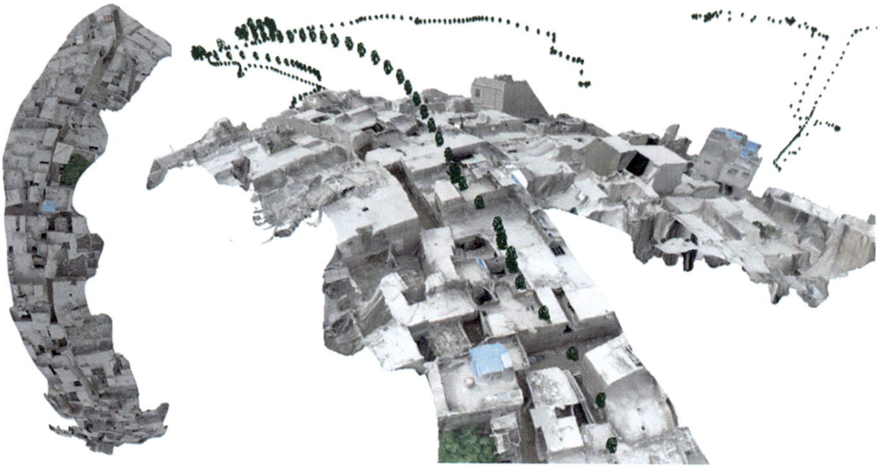

**Fig. 10.3** Photogrammetric model of Kashgar (image by Aydin 2018)

regulations and local permissions by the civil authorities, which may be subject to more strict regulations compared to those applied in other conflict-free zones.

The intricate relations between houses in Kashgar become visible when viewed from above. The mazes appear as a combination of similar components that reveal distinct differences just upon closer inspection. Interlocked combinations of ensembles reflect a historical fact that the houses are all built with traditional similar materials and construction techniques. Local adaptations break up this general homogeneity to meet the new living requirements. Aerial imaging was used to examine the complex structure of the old town from above. This documentation is applied to 3D photogrammetric modeling. A DJI Phantom 2 (mounted with a GoPro Hero4 camera) and a DJI Phantom 3 Professional (using an original built-in camera) were used for recording aerial views in Kashgar. The aerial photography process can be divided based on the followed flight path, encompassing three types of recording: (i) along the neighbourhood's perimeter, (ii) random pattern of the neighbourhood and (iii) on alleys. Prior to flights, paths on air were designed to produce results as efficiently and accurately as possible.

Figure 10.3 shows the result of the photogrammetric modeling by following one of the trails of the third flight path. High-resolution 4K videos from aerial documentation were converted into images.[11]

[11] Their size was reduced to remain manageable and reasonably accurate. Low-cost photogrammetry means less computational power required to reach a desired state of quality and resolution. In this case, 4K videos were imported to Photoshop to be converted into lower resolution images, which are then imported into photogrammetry software for the generation of real-like 3D models.

## 10.5 Representation

3D digital representations can unfold the complexity of historic constructions and their environments to simulate virtual reconstructions. To build a digital replica of the old town, non-invasive techniques are used to model the tangible character of the narrow alleys in Kashgar's old town. The purpose of using representation methods was to examine how users would react to the recreated environment.

Digital geometry is 'the geometry in digital space' (Mukhopadhyay et al. 2013). In digital heritage, different types of geometries are computed through various means of representation. Methods of representation include a range of means such as those of 'digital forensics' (e.g., Webb and Brown 2016), high-definition scanning technologies (e.g. Kenderdine 2013), 3D digital reconstruction (e.g. Datta and Beynon 2014) and photogrammetry (e.g., Dorffner and Forkert 1998). Advanced digital technologies used for architectural and archaeological heritage generate a variety of computational geometrical representations that are addressed by, e.g., Lu and Pan (2010), Zhou et al. (2012), Ioannides and Quak (2014), Münster et al. (2016) and Ippolito (2017).

### *10.5.1 Affordable Photogrammetric Surveys*

Photogrammetry is an image-based method to model sufficiently accurate 3D digital geometries, often applied when time and budget are limited. In photogrammetry, models can be produced as point clouds by marking and aligning 2D photographs. Different methods of image-based modeling and laser scanning (e.g., LIDAR—Light Detection and Ranging surveys) are used in photogrammetry, as discussed by Webb and Brown (2011b). Another term used for this type of photogrammetric modeling is Structure-from-Motion (SfM) (Fukuda et al. 2017). As a geological survey tool, photogrammetry is the science of measuring from photographs. It turns into a robust method for 3D modeling with technological progression, especially with sensitive camera lenses, advanced computers and low-cost software options. The latter demands an understanding of orientation, light and camera specs. The size and quality of details in the photographed content are essential to guarantee the quality of the model produced.

The photogrammetric surveys undertaken in this study (Table 10.3) were based on aerial and close-range techniques, requiring different understanding of photographic resources. In aerial photogrammetry, geometries can be optimized by built-in functions of the software, such as the Nadir orientation if the camera angle is zero (i.e. perpendicular to the surface of the earth). The close-range technique is more flexible in terms of camera angles, but the output may have to be improved by referencing points visible on multiple images (Nikolov and Madsen 2016).

**Table 10.3** Two main image-based photogrammetry techniques are based on the viewpoint

| Technique | Viewpoint | Resource (2D image) | Output (3D geometry) |
|---|---|---|---|
| Aerial photogrammetry | 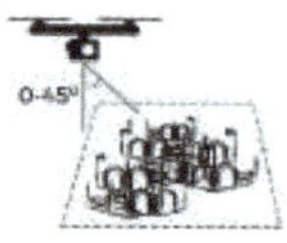 |  |  |
| Close-range photogrammetry | 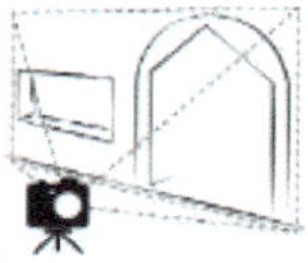 |  |  |

*Note* Aerial images were taken with GoPro Hero4, whereas close-range photographs were taken with Sony α6000. 3D outputs were modelled in Autodesk products (by authors)

Overall, the *.fbx* format could help faster and higher-fidelity data exchange through all steps of photogrammetric modeling thanks to consistency between sets of operations. Figure 10.4 shows selected images of the 3d models taken from different stages.

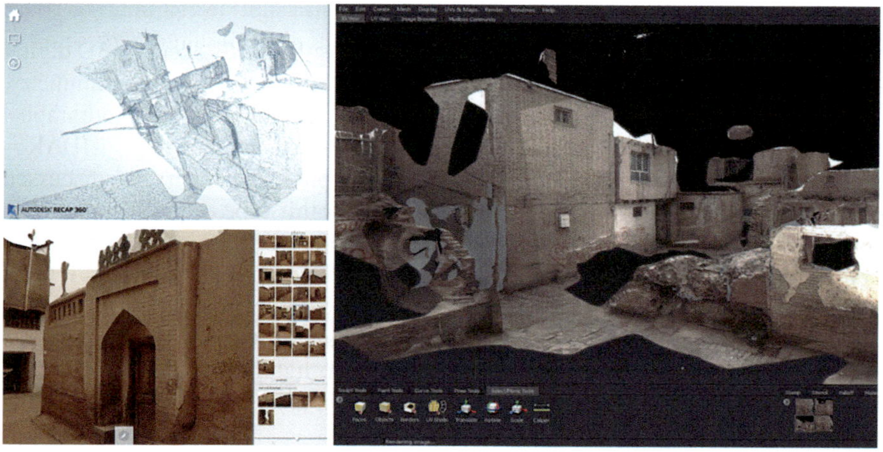

**Fig. 10.4** Photogrammetric model in Autodesk ReCap (*left*). Mesh optimization and correction on Autodesk Mudbox (*right*) (image by Aydin 2018)

### *10.5.2 Parameterization*

Texture mapping and basic operations (e.g., remeshing and decimation) are two direct applications of geometry parameterisation. 'Texture mapping' is the first application of parameterization on which visual glitches may appear if the algorithm cannot correctly map the texture on the coordinates of the 3D geometry. 'Parameterization' helps determine how to map texture on the mesh. Technically, it can be understood as a move before differential geometry in the hierarchy of processing polygon mesh. However, it is closely related to differential geometry, which is the conceptualization of discrete attributes in a parametric system. Simply put, differential geometry is the imagination of a system (e.g., Euclidean space that is already parameterized). A parametric representation of polygon mesh allows flexibility in operation between the processes of acquisition (*resource*) and application (*outcome*) (Botsch et al. 2010).

The information on the location of vertices is required to operate formulas during the conversion of 2D image-based information into 3D polygons. These formulas are handled by two complementary processes, the 'differential geometry' and 'parameterization'. Mesh polygons are built on the scalar (e.g., length, curvature and area) and discrete attributes (e.g., vector and tensor) as analyzed by Cohen-Steiner and Morvan (2006) and Botsch et al. (2010), among others. Smooth SfM surfaces of photogrammetric models stem from the derivation of discrete elements (i.e., vectors) from 2D photographs. They are then calculated as 'differential' properties in 3D. These discrete elements allow mathematical operations. This study explains the role of 'vectors' with a simple diagram. Figure 10.5 clarifies the concept of 'differential geometry.' The half-edge data structure maintains the connectivity of mesh patterns with all the algorithmic definitions shown on the left image (right). Different types of mesh errors may occur in photogrammetry.

The photographs of Kashgar were taken at different times and in different environmental conditions, such as cloudy days with evenly distributed light or sunny days.

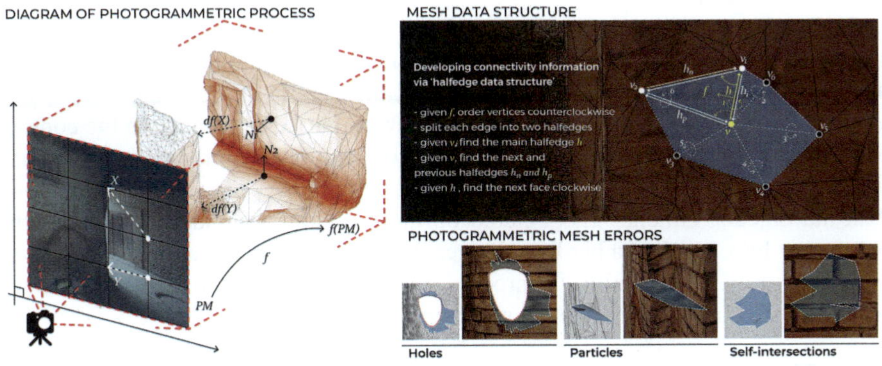


**Fig. 10.5** Differential *df* of a photographic map (PM) executes corresponding vectors $df(X)$ and $df(Y)$ on $f(PM)$. Vectors X and Y are stretched and transformed from one space to another (left) (image by Aydin)

Since these conditions excessively brightened white surfaces, parts of the geometry could not be recognized by the algorithm, which resulted in the creation of random black holes. Additionally, other errors were revealed in textures, and the photogrammetric process caused other misalignments. However, this also gave rise to its own glitch aesthetics, caused by errors in SfM modeling that misinterpret the pixels of a texture file. Software solutions provide auto-correction on glitch-like effects on photogrammetric meshes. The purpose of 'correcting' polygon mesh is to generate a 2-manifold geometry so that parameterisation is effective. Mesh connectivity held by the data structure (the *half-edge* method) is often compelled to fail by the complexity of actual heritage environments. In Kashgar, capturing reality involves minute details, such as telephone cables and power lines wiring space between houses through alleyways. These trivial details may be important elements that represent the realness. Their ordinary character can contribute to providing the last piece of a puzzle imagined in the virtuality domain. Ironically, most software options in digital heritage are oriented towards 'fixing' these real (or necessary) elements with their disappearance for a more aesthetic purified vision. This research interpreted a glitch as a force on computational geometry to go beyond algorithmic definitions. Such computational errors generate an opportunity for users to project their own understanding to complete the missing parts of 3D models.

### 10.5.3 Brief Review of Methods

Cost-effective computation has become increasingly prevalent in constructing digital, heritage-related or architectural content. Museums should integrate their decision-making workflow with new strategies to effectively leverage the large amount of user-generated content. These findings potentially generate new streams of interest; among those, virtual object restoration is a topical subject in the field of archaeology (Papaioannou et al. 2017).

In the object-centred field of archaeology, missing parts are viewed negatively as they require more interpretation and can lead to greater ambiguity. In contrast to the views of knowledge as a social construct, the criteria in these approaches aim to seek low granular information. Yet, this view might be challenged in the context of emerging curatorial museum activities to promote the transformation of information into knowledge-based more on social and participatory processes and relations than the objects. Glitches encountered during the entire computational geometry processing have reached a hardly manageable complexity that was difficult to keep track of entirely. To streamline the process, a scenario was selected that is sufficiently intelligible to conclude speculative reconstructions.[12]

[12] Glitched photogrammetric models were selected based on the criteria that the result is not too chaotic.

## 10.6 Dissemination

For dissemination, immersive media applications are customized to examine the role of users in evaluating and interpreting the cultural heritage values of the Kashgar Old Town. A hybrid virtual reality environment, branded as Hyve-3D, was uploaded with 3D digital replicas of the Kashgar old town. Hyve-3D is a representational ecosystem, which hybridizes alternate realities of media experiences (Dorta et al. 2016). The research on using Hyve-3D focused on several topical areas of user-oriented studies obtained from evaluating different aspects. For example, Schnabel et al. (2016) explored collaborative design with the system.

Hyve-3D was used in this research to deliver collaborative and real-time sketching in 3D through a user-friendly interface designed for anybody who can draw. The visualization system of Hyve-3D was an anamorphic *trompe-l'oeil* projection on a spherical concave screen that covers a five-to-five-meter physical space. One of about twenty viewers within this space controlled the navigation on the screen. The number of e-users depends on the number of tablets connected to the system, with a laptop station in the middle of the space, made by the concave screen, as shown in Fig. 10.6.

### *10.6.1 Two-Day Workshop in Melbourne (2016)*

A workshop was organized within the CAADRIA (Computer-Aided Architectural Design and Research in Asia) 2016 Conference in Melbourne. The workshop participants came from architecture-related fields and were not required to have previous software skills to participate. The data collected during the workshop includes participant observations and unstructured interviews. The instructions for using Hyve3D's hybrid system were given to eight participants[13] at the beginning of the workshop.

#### 10.6.1.1 Procedure

The workshop activities included photography and aerial imaging, SfM modeling, polygon mesh processing, 3D sketching in immersive Hyve-3D and interaction design. Figure 10.7 shows the number of participants working during different activities and the integration of the immersive Hyve-3D platform into the production line for digital heritage content-making. The deployment timeline of five different methods across two days is divided into four parts (Parts A–D: two in the morning; Parts E–H: two in the afternoon). Between Part D and Part G, SfM models of Kashgar were visualised in both the immersive and non-immersive editions of Hyve-3D.

[13] Two other participants joined from Montreal on the second day when Hyve-3D's immersive setup was used for remote collaboration. Participants were organised as individuals and groups at different stages.

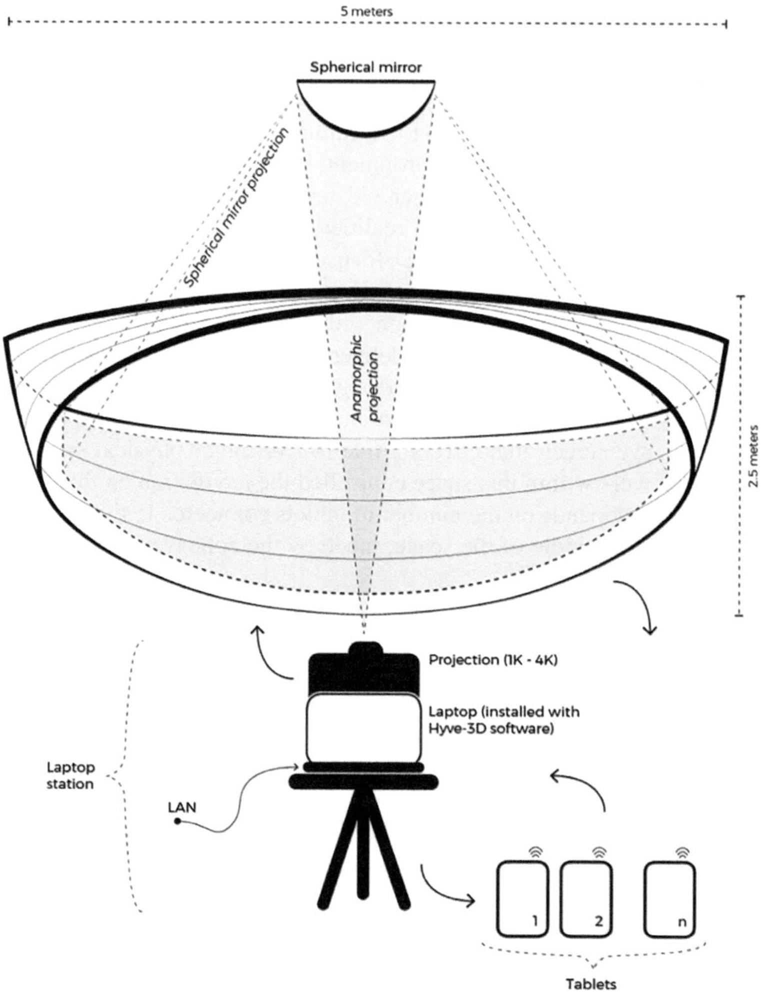


**Fig. 10.6** Hyve3D ecosystem (image by Aydin)

Table 10.4 shows the stages related to Parts D, E and F in which Hyve-3D was embedded with 3D models of Kashgar. The remote connection between Montreal and Melbourne was established in Part E.

Four lectures provided the participants with background knowledge about Kashgar and digital heritage to enrich the program. The lectures were oriented towards creative participation in digital heritage content. Before these activities, the participants were unfamiliar with Kashgar. However, all had specific theoretical and critical thinking on heritage and conservation due to their interest and background in architecture. They were asked to reflect on the knowledge gained by drawing 3D sketches. They should complete the missing geometrical information on the virtual reconstruction

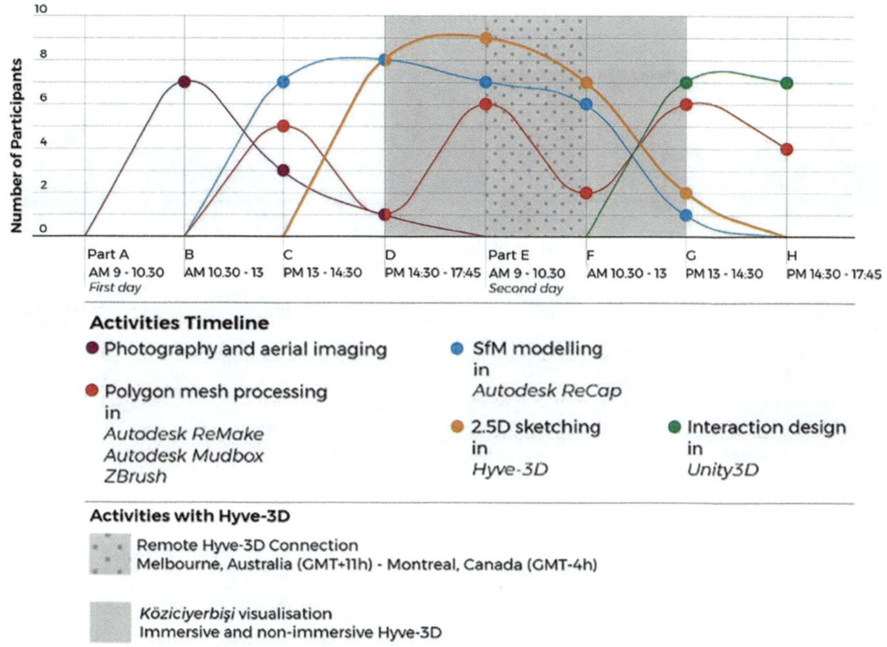


**Fig. 10.7** Activities during the two-day workshop in Melbourne and number of participants

of the historic building stock in Kashgar. Ten participants engaged interactively with the pre-modelled replicas of alleys. Navigating through narrow spaces, participants superimposed digital sketches on the model to communicate their perceptions of the pedestrian simulated experience. Figure 10.8 shows the collaborative activity of 3D sketching, followed by on-site observations and unstructured interviews by an expert panel of four workshop champions.

#### 10.6.1.2 Analysis

Kashgar is characterized by specific architectural Islamic features, such as hexagonal cobblestones. Participants in the workshop transferred this knowledge directly into the virtual world. In summary, the insight gained from the workshop is that personalized reinterpretations of heritage[14] in an immersive system produce the same desires as travellers in actual heritage sites. As studied by Urry (1990), MacCannell (1992), Leed (1991), Rojek (1997) and Staiff (2014), the perceptions by tourists include nostalgia, intellectual fantasy, imaginary power, aesthetic expression, and sensual and spiritual expositions. Evident in their 3D sketches, the essence of these desires

[14] One of them drew hexagonal patterns. Another participant added Islamic arches, influencing others to draw timber latticework for window protection (*mashrabiya*). Some participants also expressed their personality through graffiti.

**Table 10.4** Stages in Hyve-3D system with virtual Kashgar models

| Part D | Part E | Part F |
|---|---|---|
| <br>1. Introduction of the system and interface | <br>6. Set up of the content and remote connection | <br>12. On-screen expert analysis of different stages |
| <br>2. Individual participate in immersive Hyve3D | <br>7. Sketching in remote collaboration | <br>11. On-screen discussion of the content generated immersive and remotely |
| <br>3. Group work in non-immersive Hyve3D | <br>8. Individual sketching with a remote partner | <br>13. On-screen expert discussion on immersiveness |
| <br>4. Group work in immersive Hyve3D | <br>9. Sketching in groups with remote partners | <br>14. General discussion on user engagement in digital heritage via immersiveness |
| <br>5. Comparison of individuals' sketches | <br>10. Sketching non-immersive with remote partners | |

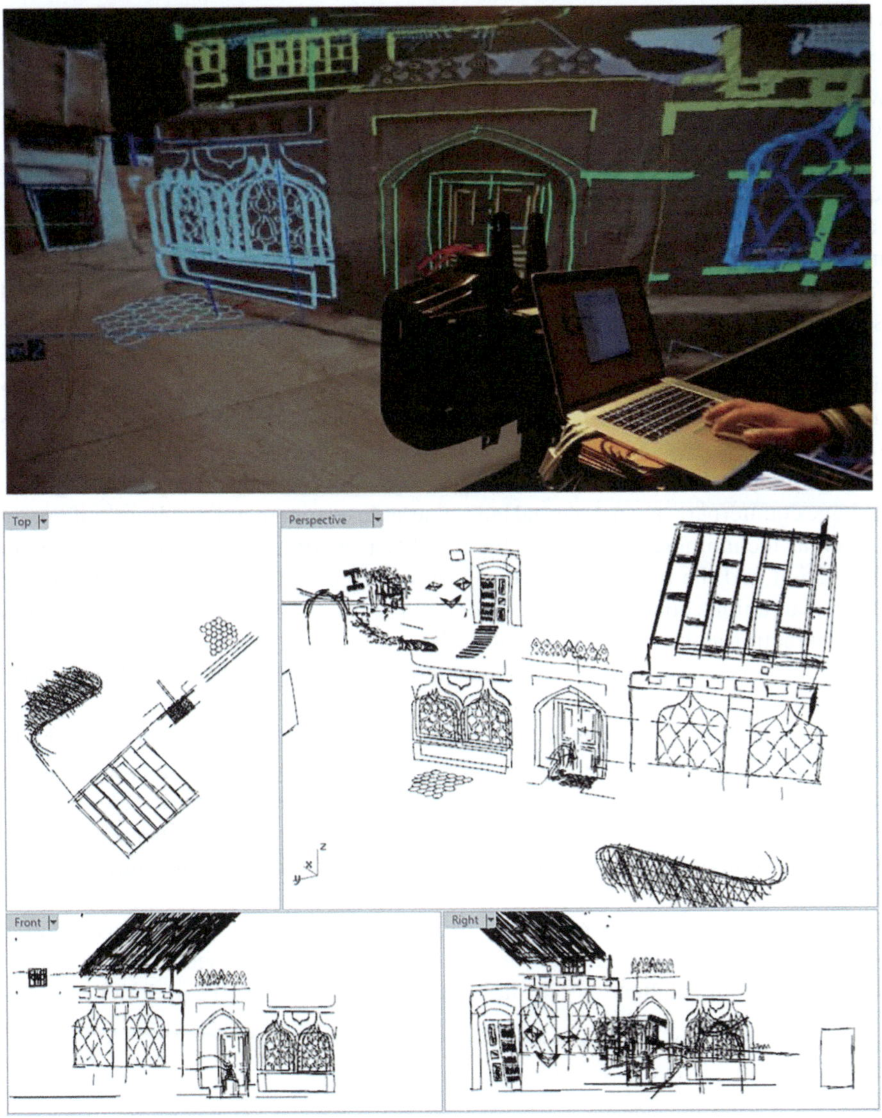


**Fig. 10.8** 3D sketches at the end of the workshop with the central laptop station of the Hyve3D system (*top*) and 3D sketches at the end of a remote collaboration session (*bottom*) (Aydin 2018)

is distilled by participants engrossed in interpretation, as shown in one example in Fig. 10.8 (*bottom*). The first activity of the user is the imitation of contour lines and edges of mesh surfaces.

## 10.7 Results and Discussion

Workshop findings that can classified into three categories (3D sketches, digital workflow, ethics of digital heritage) are shown in Table 10.5.

Creative engagement should not allow predefined personalization. This aspect is further explored in the following event. Digital design methods can be transferred to non-experts in a short time. The implication could be valuable for museum managers and curatorial staff looking for ‘citizen science’ or online crowdsourcing projects. Participatory content-making can also play a role in diversifying views on ethical issues, including authenticity.

Digitizing heritage information reflects subjective views on how to map and visualize reality in a virtual environment. Although the mapping processes of heritage are devoted explicitly to data preservation, a large amount of information can be lost, degraded and even erased entirely. These risks increase when this information is disseminated to a broad audience. In this sense, digital objects representing their heritage counterparts are not eternal but vulnerable to ephemeral conditions of reality as well as technological changes. This fragility is a stimulus for transforming both the content and the users’ perceptions. These dynamic transformations in content give rise to unique conditions in the digital realm, where metadata is generated from user interaction and critical interpretation. This relational knowledge can be searched about user-generated content to validate alternative meanings that are unknown until searched.

During the workshop, relevant information about public immersive engagement was collected, as shown in Fig. 10.9. Museum visitors were granted direct and free access to the content at the cost of complexity. Having retrieved alternative knowledge from public creative participation, the indexicality of content was further studied with an innovative application of a data mining method in digital architectural heritage research.

During the workshop, a relevant aspect of immersiveness emerged as the user began to take meaningful action. The role of agency reflects a mechanism of intelligence interpreting ‘authenticity’ in digital heritage. Conducting a correlation analysis

**Table 10.5** Workshop outcomes and classified qualitative findings

| Workshop outcome | Qualitative findings |
|---|---|
| 3D sketches | Immersive 3D sketching resulted in ‘noisy’ interpretations that are unique and grow beyond the medium’s technological infrastructure |
| Digital workflow | Training digital heritage experts can be relatively low-cost by utilizing user-friendly and affordable (or open access) software that integrates seamlessly, ensuring high interoperability among different software |
| Ethics of digital heritage | New viewpoints emerge on ethical topics, such as authenticity. These issues are topical in the digital age since we generally ponder them without formal instruction |

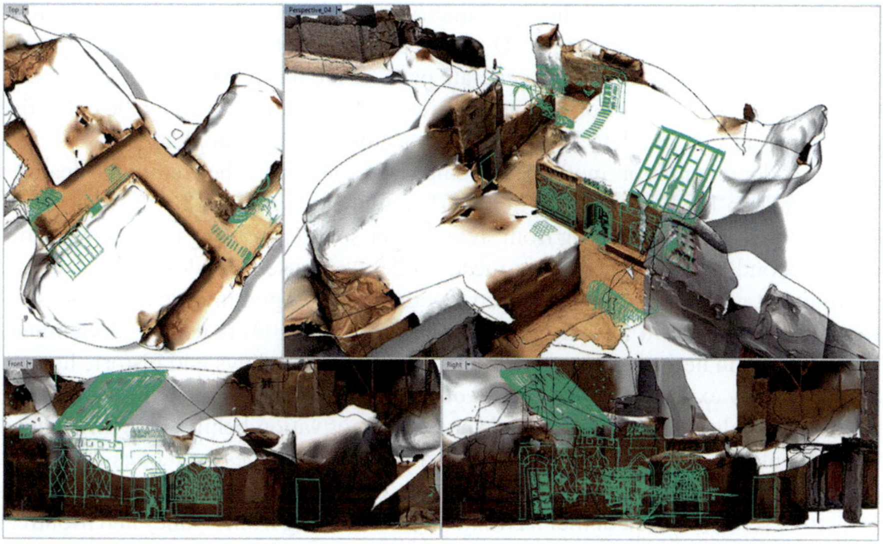

**Fig. 10.9** 3D user sketches and the 3D model of Kashgar (green) (image by Aydin)

of 3D sketches as user-generated content may reveal insight into this novel mechanism of authenticity. Associations of such indices are found to occur between the sets of user-generated content. In this sense, these correlations explain 'shared indexicality' between alternate realities based on select correlations, including horse carts, doors with eaves, lanterns, *mashrabiya* windows, flowers, gates and cats.

A correlation analysis exposes 'new standards of evidence' to define authenticity based on participation and conversation instead of singular authorship. The lack of local participation from Kashgar may result in inauthenticity. However, it should be viewed as both a limitation and a compelling opportunity. This research suggests that 'transformation of content' plays a central role in measuring alternative knowledge of virtuality in participatory content-making within conjectural reconstructions of heritage sites. In other words, the alternative knowledge of virtuality in digital heritage is intricately linked to how content is transformed through creative engagement.

## 10.8 Conclusion

New methods and digital environments are combined to visualize architectural heritage in Kashgar through digital documentation and innovative virtual reality applications. Among advanced non-invasive capturing methods of tangible architectural environments, photogrammetry is one of the most cost-effective options.

The preliminary process of photogrammetry involves the translation and parameterization of 2D photographs into 3D virtual environments. During this process, the algorithm of the software fails to generate parts of the mesh. This creates an opportunity to address gaps in information. This research is characterized by the collective interpretation of incomplete 3D environments along three main phases.

Firstly, documentation methods are employed to capture the traditional features of alleyways in Kashgar. Diverse fieldwork activities carried out by the authors are described in this study, ranging from stereo street-sound recordings to aerial photography. Secondly, photogrammetric mesh modeling is used for designing a virtual environment with photographs stitched together in photogrammetric modeling software. Thirdly, a hybrid 3D virtual reality system (Hyve3D) is used to disseminate Kashgar's urban heritage, featuring models of its narrow alleys and historic houses. A participatory experiment was carried out to collect user-generated digital heritage content for evaluation through a workshop. The motivation behind the participants' engagement was the straightforward task of drawing sketches on tablets connected to the virtual reality system, allowing them to view their drawings in real time on a panoramic screen in front of them. Eventually, connecting from Sydney and Montreal to the virtual replica of Kashgar through the hybrid virtual reality system, participants provided user-generated content to evaluate their engagement with heritage information.

Based on ephemeral, contextual and relative association rules, this research proves that digital engagement does not only conform with descriptive information, which generally conditions heritage knowledge to the past, but it is also generative. New perspectives on heritage transform heritage information into future knowledge. The type of creative engagement shown in this research suggests a causal mechanism between the material aspects and the meaningful expressions of heritage.

The experiments demonstrated how a higher level of engagement is achievable based on the creative act of completing a virtual model. Finding associations in user-generated content operates as an endless process of combining patterns, which can be appropriate or inappropriate. This paves the way for generalizing a language of visual conversation that can be sustained through a search mechanism. The participant translates architectural heritage into creative digital forms, contributing to the concept of unmediated cultural heritage.

Ultimately, this study demonstrates how the analysis of user-generated content helps interpret collective interaction with heritage knowledge. Documentation, representation and dissemination aim to search for alternative knowledge in participatory digital heritage-making. The novelty of the proposed methodology lies in exploring alternative knowledge through different realities. In architectural heritage studies, the proposed method offers a contemporary way of translating *things* into *artefacts* that can be built into digital museums and accessible to all.

## References

Adair B, Filene B, Koloski L (eds) (2011) Letting go? Sharing historical authority in a user-generated world. The Pew Center for Arts & Heritage, Philadelphia

Addison AC (2000) Emerging trends in virtual heritage. IEEE MultiMedia 7(2):22–25. https://doi.org/10.1109/93.848421

Affleck J, Kvan T (2005) Reinterpreting virtual heritage. In: Proceedings of the 10th CAADRIA, vol 1, New Delhi, 28–30 April 2005, pp 169–178. https://doi.org/10.52842/conf.caadria.2005.169

Aydin S (2018) Decoding Kashgar: a digital design approach to steer and diversify creative engagement in digital heritage (Thesis). Victoria University of Wellington. https://doi.org/10.26686/wgtn.17068574

Aydin S, Schnabel MA, Sayah I (2017) Association rule mining to assess user-generated content in digital heritage. In: Çağdaş G, Özkar M, Gül LF, Gürer E (eds) Computer-aided architectural design. Future trajectories. CAADFutures 2017. Communications in computer and information science, vol 724. Springer, Singapore, pp 231–251. https://doi.org/10.1007/978-981-10-5197-5_13

Bellér-Hann I (2008) Community matters in Xinjiang, 1880–1949: towards a historical anthropology of the Uyghur. Brill, Leiden

Bellér-Hann I (2014) The Bulldozer state: Chinese socialist development in Xinjiang. In: Reeves M, Rasanayagam J, Beyer J (eds) Ethnographies of the state in Central Asia: performing politics. Indiana University Press, Bloomington, pp 173–197. http://www.jstor.org/stable/j.ctt16gzghd.13

Bentkowska-Kafel A (2013) "I bought a piece of Roman furniture on the Internet. It's quite good but low on polygons."—Digital visualization of cultural heritage and its scholarly value in art history. Vis Resour 29(1–2):38–46. https://doi.org/10.1080/01973762.2012.761117

Borowiecki KJ, Forbes N, Fresa A (eds) (2016) Cultural heritage in a changing world. Springer, Cham. https://doi.org/10.1007/978-3-319-29544-2

Botsch M, Kobbelt L, Pauly M, Alliez P, Lévy B (2010) Polygon mesh processing. A K Peters, Natick, MA

Champion E (2011) Playing with the past. Springer London, London. https://doi.org/10.1007/978-1-84996-501-9

Charatzopoulou K, Hagedorn-Saupe M, Prehn A (2016) D6.1 access, participation, learning: digital strategies for audience engagement with cultural heritage in museums and libraries. RICHES Resources. https://resources.riches-project.eu/d6-1-access-participation-learning-digital-strategies-for-audience-engagement-with-cultural-heritage-in-museums-and-libraries/

Colley S (2015) Ethics and digital heritage. In: Ireland T, Schofield J (eds) The ethics of cultural heritage. Springer New York, New York, NY, pp 13–32. https://doi.org/10.1007/978-1-4939-1649-8_2

Cohen-Steiner D, Morvan J-M (2006) Differential geometry on discrete surfaces. In: Boissonnat, J-D, Teillaud M (eds) Effective computational geometry for curves and surfaces. Springer Berlin Heidelberg, pp 157–179. https://doi.org/10.1007/978-3-540-33259-6_4

Datta S, Beynon D (2014) Digital archetypes: adaptations of early temple architecture in South and Southeast Asia. Ashgate Publishing Company, Burlington, VT

Delve J, Anderson D (2014) Preserving complex digital objects. Facet, London

Di Giuseppantonio Di Franco P, Winterbottom M, Galeazzi F, Gogan M (2019) Ksar Said: building Tunisian young people's critical engagement with their heritage. Sustainability 11(5):1373. https://doi.org/10.3390/su11051373

Dorffner L, Forkert G (1998) Generation and visualization of 3D photo-models using hybrid block adjustment with assumptions on the object shape. ISPRS J Photogramm Remote Sens 53(6):369–378. https://doi.org/10.1016/S0924-2716(98)00020-3

Dorta T, Kinayoglu G, Hoffmann M (2016) Hyve-3D and the 3D cursor: architectural co-design with freedom in virtual reality. Int J Archit Comput 14(2):87–102. https://doi.org/10.1177/1478077116638921

Euromed (2020) Digital transformation for user engagement in cultural heritage. Europeana PRO website: https://pro.europeana.eu/event/euromed-2020. Accessed 17 June 2024

Florenzano M, Courel M-F, De Domenico F (2010) Digitally conserving an endangered built heritage in Kashgar, an Oasis City of the Taklimakan. In: Schneier-Madanes G, Courel M-F (eds) Water and sustainability in arid regions. Springer Netherlands, Dordrecht, pp 165–179. https://doi.org/10.1007/978-90-481-2776-4_11

Fukuda T, Nada H, Adachi H, Shimizu S, Takei C, Sato Y et al (2017) Integration of a structure from motion into virtual and augmented reality for architectural and urban simulation. In: Çağdaş G, Özkar M, Gül LF, Gürer E (eds) Computer-aided architectural design. Future trajectories. CAADFutures 2017. Communications in computer and information science, vol 724. Springer, Singapore, pp 60–77. https://doi.org/10.1007/978-981-10-5197-5_4

Gilad U (2009) Kashgar: GIS and spatial modeling of cultural heritage sites at the heart of the Silk Road. PhD dissertation. Monash University

Holdstock N (2015) China's forgotten people: Xinjiang, terror and the Chinese state. I.B.Tauris, London

Howard P (2003) Heritage: management, interpretation, identity. Continuum, London; New York

ICOMOS (2017) The seville principles: international principles of virtual archaeology, *19th ICOMOS General Assembly in New Delhi, December 2017*, https://icomos.es/wp-content/uploads/2020/06/Seville-Principles-IN-ES-FR.pdf

Ioannides M, Quak E (eds) (2014) 3D research challenges in cultural heritage: a roadmap in digital heritage preservation. Springer, Berlin, Heidelberg. https://doi.org/10.1007/978-3-662-44630-0

Ippolito A (ed) (2017) Handbook of research on emerging technologies for architectural and archaeological heritage. IGI Global. https://doi.org/10.4018/978-1-5225-0675-1

Kalay YE, Kvan T, Affleck J (eds) (2007) New heritage: new media and cultural heritage. Routledge, London; New York

Kenderdine S (2013) "Pure Land": inhabiting the Mogao Caves at Dunhuang. Curator Museum J 56(2):199–218. https://doi.org/10.1111/cura.12020

Kenderdine S (2015) Embodiment, entanglement, and immersion in digital cultural heritage. In: Schreibman S, Siemens R, Unsworth J (eds) A new companion to digital humanities, 1st edn. Wiley, Chichester, pp 22–41. https://doi.org/10.1002/9781118680605.ch2

Kenderdine S, Shaw J (2014) A cultural heritage panorama: trajectories in embodied museography. In: Din H, Wu S (eds) Digital heritage and culture. World Scientific, Singapore, pp 197–218. https://doi.org/10.1142/9789814522984_0014

Leed EJ (1991) The mind of the traveler: from Gilgamesh to global tourism. Basic Books, New York

London Charter ([2006] 2009) The London Charter for the computer-based visualisation of cultural heritage. First drafted at an expert seminar on "Making 3D visual research outcomes transparent". King's College London, London, February 25, 2006. Accessed 6 June 2024. http://www.londoncharter.org/introduction.html

Lu D, Pan Y (2010) Digital preservation for heritages. Springer, Berlin, Heidelberg. https://doi.org/10.1007/978-3-642-04862-3

MacCannell D (1992) Empty meeting grounds: the tourist papers. Routledge, London; New York

Milgram P, Takemura H, Utsumi A, Kishino F (1995) Augmented reality: a class of displays on the reality-virtuality continuum. In: Proceedings of the SPIE 2351, telemanipulator and telepresence technologies, 21 Dec 1995. Boston, MA, pp 282–292. https://doi.org/10.1117/12.197321

Mukhopadhyay J, Das PP, Chattopadhyay S, Bhowmick P, Chatterji BN (2013) Digital geometry in image processing. Chapman and Hall/CRC, Boca Raton, FL. https://doi.org/10.1201/b14786

Münster S, Pfarr-Harfst M, Kuroczyński P, Ioannides M (eds) (2016) 3D research challenges in cultural heritage II: how to manage data and knowledge related to interpretative digital 3D reconstructions of cultural heritage. Springer, Cham. https://doi.org/10.1007/978-3-319-47647-6

Nikolov I, Madsen C (2016) Benchmarking close-range structure from motion 3d reconstruction software under varying capturing conditions. In: Ioannides M, Fink E, Moropoulou A, Hagedorn-Saupe M, Fresa A, Liestøl G et al (eds) Digital heritage. Progress in cultural heritage: documentation, preservation, and protection, vol 10058. Springer, Cham, pp 15–26. https://doi.org/10.1007/978-3-319-48496-9_2

Papaioannou G, Schreck T, Andreadis A, Mavridis P, Gregor R, Sipiran I, Vardis K (2017) From reassembly to object completion: a complete systems pipeline. J Comput Cult Herit 10(2):1–22. https://doi.org/10.1145/3009905

Pavlidis G, Koutsoudis A, Arnaoutoglou F, Tsioukas V, Chamzas C (2007) Methods for 3D digitization of cultural heritage. J Cult Heritage 8(1):93–98. https://doi.org/10.1016/j.culher.2006.10.007

Pawan S, Niyazi A (2016) From Mahalla to Xiaoqu: transformations of the urban living space in Kashgar. Inner Asia 18(1):121–134. https://doi.org/10.1163/22105018-12340056

Prince S (2012) Digital visual effects in cinema: the seduction of reality. Rutgers University Press, New Brunswick, NJ. https://www.jstor.org/stable/j.ctt5hj5pv

Rahaman H (2012) A framework for digital heritage interpretation (Thesis). National University of Singapore

Rainey J, Macfarlane S, Puussaar A, Vlachokyriakos V, Burrows R, Smeddinck JD et al. (2022) Exploring the role of paradata in digitally supported qualitative co-research. In: CHI conference on human factors in computing systems. ACM, New Orleans, LA, pp 1–16. https://doi.org/10.1145/3491102.3502103

Richens P (2014) Virtual reality and cultural landscapes. Keynote at CAADRIA 2014, 14–17 May 2014

Rogers J, Schnabel MA, Moleta T (2018) Future virtual heritage-techniques. In: New realities: authenticity & automation in the digital age, 3rd digital heritage international congress (DigitalHERITAGE) held jointly with 2018 24th international conference on virtual systems & multimedia (VSMM 2018). IEEE, pp 70–73. https://doi.org/10.1109/DigitalHeritage.2018.8810119

Rojek C (1997) Indexing, dragging and the social construction of tourist sights. In: Rojek C, Urry J (eds) Touring cultures: transformations of travel and theory. Routledge, London, pp 52–74

Rushton H, Schnabel MA (2022) Immersive architectural legacies: the construction of meaning in virtual realities. In: Ch'ng E, Gaffney V, Chapman H (eds) Visual heritage: digital approaches in heritage science. Springer series on cultural computing. Springer, Cham, pp 243–269. https://doi.org/10.1007/978-3-030-77028-0_13

Schettino P, Kenderdine S (2011) Place-Hampi: narratives of inclusive cultural experience. Int J Inclus Museum 3(3):141–156. https://doi.org/10.18848/1835-2014/CGP/v03i03/44338

Schnabel MA, Aydin S, Moleta TJ, Pierini D, Dorta T (2016) Unmediated cultural heritage via Hyve-3D: collecting individual and collective narratives with 3D sketching. In: Proceedings of the 21st CAADRIA, 30 March–2 April 2016, Melbourne, pp 683–692. https://doi.org/10.52842/conf.caadria.2016.683

Smith L (2006) Uses of heritage, 1st edn. Routledge. https://doi.org/10.4324/9780203602263

Staiff R (2014) Re-imagining heritage interpretation. Routledge, London. https://doi.org/10.4324/9781315604558

Steenberg R (2014) Transforming houses—the changing concept of the house in Kashgar. Int Asienforum 171–191. https://doi.org/10.11588/IAF.2014.45.3983

Tang J, Zhou W (2013) Research of national historic city dynamic monitoring by remote sensing: a case study of Kashgar historic urban area. In: Lu W, Cai G, Liu W, Xing W (eds) Proceedings of the 2012 international conference on information technology and software engineering, vol 211. Springer, Berlin, Heidelberg, pp 329–337. https://doi.org/10.1007/978-3-642-34522-7_36

Urry J (1990) The tourist gaze: leisure and travel in contemporary societies. Sage Publications, London

Wang XD, Song H, Liu J, Zhu NY (2014) 喀什高台民居 [Kashi gao tai min ju = terraced household Kashgar]. Southeast University Press, Nanjing

Webb N, Brown A (2011a) Augmenting critique of lost or unbuilt works of architecture using digitally mediated techniques. In: Proceedings of the 29th eCAADe, Ljubljana, 21–24 Sep 2011, pp 942–950. https://doi.org/10.52842/conf.ecaade.2011.942

Webb N, Brown A (2011b) Digital forensics as a tool for augmenting historical architectural analysis: case study: the student work of James Stirling. In: Proceedings of the 16th CAADRIA, Newcastle, 27–29 April 2011, pp 505–514. https://doi.org/10.52842/conf.caadria.2011.505

Webb N, Brown A (2016) Digital re-analysis of lost architecture and the particular case of Lutyens' Liverpool Metropolitan Cathedral. Front Arch Res 5(2):265–275. https://doi.org/10.1016/j.foar.2016.01.004

Zhou M, Geng G, Wu Z (2012) Digital preservation technology for cultural heritage. Springer, Berlin, Heidelberg. https://doi.org/10.1007/978-3-642-28099-3

# Afterword

Sarah Irene Brutton Kenderdine

As we conclude this expansive journey through the diverse landscapes of cultural heritage and digital archaeology, it becomes clear that integrating advanced technologies with traditional architectural, conservation, and preservation methods is a burgeoning frontier of innovative practices. *Endangered Heritage Sites—Using Enhanced Representations for Informed Solutions* underscores the urgency and complexity of safeguarding our tangible heritage amid escalating global challenges—armed conflicts, natural disasters, and the rapid pace of urban development with its often-destructive consequences. Collectively, the contributions made to this volume reveal a field that is underscored by interdisciplinary, merging the arts and humanities with science and technology. The adoption of computational tools, remote sensing, virtual and augmented reality alongside participatory approaches, signals a paradigm shift in how we approach the past, informing more resilient and informed paths into the future.

Building on the insights presented in the chapters, the outlook for digital cultural heritage technologies is also poised for transformative growth. Rapid advances in computational design, semantic technologies, and immersive visualization are driving innovations that support advanced analysis reinforced through increasingly accurate datasets. Parametric and procedural modeling enable precise reconstructions of historic structures—particularly powerful when coupled with machine learning for predictive modeling and data-driven preservation strategies. Knowledge graphs and ontologies unify disparate data, fostering cross-disciplinary collaboration. Remote sensing techniques, including satellite imagery and drone surveys, bolster climate change adaptation and risk assessment, ensuring heritage remains resilient in the face of disasters.

The potential for research in this arena is exhilarating and empowering. Generative and procedural modeling refines large-scale, flexible digital reconstructions, while semantic integration and knowledge graphs offer more sophisticated analyses workflows. Predictive analytics and machine learning hold promise for structural health



S. Stellacci and S. Aydin (eds.), *Endangered Heritage Sites*, Springer Series on Cultural Computing, https://doi.org/10.1007/978-3-031-91949-7

monitoring, climate impact forecasting, and proactive conservation, as community-centric initiatives continue to promote citizen science, user-generated content, and inclusive preservation. Enhanced HBIM solutions—supported by AI, AR visualizations, and robust data management are promising comprehensive heritage site documentation and management.

Alongside these developments, AR and VR technologies are revolutionizing heritage interpretation, offering immersive visitor experiences and potent educational platforms. Community engagement—through participatory practices and tools like 3D printing—deepens public involvement and broadens the scope of cultural stewardship. As policy guidelines and international cooperation continue to shape ethical, sustainable strategies for preservation, emphasis on adaptive reuse, digital fabrication, and expanded educational initiatives will only grow.

This volume highlights the ethical responsibilities that the custodians of cultural heritage have, reminding us to balance technological progress with respect for the historical and cultural dimensions of the sites we seek to protect. At the frontiers of digital cultural heritage, we must remain vigilant about biases in our datasets, data security, ethics, copyright and preserving cultural authenticity. Navigating these challenges will require those interdisciplinary efforts that unite technologists, conservators, policymakers, and local communities in open dialogue and ongoing knowledge exchange. Climate change, urbanization, and socio-political conflicts will continue to threaten our shared past, yet the methods described in this volume offer informed optimism. By embracing emerging tools and methodologies, the field of cultural heritage demonstrates a steadfast commitment to preserving cultural legacies, creating resilient systems well-positioned to protect and celebrate our shared history, ensuring that it endures for generations to come.

GPSR Compliance

*The European Union's (EU) General Product Safety Regulation (GPSR) is a set of rules that requires consumer products to be safe and our obligations to ensure this.*

*If you have any concerns about our products, you can contact us on ProductSafety@springernature.com*

In case Publisher is established outside the EU, the EU authorized representative is:

Springer Nature Customer Service Center GmbH
Europaplatz 3
69115 Heidelberg, Germany

**Batch number: 10755227**

Printed by Printforce, the Netherlands